PATERNOSTER THEOLOGICAL M

The Bonds of Freedom

Vows, Sacraments and the Formation of the Christian Self

PATERNOSTER THEOLOGICAL MONOGRAPHS

A full listing of titles in this series and Paternoster Biblical Monographs appears at the end of this book

PATERNOSTER THEOLOGICAL MONOGRAPHS

The Bonds of Freedom

Vows, Sacraments and the Formation of the Christian Self

Garry J. Deverell

MILTON KEYNES · COLORADO SPRINGS · HYDERABAD

Copyright © Garry J. Deverell 2008

First published 2008 by Paternoster

Paternoster is an imprint of Authentic Media
9 Holdom Avenue, Bletchley, Milton Keynes, MK1 1QR, UK
1820 Jet Stream Drive, Colorado Springs, CO 80921, USA
OM Authentic Media, Medchal Road, Jeedimetla Village,
Secunderabad 500 055, India
Authentic Media is a division of IBS-STL UK, a company limited by guarantee
(registered charity no. 270162)

14 13 12 11 10 09 08 7 6 5 4 3 2 1

The right of Garry J. Deverell to be identified as the Author of this Work
has been asserted by him in accordance with the Copyright, Designs
and Patents Act 1988.

All rights reserved. No part of this publication may be reproduced, stored in a retrieval system, or transmitted, in any form or by any means, electronic, mechanical, photocopying, recording or otherwise, without the prior permission of the publisher or a license permitting restricted copying. In the UK such licenses are issued by the Copyright Licensing Agency, 90 Tottenham Court Road, London W1P 9HE.

British Library Cataloguing in Publication Data
A catalogue record for this book is available from the British Library

ISBN 978-1-84227-527-6

Unless otherwise stated, Scripture quotations are taken from
THE HOLY BIBLE: NEW REVISED STANDARD VERSION, Anglicised ed.
Copyright © 1989, 1995 Division of Christian Education of the National Council
of the Churches of Christ in the United States of America.
Used by permission. All rights reserved.

Typeset by the Author
Printed and bound in Great Britain
for Paternoster
by Nottingham Alpha Graphics

PATERNOSTER THEOLOGICAL MONOGRAPHS

Series Preface

In the West the churches may be declining, but theology—serious, academic (mostly doctoral level) and mainstream orthodox in evaluative commitment—shows no sign of withering on the vine. This series of *Paternoster Theological Monographs* extends the expertise of the Press especially to first-time authors whose work stands broadly within the parameters created by fidelity to Scripture and has satisfied the critical scrutiny of respected assessors in the academy. Such theology may come in several distinct intellectual disciplines—historical, dogmatic, pastoral, apologetic, missional, aesthetic and no doubt others also. The series will be particularly hospitable to promising constructive theology within an evangelical frame, for it is of this that the church's need seems to be greatest. Quality writing will be published across the confessions—Anabaptist, Episcopalian, Reformed, Arminian and Orthodox—across the ages—patristic, medieval, reformation, modern and counter-modern—and across the continents. The aim of the series is theology written in the twofold conviction that the church needs theology and theology needs the church—which in reality means theology done for the glory of God.

PATERNOSTER THEOLOGICAL MONOGRAPHS

Series Editors

David F. Wright, Emeritus Professor of Patristic and Reformed Christianity, University of Edinburgh, Scotland, UK

Trevor A. Hart, Head of School and Principal of St Mary's College School of Divinity, University of St Andrews, Scotland, UK

Anthony N.S. Lane, Professor of Historical Theology and Director of Research, London School of Theology, UK

Anthony C. Thiselton, Emeritus Professor of Christian Theology, University of Nottingham, Research Professor in Christian Theology, University College Chester, and Canon Theologian of Leicester Cathedral and Southwell Minster, UK

Kevin J. Vanhoozer, Research Professor of Systematic Theology, Trinity Evangelical Divinity School, Deerfield, Illinois, USA

*To Lil, Erin and Gretel
with all my love.*

Contents

Acknowledgements	xv
Introduction	1

Chapter 1
If It Be Your Will:
Making Promises with Derrida, Ricoeur and Chauvet	5
1. Vows or Promises are Performances of the Self in Favour of Another	6
1.1 The Performative	6
1.2 The Performative as 'Peverformative'	9
1.3 The Self in Favour of the Other	10
1.4 Are Derrida and Ricoeur Compatible on the Responsible Self?	17
2. Vows or Promises Inscribe a Peculiarly Jewish or Christian Sense of the Real	18
3. Christian Worship is an Exemplary Performance of the Vow	21
3.1 Symbols and Method in Sacramental Theology	22
3.2 The Liturgy as a Vow in Favour of the Christic Other	26

Chapter 2
Divine Metamorphoses:
Thinking about God in Late Modernity	31
1. God and Being	31
1.1 Heidegger's Critique of Onto-theology	31
1.2 Lévinas: God is not Being	33
1.3 Marion: God is not an Idol	34

1.4 Jüngel: God is not the Most Perfect Being	35
2. 'God is Dead': On the Possibilities of 'Atheism' for Faith	37
2.1 Which 'God' is Dead?	37
2.2 The Promise of Nietzschean Atheism	39
3. (Re)turn to the Self-revealing God?	40
3.1 Heidegger and Luther	40
3.2 Theology and Philosophy	41
3.3 God and the Thought of God	42
3.4 The Thought of God as a Faithful Response to Mystery	44

Chapter 3
The Beyond in the Midst:
The God Who is Love

	49
1. A God Who (Never Entirely) Arrives in the 'Other'	50
1.1 Lévinas: God is the Infinite	50
1.2 Derrida: God is the Secret (or, the Secret is God)	54
2. Marion: The God who Arrives in the Gift of Christ	58
2.1 God and the Icon	59
2.2 God is Distance	60
2.3 The Eminent, Excessive God	60
2.4 Outwitting Being by the Gift	62
2.5 God is Trinitarian Filiation	64
2.6 Theology as a logos *of the* Logos	65
2.7 The Gift in Sacramental Form	66
2.8 Is Marion's God too Domineering to Enter into Covenant?	67
3. Jüngel: God in Becoming	69
3.1 Theology Thinks after Faith	69
3.2 Thinking God from God	70
3.3 Beyond the Necessary God	71
3.4 The Cross of Christ: God's Perishability and Possibility	73
3.5 The Cross of Christ: Creating New Human Selves	74
3.6 Humanity Becomes Itself in God's Becoming	75
3.7 The Trinity: Covenant Love Embodied	77
4. Kearney: The God of Passage	78
4.1 The God Who May Be	78
4.2 God Becomes God With and For Us	80
4.3 God as Pure Passage	81

Contents xi

4.4 The Face: Where Spirit and Flesh Meet	81
4.5 God is Pure Possibility	83
4.6 The Trinity: God as Giving Place	84

Chapter 4
The Desire of God — 89

1. Desire and the Body	91
1.1 The Body: The Desirable before Desire	91
1.2 The Face to Face: Desire as a Pre-lingual Ethics	93
1.3 Asymmetry and Covenant: Friends or Antagonists?	95
1.4 Body-language: A Speech before Interlocution	99
1.5 The 'Saying' and Grace: Two Kinds of Substitution	100
1.6 The Body as the Site of Covenant	102
2. Biblical Poetry: Covenant Relations Embodied	103
2.1 Psalms: Covenanting through Antiphonal Speech	104
2.1.1 LAMENT: OTHERING PAIN	105
2.1.2 PRAYER: THE SELF AS ANOTHER	106
2.1.3 PRAYER: ANOTHER WITH THE SELF	108
2.1.4 PRAYER: ANOTHER AS THE SELF	109
2.1.5 THE NON-SYNCHRONOUS SELFHOOD OF GOD	110
2.2 The Song of Songs: Finding Oneself in God	113
2.2.1 AN EROTIC ALLEGORY OF DIVINE-HUMAN LOVE	114
2.2.2 INDETERMINACY OF IDENTIFICATION	114
2.2.3 THE NUPTIAL METAPHOR: LOVE INCARNATE	115
2.2.4 HUMAN LOVE AS THE PASSAGE FOR AN ESCHATOLOGICAL DIVINITY	116

Chapter 5
Written on the Heart:
Covenant in Israel and in Christian Worship — 119

1. The Covenant in Israel	121
1.1 The Covenant as a Mutual Choosing	121
1.2 The Conditional Covenant	122
1.3 The Unconditional Covenant	123
1.4 An Unfolding Covenant: Both Conditional and Unconditional	124
1.5 The Covenant Formulated in Worship	127

2. The Covenant in the Worship of the Church	127
2.1 The Church as a New Covenant	127
2.2 The Covenant as Summons and Gathering	129
2.3 The Covenant as Address and Listening	135
2.4 The Covenant as Embodiment and Transfiguration	139
2.5 The Covenant as Sending and Mission	143

Chapter 6
The Baptised Self:

Formation 'in Christ' as Parable	**149**
1. A Biblical Theology of Baptism: Covenanting with God through Immersion in the Pasch of Christ	150
1.1 Baptism for Repentance and Forgiveness of Sins	151
1.2 Baptism as the Arrival of An/other Self or Vocation	152
1.3 Baptism as an Immersion in the Pasch of Christ	153
1.4 Baptism as Transfiguration	154
1.5 Baptism as the Formation of a New Covenant in God as Trinity	156
1.6 Baptism as the Formation of a New Bond with Others	157
1.7 Baptism as In/corporation into the Church as the Body of Christ	158
2. Baptism, Parables and the 'Other'	159
2.1 Parables as Destabilising Agents	159
2.2 Parable Transforms Myth	159
2.3 Sacraments are Parables	160
2.4 Parable is God's Excessive Address	161
2.5 Baptism Reveals the Self as More than Itself	162
2.6 The Pasch of Jesus as the Parable of God	163
2.7 'Fools for Christ': Living Parables	164
2.8 Christ the Lacunae *of God*	164
2.9 Baptism as a Singular Event	166

Chapter 7
The Baptised Self:

Formation 'in Christ' as the Church	**169**
1. The Idea of a Liturgical Theology: Interpreting Christian Existence in and through Worship	169

2. The Ecumenical Liturgy of Baptism: A Commentary	173
2.1 The Placement of Baptism in the Ordo *and the Sacred Calendar*	174
2.2 The Significance of Sponsors	176
2.3 The Turning from Evil to Christ	176
2.4 The Declaration of Faith	177
2.5 The Immersion in Water	178
2.6 The Signing and Anointing	180
2.7 The Welcoming and Responsibilities	181
2.8 Participation in the Eucharistic Meal	182
3. The Formative Context of Baptismal Liturgy: The Catechumenate	185
4. Critical Remarks toward a Contemporary Practice of Baptismal Formation	188

Epilogue
Trauma and Joy:

A Meditation on Mark's Baptism of Jesus	**199**
1. The Holy Ambiguity of Baptism	199
2. Water is Dangerous: It can take One's Life Away	200
3. Derrida: Mourning as the Work of any Life Lived before the Other	200
4. The Rite of Baptism Today: Legitimization or Subversion of the *Status Quo*?	202
5. Mourning and Hope	204
Bibliography	**207**
Author Index	**213**

Acknowledgements

This book could not have been completed without the generous help and expertise of my doctoral supervisors, Peter Howard (Monash University) and Robyn Horner (Australian Catholic University). The Centre for Theology and Ministry of the Uniting Church in Australia (Synod of Victoria and Tasmania) granted a Sanderson Fellowship which enabled the project to be completed.

Writing a book can be a lonely experience. That it was not particularly so, I owe to the support and understanding of a number of friends and colleagues. From the Monash Research Graduate Centre I wish to thank Mark Manolopoulos, Ildiko Domotor, George Somers, David Tegart, Rodney Ling, and especially Amelia Church and Antonella Refatto. My church communities at Monash, South Yarra and Mount Waverley provided a fertile field for the practice of faith, hope and love. I am profoundly grateful to each of them for welcoming my family and I into their fold. Especial thanks are reserved for the members of the Otira Reading Group for many deeply enriching theological conversations.

Finally, I should like to dedicate this work to my partner in life, Lil, and to our children, Erin and Gretel. Each day they call me anew to the vowed life, and show me how to live it.

Garry J. Deverell
Melbourne
October 2007

Introduction

This is a book about the vow or covenant dimension of sacramental worship in the Christian tradition. It argues that sacraments, particularly baptism and the Eucharist, may be understood as fundamental performances of the mutual *promising* of God and human beings.

In baptism and Eucharist, the eschatological mission of God in and for the world takes a uniquely communicative form. The sacraments *proclaim and interpret* God's promise and call towards liberation, and they do this in ways that implicate and order the embodied existence of human beings. Thus, the sacraments are also the primary means by which the mission of God is understood, owned and co-performed by human beings. By choosing to participate in sacramental action, human beings are inscribed, and inscribe themselves, for a specifically Christian vocation and future. By submitting to baptism and participating in the Eucharist, human beings respond freely to God's call and promise, offering themselves for service in the vocative prayer 'Here I am; send me.' The sacraments should therefore be understood as liminal or 'hinge' realities between divine and human action. As such, they are the pivotal site for the formation of the Christian self, and this precisely because of their performative power, as vows, to *make things happen*, to change reality.

Chapter one begins with a phenomenological definition of the vow as an ever-new performance of the self in favour of its 'other'. One hears a 'call' in the face of another, any other, which is experienced as more original than even one's own sense of self. The call has a particularly apocalyptic or eschatological dimension to it, unsettling and destabilising in the same movement as it produces and makes real. It therefore has a power to destabilise the self such that the self may only come to be by making room for its other. The chapter is concluded by suggesting that Christian worship may well be an exemplary performance of the vowed self, so described. For Christian worship is promissory in structure, from beginning to end. The community gathers in response to a call and promise from God toward transformation into the image and likeness of that particular other known as Christ.

The second chapter will ask critical questions about the implications of this language for a doctrine of God. In what I will call its dominantly 'metaphysical' or 'onto-theological' mode, theology has often imagined God to be some kind of omnipotent 'First Cause', who set the universe on its course as a self-perpetuating entity, but now has little or nothing to contribute. For much of this theology, it is almost as though creation were somehow unavoidable or predestined, unfolding according to a logic of *necessity* in which neither divine or human decision is of any affective consequence. I will offer an extensive critique of this theology, noting that it is produced by an essentially *human-centred* kind of thinking which has little or nothing to do with the experience of *God* recorded and promised by both the Christian Scriptures and the experience of Christian worship.

Chapter three will follow on with an evaluation of three newer models of God, models more open to the idea that God and human beings may actually *change* or *affect* each other, precisely through their covenantal relations. Here I will argue that the commonplace theologemes of 'creation,' 'covenant' and 'redemption' are all predicated upon the idea that God is essential and primordial hospitality, that God makes room within the divine reality for that which is *not* God. By attending to a number of recent Trinitarian theologies, I will argue that God's own being is accomplished through a relationship with the other-in-Godself, that God *becomes* Godself through the dynamism of covenant.

The fourth chapter will propose a theology of Christian personhood that takes this *interlocutionary* action of God as its point of origin. I will show that the human body is a primary site for the constant negotiation between personal desire and the desire of a divine other, and is therefore capable of becoming a symbol that participates in God's becoming. Considerable energy will be devoted to Jacques Derrida's suggestion that a person's desire for some kind of not-yet-arrived 'other' may well be read as the prior sign or promise of that *other's* desire or love. Could our desire for God *already* be God's desire for us? I will answer, 'yes,' and argue further that the human body is the privileged site for the negotiation of these two kinds of desire. For the human self is not at one with itself, any more than God is at one with Godself. The self is present and identifiable in a body, yet it is still arriving, as from some other place or time, in a mode that has been called *persona* or *spirit*.

The fifth chapter will return to the claim that *Christian worship* is the place of a unique 'face to face' encounter between human beings and God such that both human beings and God are transformed. Beginning with an examination of the development of covenantal theology in the Hebrew Bible, I will go on to show how Christian worship *performs* that covenant through its non-identical repetition of Christ's Pasch—his life, death, resurrection and sending of the Spirit. Particular attention will be given to the conjunction of Word and Sacrament in the interlocution of God with human beings.

Chapters six and seven, which are all of a piece, will claim that the formation of Christian identity is intimately related to that 'othering' of the Christian in Christ known as baptism. In baptism the promise of God toward forgiveness and salvation is received by a 'sacrifice' or displacement of the human self in favour of its other, here identified as the crucified and risen Christ who is present in the Spirit. Such displacement, being a repetition in the self of Christ's own self-sacrifice in the Trinity and on the cross, establishes the Christian in the liminal identity of covenant responsibility. Baptism therefore reconfigures the human self for a Christ-like identity and mission whereby the love of God is written upon the human and material body of Christians. It is recognised, of course, that such a self may not be accomplished by ritual alone. Ritual is effective only insofar as it interprets or performs a *way of life*. The final chapter therefore culminates in a plea for a more radical implementation of the baptismal *catechumenate*, that process by which candidates learn *how* to be Christians as an indispensable prolegomena to their baptismal vows.

A brief epilogue will meditate upon the *traumatic* and yet *healing* nature of the Christian avowal through a series of 'Derridean' reflections on the story of Jesus' baptism in the Jordan River, as it is told by Mark.

CHAPTER 1

If It Be Your Will:
Making Promises with Derrida, Ricoeur and Chauvet[1]

If it be your will
That a voice be true
From this broken hill
I will sing to you
From this broken hill
All your praises they shall ring
If it be your will
To let me sing.

Leonard Cohen[2]

Introduction

In this chapter I should like to explore the meaning of making vows or promises, particularly as this relates to the Christian experience of worship. Along the way I will be making three claims: first, that vows or promises are performances of the self in favour of another; second, that in the West at least, vows or promises inscribe a fundamentally Jewish or Christian sense of the real; and third, that the weekly gathering of Christians to perform the Scriptures and celebrate the rites of baptism and/or Eucharist is essentially promissory in structure and effect, and may therefore be described as an exemplary experience of the vow so defined. I will substantiate my claims by engaging a number of contemporary French thinkers. Chief amongst these are two philosophers, Jacques Derrida and Paul Ricoeur, and a theologian, Louis-Marie Chauvet. Derrida has written about a 'performative self' which is always already 'responsible,' and about Western religion as an 'exemplary' instance of the performative as such. Paul Ricoeur organises his philosophy around the thought of 'oneself as another' and locates that self in a sense of conviction or decision that he calls 'attestation' or 'testimony'. Chauvet writes about

---

[1] An earlier version of this chapter was published as Garry J. Deverell, '"If It Be Your Will": Making Promises with Derrida, Ricoeur and Chauvet,' *Pacifica: Australasian Theological Studies* 16.3 (2003): 271-94.

[2] From the song 'If It Be Your Will' on *Various Positions* (Columbia Records, 1987).

Christian worship as a symbolic performance of the 'body of Christ,' that is, a body constituted as a self only through the trial of suffering and death out of love for the other. Placed together in this way, 'intertextually' as it were, the resonances between these three rather different thinkers will help me to inaugurate some new thoughts concerning the vow.

What is a vow, exactly? And what kind of analysis would yield an answer to this question? Taking the second question first, I would argue for a multi-disciplinary interrogation of the vow which is nevertheless capable of gathering the results together into some kind of analogical or even narrative answer. This approach puts into play two invaluable intellectual virtues at the same time: the virtue of a fair and attentive *listening* to many voices, and the virtue of resolute *argument*, by which these views are repeated otherwise, so that the new perspective is given a prominence born of conviction.[3] I would therefore ask questions of the vow in the same way in which Ricoeur asks questions of the self. With Ricoeur, I confess from the beginning that any conclusion I might formulate could never possess the status of objectivity in a foundationalist sense. Rather, the status of what I propose here is that of an *attestation* or *testimony* which lacks the hypercertainty of epistemic or foundationalist accounts.[4] Nevertheless, I would also follow Ricoeur in claiming that 'there is no recourse against false testimony than another that is more credible; and there is no recourse against suspicion than a more reliable attestation'.[5] Indeed, what is said here about listening, argument, and attestation can also be said of the vow or promise: the vow, no less than intellectual attestation, is 'a performance of the self' that seeks to both address and respond to others.

1. Vows or Promises are Performances of the Self in Favour of Another

1.1 The Performative

Let us begin by examining the nature of 'performance' or 'the performative'. The term, as first coined by J.L. Austin, denotes a statement which, despite appearances to the contrary, is not about truth or falsity in a descriptive or constative sense, but rather, as an utterance, performs the very action it seems to represent.[6] For Austin, vows or promises are performatives in this sense. They should not be taken as 'outward and visible signs' of internal mental or spiritual states, but rather as words which *are themselves* the accomplishment

---

[3] Here I am indebted to the ethics of conversation proposed in David Tracy, *Plurality and Ambiguity: Hermeneutics, Religion, Hope* (Chicago: Chicago University Press, 1987), especially chapter 1.

[4] Paul Ricoeur, *Oneself as Another*, trans. Kathleen Blamey (Chicago: University of Chicago Press, 1992), pp. 19, 20.

[5] Ricoeur, *Oneself as Another*, p. 22.

[6] John Langshaw Austin, *How to Do Things with Words*, William James Lectures, 2nd ed. (Oxford: Clarendon Press, 1975), pp. 4-6.

If It Be Your Will

of a bond.[7] So that when one says, in a wedding ceremony, 'I take this man as my lawful wedded husband,' it is the *words themselves* that accomplish or effect the marriage. Austin did not wish to imply by this that promissory words have a power in and of themselves, apart from the context in which they are uttered. On the contrary, performatives are said to be 'conventional acts' in the sense that they imply and refer to 'the total situation in which the utterance is issued—the total speech-act'.[8] It is essential for our purposes that we understand what Austin meant by this.

In the early chapters of *How To Do Things With Words,* Austin argues that in order for performatives to be 'successful,' the speaker or speakers need both to 'intend' and 'actually conduct themselves' in a manner 'appropriate' to the context in which they are speaking.[9] So, to invoke our marriage example again, the words 'I take this man to be my lawful wedded husband' would not *successfully* perform a marriage unless they were spoken within the context of a conventional wedding ceremony with witnesses, an authorized celebrant, the lawful paperwork etc. The participants would also have to *mean* what they say when they say it. For that reason, Austin distinguishes between 'happy' and 'unhappy' performatives, that is, performatives that are successful because of right intention and procedural fidelity, and those which are not. A good example of the 'unhappy' performative would be a promise made in the context of a piece of theatre, where both the promiser and the promisee are playing roles which begin and end with the play itself.[10]

Performatives, then, are statements which ultimately entail, imply, or presuppose what may only be described as 'other performatives' in a total contextual situation, a total 'speech-act' in which even apparently constative utterances are made to function in a performative manner.[11] It is important to recognise what this move ultimately meant for Austin: *the breakdown of any real distinction between performative and constative utterances.* In the later parts of his book Austin describes a new taxonomy that sees *all* language as performative in some way or another. All language, he says, whether it is uttered in the explicitly performative 'first person indicative active' or not, is essentially action-oriented, making explicit the '*force* or meaning' in an utterance, 'how it is to be taken'.[12]

From there he divides language into three kinds of performative action: the locutionary (doing something *as* saying something), the illocutionary (doing something *in* or *by* saying something), and the perlocutionary (saying

---

[7] Austin, *How to Do Things with Words*, p. 10.
[8] Austin, *How to Do Things with Words*, pp. 18, 52.
[9] Austin, *How to Do Things with Words*, pp. 8, 15.
[10] Austin, *How to Do Things with Words*, p. 22.
[11] Austin, *How to Do Things with Words*, pp. 47-9, 52.
[12] Austin, *How to Do Things with Words*, p. 73.

something in order to *produce effects* in other people).[13] Finally, then, there is a recognition that every statement, even those that appear to be about some kind of pre-existing truth or falsity, are themselves also ways of establishing or *accomplishing* that truth or falsity. In that sense, truth is utterly dependent on a sense of the context in which that truth is being discussed.[14] While constative statements might be more locutionary in character, and explicit performatives more illocutionary, each is made possible by the other in a total speech context which is, itself, ultimately performative.[15]

Now, there are a number of well-rehearsed objections to this theory of the performative utterance, many of them anticipated by Austin himself. Derrida points to a contradiction in Austin's determination of *conventional context* as a criteria for 'happy' performance. The requirement of a 'conscious presence of the intention of the speaking subject in the totality of his speech act' implies that the speaking subject is able to *master the meaning* of his or her performance in its specifically determined context. No residue of meaning may overflow or transgress that sense of context.[16] The conventions that authorize are therefore made coextensive with, and transparent to, the intention of the speaking subject. Derrida is right to say that such a situation represents not the reality of the ordinary speech-situation, but rather a philosophical reduction imposed upon that situation by Austin.[17] One may note the way in which Austin rules 'out of play' a whole variety of 'infelicities' which nevertheless, he admits, inhere in '*all*' conventional acts![18] He recognises, at one point, that it is often extremely difficult to determine how far a particular procedure or convention extends. 'Can a dog or a penguin be baptised?' he asks.[19] While acknowledging that innovations in conventional understanding are a potential problem for contextual delimitation, Austin chooses to rule such innovations 'out of play'.[20] Surely this represents an implicit recognition that performatives are not finally subject to the rule of either convention or intention? Derrida believes so. Indeed, he argues that it is *what Austin excludes* that makes the performative work as performative. Paradoxically, 'a successful performative is necessarily an 'impure' performative'. What makes the performative possible is its citational doubling [*doublure*], its dissociation from itself in 'the pure

---

[13] Austin, *How to Do Things with Words*, pp. 99-101.
[14] Austin, *How to Do Things with Words*, pp. 143, 146.
[15] Austin, *How to Do Things with Words*, p. 146.
[16] Jacques Derrida, 'Signature Event Context,' trans. Samuel Weber and Jeffrey Mehlman, *Limited Inc.*, ed. Gerald Graf (Evanston, Illinois: Northwestern University Press, 1988), p. 14. Austin defines an *infelicity* as either a '*misinvocation* or *misexecution*' of procedural rules stemming from the conventional setting in which a performative utterance takes place (*How To Do Things with Words*, p. 17).
[17] Derrida, 'Signature Event Context,' p. 17.
[18] Austin, *How to Do Things with Words*, pp. 18-19.
[19] Austin, *How to Do Things with Words*, p. 31.
[20] Austin, *How to Do Things with Words*, pp. 29-31.

If It Be Your Will

singularity of the event'.[21] What does Derrida mean by this?

1.2 The Performative as 'Peverformative'

Derrida's engagement with the 'performative' is at the heart of all he has written. In the 1966 essay 'Signature Event Context,' which I have cited already, Derrida built a theory of performance around the idea of the 'iterable' (from the Sanskrit, *itar*, or 'other'), that sense in which language is said to repeat itself by also differing from itself. In order for language to be language, in order for language to actually communicate, it must retain that capacity in the absence of either its supposed 'author' (speaker) or its 'reader' (hearer). At the scene of writing, an author presumes that his or her text will be readable by absent readers, whether that absence be a consequence of time or space. Similarly, in the scene of reading, a reader presumes that a text is readable apart from the presence of an authorial intention. This means that writing, or the possibility of meaningful communication in general, is predicated not upon the *presence* of meaning, but upon its *absence*:

> For a writing to be a writing it must continue to 'act' and to be readable even when what is called the author of the writing no longer answers for what he has written, for what he seems to have signed, be it because of a temporary absence, because he is dead, or, more generally, because he has not employed his absolutely actual or present intention or attention, the plenitude of his desire to say what he means, in order to sustain what seems to be written 'in his name'.[22]

In this sense, the situation of the writer or signer is exactly the same as that of the addressee or reader. In either case, there is a *'drift'* [*dérive*] in writing that takes it away from human intention and consciousness as the 'authorizing authority'. There is a double movement here, inscribed and represented in the notion of iterability. On the one hand, language must be repeatable in order to communicate. On the other hand, that very repetition is made possible only by a movement of 'absolute différance' (both difference and deferral) which ruptures the totalising genealogy of ontological presence.[23] The implications of these findings go well beyond a simple analysis of communication in language:

> Every sign, linguistic or non-linguistic, spoken or written (in the current sense of this opposition), in a small unit or a large unit, can be *cited,* put between quotation marks; in so doing it can break with every given context, engendering an infinity of new contexts in a manner which is absolutely illimitable. This does not imply

---

[21] Derrida, 'Signature Event Context,' p. 17.
[22] Derrida, 'Signature Event Context,' p. 8.
[23] Derrida, 'Signature Event Context,' p. 8.

that the mark is valid outside of a context, but on the contrary that there are only concepts without any centre or absolute anchorage.[24]

Iterability means that contexts and intentions can no longer be seen as stable horizons by which the meanings of performatives are fixed. Iterability implies that performatives are really 'peverformatives,'[25] creations of meaning that constantly escape such controls by virtue of the movement of *différance*, classically defined in *Of Grammatology* as that which 'produces what it forbids, makes possible the very thing that it makes impossible.'[26] In this perspective, the stabilization of meaning in vows would appear to be at issue as well, and this because of the interrupting movement within the promising intention of something which is 'other,' something that is 'alter-ego'.[27] On the one hand, a promise could not be a promise without being repeatable, as an event, in another context. On the other hand, such repeatability is necessarily at odds with itself, giving place to a difference that Derrida likens to the work of a parasite. A parasite (promise) depends on the hospitality of its host (a self). It 'takes place' in a space the host provides (if unintentionally), but it never entirely *takes* the place of the host. Thus, a promise can only 'take place' as an event whose meaning is never entirely completed, or whose meaning could always be something other than it is.[28] It implicates the self in ways that the self does not intend, and cannot ultimately control. It is to this sense of otherness at the heart of the vowing self that we now turn.

1.3 The Self in Favour of the Other

In his own discussion of speech-acts, Paul Ricoeur emphasises that the performative effect of language would not be possible apart from the action of human selves. The performative requires that for every speech-act there is a self or agent who gives that speech its force. This is particularly clear in the context of illocutionary speech, where the force of utterance implies that the words 'I affirm' might be placed at the beginning of every statement, making the involvement of a self explicit. But there is a second implication as well. The words 'I affirm that . . .' would be completely unnecessary were there not *another* person to whom the words are being addressed. This means that illocutionary speech is also *interlocutionary*.[29] Performative speech may

---

[24] Derrida, 'Signature Event Context,' p. 12.
[25] Jacques Derrida, *The Post Card: From Socrates to Freud and Beyond* (Chicago: University of Chicago Press, 1987), p. 136.
[26] Jacques Derrida, *Of Grammatology*, trans. Gayatri Chakravorty Spivak, corrected ed. (Baltimore: John Hopkins University Press, 1997), p. 143.
[27] Jacques Derrida, 'Limited Inc. A B C,' trans. Samuel Weber and Jeffrey Mehlman, *Limited Inc.*, ed. Gerald Graf (Evanston, Illinois: Northwestern University Press, 1988), p. 76.
[28] Derrida, 'Limited Inc. A B C,' p. 90.
[29] Ricoeur, *Oneself as Another*, p. 43.

If It Be Your Will

therefore be described as an essentially 'bi-polar phenomenon: it assumes, simultaneously, an 'I' that speaks and a 'you' to whom the former addresses itself.' Here 'I affirm that' equals 'I declare to *you* that' and 'I promise that' equals 'I promise *you* that'. The axiom Ricoeur draws from this analysis will prove decisive for my argument in this book: 'every advance made in the direction of the selfhood of the speaker of the agent has as its counterpart a comparable advance in the otherness of the partner'.[30]

But who and what is this self that speaks? And who or what is the other that is addressed? These questions are unanswerable, says Ricoeur, unless one first recognises, with Heidegger, that a self is always already embedded in *temporality* and therefore in a kind of *historical narrative* which orients itself toward the future.[31] A discussion about the problematics of the self would then be oriented, necessarily, towards the question of how it is that personal identity may be established and maintained through time.[32] Here Ricoeur proposes what he calls a 'narrative' theory of the self, gathered around the polar concepts of *character* and the *keeping of one's word*. Let us examine each of these in turn, noting the ways in which the self and the other are mutually implicated.

Character designates 'a set of distinctive marks which permit the reidentification of a human individual as being the same'.[33] It is formed through a continual and ongoing negotiation between sedimentation and innovation in bodily praxis, but more significantly between relationship to the other and the internalisation of such relations. In the context of my book, I wish to emphasise the second of these processes, because here the constitution of the self is predicated upon a fundamental recognition of values, norms, ideals, even heroes, in the 'other' by which the self comes to identify itself with a proper name. Despite the inevitable appropriations and projections involved in such a process at the psychological level, Ricoeur notes that a certain kind of un-erasable loyalty and fidelity is implied, such that what others say about the self becomes an indispensable source of *stability* in character.[34] Why am I a self that perseveres through time? Because others recognise me as such, and because I identify myself in stable characters beyond myself.

Character is of course a narrative concept. In narrative, according to Ricoeur, personal identity is not identical with character, but is constructed in the relationship between character and *plot*. Narrative identity therefore has a distinctively *event* nature. It is performed as a 'discordant concordance,' in which heterogeneous elements are synthesized into the unitary whole that is narrative itself. 'The paradox of emplotment,' says Ricoeur, 'is that it inverts the effect of contingency, in the sense of that which could have happened

---

[30] Ricoeur, *Oneself as Another*, pp. 43-44.
[31] Ricoeur, *Oneself as Another*, p. 113.
[32] Ricoeur, *Oneself as Another*, p. 117-18.
[33] Ricoeur, *Oneself as Another*, p. 119.
[34] Ricoeur, *Oneself as Another*, pp. 121-22.

differently or might not have happened at all, by incorporating it in some way into the effect of necessity or probability exerted by the configuring act'.[35] In the context of narrative strategy, identity is established by a transference of the event-nature of the unfolding plot onto individual characters, such that characters become, themselves, correlative versions of the larger story. Indeed, the event-forces cut both ways in this situation, because character produces plot as much as plot produces character.[36] There is a dialectical notion of freedom here, in the Kantian rather than the Hegelian sense. While the self is constituted by the force of a larger history in which it simply arrives, or is 'thrown,' it also possesses a performative power of initiative, whereby it can reinscribe what it receives in genuinely original ways.[37] In the language of narrative, such a self might be called a 'character' or a 'narrator,' or perhaps even a 'co-author'.[38] But there is another implied in this taxonomy, an 'other' who is not simply another person, another character, but also the force of the 'story' in which the self finds itself. But what 'is' this story, and does it have an identifiable author? These are important questions indeed! We shall delay that particular discussion until we turn to Chauvet and the liturgy in the final section of the chapter. But now we must turn to that other source of narrative identity, the *keeping of one's word*.

With *the keeping of one's word*, we discover that there is yet another 'other' at the heart of the self, this time in the form of an ethical obligation. According to Ricoeur, the question 'who is the self?' may only be answered in the singularity of an 'I' who 'has the obligation to safeguard the institution of language and to respond to the trust that the other places in my faithfulness'.[39] This statement carries further that emerging sense we have from Ricoeur in which the 'real' or narrative self is a *unique event* in the negotiation between the 'same' (character) and the 'other' (plot, author, theme, other characters). From the side of the other, Ricoeur develops a theory of *self-constancy* as the ethical fulfilment or completion of narrative. Citing Walter Benjamin, he notes the way in which narratives facilitate exchanges of experience that are inevitably assessed in terms of praise or blame, approval or disapproval. Even where specific values are transformed through the course of a narrative, one may never escape the fact of valuation. Even with history, that mode of narrative that seeks to be the least polemical with regard to values, the historian cannot help but be drawn into the evaluating universes which he or she is investigating. So much so that 'At least in the mode of imagination and sympathy the historian brings back to life ways of evaluating which continue to belong to our deepest humanity,' and this is the case even where historical

---

[35] Ricoeur, *Oneself as Another*, p. 142.
[36] Ricoeur, *Oneself as Another*, pp. 143-44.
[37] Ricoeur, *Oneself as Another*, p. 147.
[38] Ricoeur, *Oneself as Another*, pp. 159-60.
[39] Ricoeur, *Oneself as Another*, p. 124.

research reveals only monsters and victims. In this last instance, the relation of debt to the past is transformed into 'the duty never to forget'.[40]

Valuation in narrative therefore inscribes an originary sense of the other who 'calls' the self to account, in the Lévinasian sense. Here there is both an 'other' who counts on me, who calls out 'Where are you? I need you!' and a 'me' who becomes accountable, who answers 'Here I am!' Lévinas' term 'responsibility' unites these two senses. In responsibility, says Ricoeur, there is a constancy that cannot be reduced to a perpetuation of the same.[41] In the 'Here I am' the self responds to the call of the other with a sense of resolute decision, not as a repression of the awareness that things may be otherwise (in the midst of a story, things may *always* be otherwise), but rather with that sense that 'sure, I could do things differently, but here is where I stand'.[42] This is the moment of *promising,* of *attestation,* of *testimony,* the moment at which the self is posited or performed *as a self.* Now, let us be clear about what this means. *Attestation* is not, in Ricoeur, the adding of another to the self after that self has been established in some kind of monadic unity. Rather, the self is *always already* that tension between the other and the same that he calls responsibility. In phenomenological terms, the self is constituted in a threefold experience of *passivity*: a passivity towards one's body, a passivity towards someone or something other than oneself, but also the passivity experienced in that self-relation that Heidegger called *Gewissen* or 'conscience'.[43] I should like to conclude my discussion of Ricoeur with a brief reflection on the way in which each of these categories might shed light upon the vow.

The body, says Ricoeur, has a two-fold adherence: to the world of things and to the self.[44] This means that the body represents the other *in* the self, a self that may not be posited apart from the resistance which the body offers in the form of *suffering.* Suffering, says Ricoeur, is not simply physical pain, though it is that too. It is also the experience of aporias in the narrative of one's life, 'the incapacity to tell a story, the refusal to account, the insistence of the untellable'. As we have noted, the power to tell a story is also an experience of the power to *act,* to posit the self as a narrative event unfolding through time. Ricoeur cites Husserl, who said that the body even appears to precede the distinction between the voluntary and the involuntary. Thus, the experience of suffering might be understood as the moment when embodied *existence* appears to resist the power to tell a particular story *about* that existence.[45] Still, there is an implicit

---

[40] Ricoeur, *Oneself as Another,* p. 164.
[41] Ricoeur, *Oneself as Another,* p. 165.
[42] Ricoeur, *Oneself as Another,* pp. 167-68.
[43] Ricoeur, *Oneself as Another,* p. 318.
[44] Ricoeur, *Oneself as Another,* p. 319.
[45] Ricoeur, *Oneself as Another,* p. 320. A similar perspective is developed in Elaine Scarry, *The Body in Pain: The Making and Unmaking of the World* (New York: Oxford University Press, 1985), pp. 4, 5.

recognition in this account that another story may be told, a story about 'evil'. Most of the 'evil' in the world, says Ricoeur, is inflicted by humans on other humans, and thus the experience of pain in one's own body, and the experience of another's power over that body, coincide to the point of becoming virtually 'indistinguishable'.[46] One might conclude, then, that while suffering offers a serious resistance to the ambition to tell a *particular* story, it does not appear to prohibit the possibility of telling stories altogether. Having suffered, one must tell one's story *differently* or *otherwise*. Vows, as performances of the self, would therefore require that the experience of suffering, and even of the resistance of suffering to certain kinds of performance, be taken seriously. This, I think, is precisely what Christian baptismal vows do most excellently, with their two-fold insistence on the *undergoing* of suffering and the *resistance* before evil.[47]

In turning to the otherness of other people, we note, again, the confrontation—at once admiring and critical—that Ricoeur makes with Emmanuel Lévinas. Lévinas had argued, in *Totality and Infinity,* that the injunction from the 'Other' takes place in a space which is inherently asymmetrical. The Other is the teaching master who the 'I' is powerless to objectify. The 'I' and the 'Other' cannot, therefore, be correlated within a pre-existing framework or ideological system. The Other is above and beyond correlation because he or she is from infinity.[48] Ricoeur interprets this talk of 'asymmetry' and 'relation without relation' as hyperbolic, and therefore overstated. 'The Other absolves itself from relation in the same movement by which the Infinite draws free from totality'. Ricoeur argues that Lévinas found this move necessary only because he had *already* identified the Platonic category of the 'same' with the 'self' in an equally hyperbolic way. Here the ego is locked up in itself, absolutely incapable of the Other.[49] Ironically, the later writings correct this disingenuousness, not by a withdrawal from hyperbole, but by the use of an even more radical hyperbole. In *Otherwise Than Being,* Lévinas wrote of the Other not as a master teacher but as an offender or

---

[46] Ricoeur, *Oneself as Another*, p. 320.
[47] See chapter 6 below.
[48] Emmanuel Lévinas, *Totality and Infinity: An Essay on Exteriority*, trans. Alphonso Lingis (The Hague: Martinus Nijhoff Publishers, 1979), p. 216.
[49] Ricoeur, *Oneself as Another*, p. 337. The passage Ricoeur has in mind is from *Time and the Other*, where Lévinas speaks about the ego as insomnia: a wakefulness in which there is not yet anything that could be called conscious agency or intention, a moment between simple being and personal willing or knowing: 'One is detached from any object, any content, and yet there is presence'. At this moment, the sheer fact of presence is oppressive because one is 'held by being, held to be'. Wakefulness, insomnia, is utterly anonymous because there is not yet subjective agency: 'I am, one might say, the object rather than the subject of anonymous thought' [Emmanuel Lévinas, *Time and the Other (and Additional Essays)*, trans. Richard A. Cohen (Pittsburgh: Duquesne University Press, 1987), pp. 65-6].

persecutor in need of pardon, and that such a thing might only be effected by the willingness of the 'I' to substitute itself for the Other. Here it is an 'expiation,' or substitution, which makes the relation between alterity and identity possible. Thus, Lévinas can speak of a 'gestation' of the Other in the same whereby I am bound in relation to the Other before I am bound to even my own body.[50] In this Ricoeur discerns a welcome shift in Lévinas' conception of the self. Here the self is no longer the Same, but its contrary, Substitution, a reflexive self in which the otherness of the Other is always already present, not as a suspect representation, but as the 'trace' of infinity. This implies, of course, a self which possesses a capacity for the Other—a native openness to address and discovery—from the very beginning.[51] In this perspective, the vow or performance of self would become the 'mode of truth' by which the self bears witness to the other-in-the-self. Far from positing the self as some kind of Cartesian foundation, the vow becomes the evidence that an eternal return of the Same is simply not possible.

The closest proximity of the other in the self is what Ricoeur calls, after Heidegger, *Gewissen*, or conscience. In *Being and Time*, Heidegger had spoken of conscience as the awakening of a self that could be distinguished from the 'they'. The awakening happens when a 'call' [*Ruf*] or 'summons' [*Anruf*] is heard.[52] There are two agencies here, and there is a dissymmetry in favour of the agency that calls. Lest we hear these words in a moralistic sense, or press them into the service of a dialectic between 'good' conscience and 'bad' conscience, Ricoeur reminds us that the call in Heidegger actually 'says' nothing, indeed, the caller is none other than *Dasein* itself! Yet the call is experienced as from somewhere else, '*from beyond me and over me*' [*aus mir und doch über mich*],[53] reminding Dasein of its thrownness, and therefore of its debt to all that is more primordial than itself. While this doctrine of being guilty, or indebted, certainly calls for action on the part of Dasein, Heidegger, it seems, refrained from speculating on precisely what that action ought to be.[54] While Heidegger's theory has the advantage of being free of moralism, it has the disadvantage of promulgating a 'demoralization' of human behaviour. For that reason Ricoeur explores, instead, a model of conscience that joins '*injunction*' and '*attestation*'. Here 'Listening to the voice of conscience would signify being-enjoined by the Other. In this way, the rightful place of the notion of *debt* would be acknowledged, a notion too hastily ontologized by Heidegger

---

[50] Emmanuel Lévinas, *Otherwise Than Being or, Beyond Essence*, trans. Alphonso Lingis (Pittsburgh: Duquesne University Press, 1981), pp. 15, 84, 76.
[51] Ricoeur, *Oneself as Another*, pp. 339-40.
[52] Martin Heidegger, *Being and Time: A Translation of Sein Und Zeit*, trans. Joan Stambaugh (Albany: State University of New York Press, 1996), pp. 248-55.
[53] Ricoeur, *Oneself as Another*, p. 348.
[54] Ricoeur, *Oneself as Another*, p. 350.

at the expense of the ethical dimension of indebtedness'.[55] But how does one retain the ethical injunction inscribed in responsibility, without becoming moralistic at the same time?

Derrida, for his part, opts for a 'mystical'[56] kind of responsibility, a duty 'beyond' either debt *or* duty as they are ordinarily understood: 'In order to fulfil my duty towards God (Derrida's name for the other who calls, *any* other), I must not act *out of duty*, by means of that form of generality that can always be mediated and communicated and that is called duty. The absolute duty that binds me to God himself, in faith, must function beyond and against any duty I have'. This absolute duty appears to operate, in Derrida, as a gift or sacrifice that is beyond 'both debt and duty, beyond duty as a form of debt'.[57]

In a Kierkegaardian meditation upon the story of the sacrifice of Isaac (Gen 22.1-19), Derrida claims that the duty 'beyond' duty is nothing other than the necessity of choosing, like Abraham, between many goods, many 'others' for whom I am originally responsible: *to be prepared to choose between the other and the other, to give to one the gift of death, and to another life.* Paradoxically, the willingness to accomplish this 'absolute duty' also absolves us of every ordinary debt and releases us from every moral duty. And all this *without our knowing why.* Derrida makes Abraham a 'witness' of these things, but a necessarily silent witness who must keep the 'secret' of the absolute because it can never be understood, even by the one witnessing.[58] 'Such, in fact, is the paradoxical condition of every decision: it cannot be deduced from a form of knowledge of which it would simply be the effect, conclusion, or explication. It structurally breaches knowledge and is thus destined to nonmanifestation; a decision is, in the end, secret. It remains secret in the very instant of its performance'.[59] Citing Kierkegaard, who said that if he were to speak of the duty to God he would need to speak in tongues, Derrida claims that the witness to absolute duty is at the essence of that performative he calls, alternatively, 'testimony' or 'faith'.[60] Here the vow is a performative decision which testifies to both the possibility of moral life and the impossibility of a total ethical code. This squares quite nicely, I think, with Ricoeur's citation from Rosenzweig's *Star of Redemption*, where he finds in the *Song of Songs* a form of commandment that is not yet a law, in the pleading of the lover to his beloved:

---

[55] Ricoeur, *Oneself as Another*, p. 351.

[56] Jacques Derrida, 'Force of Law: The Mystical Foundation of Authority,' *Cardozo Law Review* 11 (1990): 919-1045.

[57] Jacques Derrida, *The Gift of Death*, trans. David Wills (Chicago: University of Chicago Press, 1995), p. 63.

[58] Derrida, *The Gift of Death*, pp. 72-3.

[59] Derrida, *The Gift of Death*, p. 77.

[60] Jacques Derrida, 'Faith and Knowledge: The Two Sources Of "Religion" At the Limits of Reason Alone,' trans. Samuel Weber, *Acts of Religion*, ed. Gil Anidjar (London/New York: Routledge, 2002), p. 98.

'love me'.[61] The moment of conviction and of attestation appeals to the power of this singular pleading in conscience, even as it is unable to stabilize some kind of moral *code* by way of response.

1.4 Are Derrida and Ricoeur Compatible on the Responsible Self?

I am creating my discourse on the vow by weaving together the thought of Ricoeur and Derrida. But is this really possible? From a Derridean point of view, does not Ricoeur, with his positing of a 'narrative self' which negotiates the difference between the other and the same, simply repeat the 'Hegelian' dialectic of thesis and anti-thesis which resolves itself into a synthesis? Does he not, therefore, simply repeat the delusory march of metaphysical self-presence through history, thus failing to seriously address that history's aporias? I think not. On the contrary, like Derrida, Ricoeur suspects that history and the self and everything are ultimately resistant to such monadic topologies. This may be seen in what he says about the self in 'postmodern' literature or science fiction, where the classical features of character are all but erased in favour of some kind of stream of consciousness. The effect of such writing is to *erase* a sense of the self as the same through time (character) in favour of a self which is far more contingent and far less accomplished.[62] Ricoeur notes that while these literatures are less 'realist,' in the sense that a self cannot really be a self apart from the permanence inscribed through characterisation, they nevertheless expose our thinking to the question of what the 'existential conditions' might be which make the performance of a self possible in ontological terms. Here he speculates that such literature may reveal an 'inviolable' difference between the self as a singularity and the self as the same through time, even on the level of corporeality.[63]

This is a significant statement, because it shows that Ricoeur, no less than Lévinas or Derrida, is cautious about any attempt to dissolve the thought of self into either narrative *or* metaphysics, if these are conceived as totalities. That is why he ultimately rejects the suggestion of Alistair MacIntyre in *After Virtue*, that a life must be grasped as a singular totality if it is to be experienced as successful or complete. Real life is messy, says Ricoeur. The capacity of a self to master his or her own story in the fashion of a Cartesian *cogito* is virtually impossible on several fronts. First, the memory of origins are hazy at best. Second, one may never experience and assimilate one's own death. Third, many of the key elements of one's life properly belong to the stories of others, such that it is almost impossible to distinguish what is mine from what is another's. Finally, the self can tell a number of different stories about itself at the same time, and each of these may contradict and fracture the others at

---

[61] Ricoeur, *Oneself as Another*, p. 351.
[62] Ricoeur, *Oneself as Another*, pp. 148-50.
[63] Ricoeur, *Oneself as Another*, p. 151.

multiple points.[64]

Why, then, a *narrative* theory? Does not the very idea suggest a totalising intention? Well, no. Of all the models of the real available to us, the category of narrative would seem the most open-ended. Ricoeur's argument here is, I think, undeniable. Narrative cannot, and does not, totalise the real. Rather, it creates a habitable, but always provisional, space in which life may actually be lived. It helps us to organise our experiences and thoughts retrospectively, thus creating patterns of expectation for the future without fixing these in place. In doing this, narrative does not set one individual's monologue over and against others, but forms a discourse in which there are many protagonists and projects, sometimes competing, sometimes agreeing, but always enmeshed.[65] Is this account really all that *crucially* different from the Derridean belief that all of us are always already *inside* a field of meaning—a field which Derrida does not hesitate to call 'ritual'? Even the one who studies the ritual, he says, is 'playing a role' which the ritual allows for, so that the boundary between the critic and the actor is both 'uncertain' and 'permeable'.[66] Perhaps the only significant difference between these two thinkers is, therefore, simply one of emphasis: that Derrida is more interested in the instability of performance, while Ricoeur is more interested in its stability.

2. Vows or Promises Inscribe a Peculiarly Jewish or Christian Sense of the Real

The great etymologist of European languages, Emile Benveniste, testifies to the profound affinity in European thought between the ideas of religion, responsibility, and the vow. In each he locates a deep sense of paradoxical duality. The Latin *sacer* can mean both 'consecrated to a god' and 'affected with an eradicable pollution'.[67] In time, the two concepts attracted two different words. *Sacer* was reserved for a sense of 'implicit sacredness,' while a related word, *sanctus,* was used to denote 'explicit sacredness,' or that which is set aside by human beings as sacred.[68] Similarly, the Greek term *hierós* has to do with an original sacredness in holy things which were believed to be charged with divine presence, while *hósios* was reserved for objects which had more to do with human law and activity, even if that sphere was set apart by the gods.[69] The Latin *religio* has a similarly ambivalent history. Cicero and his followers

---

[64] Ricoeur, *Oneself as Another*, pp. 160-61.
[65] Ricoeur, *Oneself as Another*, p. 162.
[66] Jacques Derrida, *On the Name*, trans. David Wood, Jr. John P. Leavey and Ian McLeod (Stanford, California: Stanford University Press, 1995), p. 3.
[67] Emile Benveniste, *Indo-European Language and Society*, trans. Elizabeth Palmer (London: Faber and Faber, 1973), p. 451.
[68] Benveniste, *Indo-European Language and Society*, p. 455.
[69] Benveniste, *Indo-European Language and Society*, p. 461.

trace it from *legere*, to gather or collect, but Tertullian and his disciples preferred *ligare*, to bind. Buried in the first meaning is the idea of *scruple*, a sense in which there is re-collection, a starting again after careful consideration. The second tradition is more confident, designating a positive *bond* or *obligation* between human beings and God.[70] The bond idea comes up again in the Greek *sponde* or 'responsibility,' which originally meant to give a personal pledge on someone else's behalf. In the Latin *respondeo* there is a drift into the sense of a pledge or bond which responds to another's bond, while the Gothic *swaran* took on the explicit meaning of a vow.[71] But it is the Greek term *eúkhesthai* that interests me most for the investigation at hand. In Benveniste's opinion, the word combines a dual notion: to pray and to make a vow. It gathers together that sense in which a pledge is offered and addressed to the divine, in the expectation that the divine will respond with blessing or a favour.[72]

Derrida recently revisited exactly this etymology in attempting a definition of religion for our contemporary age. Religion today, he says, is a universalising phenomenon that is deeply associated with the Latin language and culture, particularly as it is played out in its Anglo-American manifestation. This 'hyper-imperialist appropriation,' provocatively named '*Globalatinization*,' has, he says, been going on for centuries, but is now absolutely dominant, even as it begins to 'run out of breath' [*essoufflée*]. Interestingly, Derrida avoids the temptation to speak about the more plastic end of this phenomenon ('McDonaldisation,' 'Disneyfication' etc.), noting only that international law and the global political rhetoric are dominated by the Latin sense of religion in general, and Christianity in particular. And what is the essential structure of this religious language and culture? Answer: *sacramentality*, an alliance and 'promise' to testify to a future truth which has itself been promised, and, indeed, has already arrived in the testimony itself. 'The promise promises *itself*, it is *already* promised, that is the sworn faith, the given word, and hence the response'.[73] This is to speak, as Derrida often does, of an essentially 'messianic' or 'apocalyptic' structure to Western thinking. Following Lévinas, Derrida locates in language a sense of promise and expectation which issues, ultimately, in an inbreaking of hyperbolic justice in the face of an 'other'. This inbreaking 'inscribes itself in advance in the promise, in the act of faith or in the appeal to faith that inhabits every act of language and every address to the other'.[74] If Derrida is right (and I wager that he is) then every vow or promise made in a European language is always already inscribed with a fundamentally Jewish or Christian sense of the real. This means, further, that the 'performative' as such—which we have already

---

[70] Benveniste, *Indo-European Language and Society*, pp. 517-22.
[71] Benveniste, *Indo-European Language and Society*, pp. 474-75.
[72] Benveniste, *Indo-European Language and Society*, pp. 489-96.
[73] Derrida, 'Faith and Knowledge,' pp. 66-7.
[74] Derrida, 'Faith and Knowledge,' pp. 56-7.

described as a positing of self in favour of the other—must be seen as an idea indigenous to the Judaeo-Christian tradition. I would like to take a moment or two to explore this thesis.

Hent de Vries believes that Derrida's entire project might be justly characterised as a 'being *on the way* (an *unterwegs* of sorts), not to language (*Sprache*), not to the essence of language, and not to writing, let alone to a science of writing, but rather, to 'God' (*á dieu*) or to what comes to substitute for this name for the totally other, yet another totally other (an incommensurable, totally other 'totally other')'.[75] This is borne out, I think, in Derrida's writings on what is called 'negative theology'. In *On the Name*, Derrida defines negative theology as a language that casts suspicion on the very essence and possibility of language. As a language of *kenosis*—a language which constantly empties itself of final or definitive meaning, even as it produces an infinite number of meanings through iterability—negative theology is also 'the most exacting, the most intractable experience of the 'essence' of language: a discourse on language, a 'monologue' . . . in which language and tongue speak for themselves'.[76] Negative theology 'launches or carries negativity as the principle of auto-destruction in the heart of every thesis,' and yet, paradoxically, 'nothing is more faithful than this hyperbole to the original ontotheological injunction'.[77] This talk of 'faithfulness' implies a promise and an injunction which is always already there, in the language, before the self even has a chance to constitute itself:

> I will speak of a promise, then, but also within the promise. The experience of negative theology perhaps holds *to* a promise, that of the other, which I must keep because it commits me to speak where negativity ought to absolutely rarefy discourse . . . Why can't I avoid speaking, unless it is because a promise has committed me even before I begin the briefest speech? If I therefore speak of the promise, I will not be able to keep any metalinguistic distance in regard to it. Discourse on the promise is already a promise: *in* the promise. I will thus not speak of this or that promise, but of that which, as necessary as it is impossible, inscribes us by its trace in language—before language. From the moment I open my mouth, I have already promised; or rather, and sooner, the promise has seized the *I* which promises to speak to the other, to say something, at the extreme limit to affirm or confirm by speech at least this: that it is necessary to be silent; and to be silent concerning that about which one cannot speak . . . This promise is older than I am.[78]

---

[75] Hent De Vries, *Philosophy and the Turn to Religion* (Baltimore: John Hopkins University Press, 1999), p. 26.
[76] Derrida, *On the Name*, pp. 48-54.
[77] Derrida, *On the Name*, pp. 67-8.
[78] Jacques Derrida, 'How to Avoid Speaking: Denials,' trans. Ken Frieden, *Language of the Unsayable: The Play of Negativity in Literature and Literary Theory*, eds. Sanford Budick and Wolfgang Iser (New York: Columbia University Press, 1989), p. 14.

If It Be Your Will

Here, in negative theology, Derrida locates the source or exemplary instance (he can't decide which)[79] of that doubling or splitting of allegiance to self and other that I have called the 'vow'. On the one hand, negative theology is tied to a faithful repetition of traditional Christian texts. On the other hand, there is an attempt to slough off this sedimentation in response to a call and gift (of Christ?) which seems to come from a 'place' beyond that which the tradition inscribes.[80] In this way, the faithful performance inherent in a vow seems tied to a kind of *un*faithfulness. As we noted in our discussion of otherness, the vow necessarily performs the sacrifice of the other for the sake of another other: this as responsibility, an act and a decision in response to the injunction which comes from 'God' as the wholly Other who is also 'any other'. The *à dieu*, of course, is both a movement towards and a movement away from God, and at the same time.[81] It is a renouncing of God as idol for the sake of loving a God beyond being, an 'other' whose proper name is no more than a trace of a trace, in the tradition of Eckhart's *gelâzenheit*.[82] According to Derrida, the performative is always a participation in this double movement of affirmation and denial, which means, for our purposes, that *the vow* is the example, par excellence, of the 'becoming theological of all discourse'.[83]

3. Christian Worship is an Exemplary Performance of the Vow

Until now, Christian theology has exhibited a distinct indifference to the vow as I have described it. Most of the works written about vows have concentrated on either occasional rites (ordination, vows to become members of canonical religious congregations) or else upon the social or psychological implications of making such vows. As far as I am aware, no work has yet explored the possibility that the ordinary Sunday liturgy of the church, with or without a particular baptismal rite, might be considered a 'performance of the self in favour of the other' in the way that I have described it. The works that come closest to our purpose, not surprisingly, are those that engage the French phenomenological tradition in a redefinition of liturgical action. Amongst these, the most important are works by Jean-Luc Marion, David Power, Kenan Osborne, and Louis-Marie Chauvet.[84] For the purposes of this chapter, I will

---

[79] Derrida, 'How to Avoid Speaking,' pp. 61-2; Derrida, *On the Name*, p. 75.
[80] Derrida, *On the Name*, pp. 71-2.
[81] Emmanuel Lévinas, *Of God Who Comes to Mind*, trans. Bettina Bergo (Stanford, California: Stanford University Press, 1998), p. xv.
[82] Derrida, *On the Name*, p. 74.
[83] Derrida, 'How to Avoid Speaking,' p. 6.
[84] Jean-Luc Marion, *God without Being: Hors-Texte*, trans. Thomas A. Carlson (Chicago: University of Chicago Press, 1991), Jean-Luc Marion, *The Idol and Distance: Five Studies*, trans. Thomas A. Carlson (New York: Fordham University Press, 2001), David Noel Power, *Sacraments: The Language of God's Giving* (New York: Crossroad/Herder & Herder, 1999), Kenan B. Osborne, *The Christian Sacraments of Initiation:*

confine myself to a conversation with Chauvet, beginning with an outline of his theological method, and concluding with an appropriation of his thinking for my thesis concerning the vow.

3.1 Symbols and Method in Sacramental Theology

Chauvet's book *Symbol and Sacrament* presents a theory of sacramental action which listens, attentively, to the thought of the performative. In a statement reminiscent of Derrida's comments on ritual, Chauvet says that 'It is impossible to really comprehend anything without recognizing oneself as always-already involved in what one is trying to comprehend; this is the clearest description we can give of the method of our project.'[85] Out of this conviction, Chauvet proposes what he calls a 'symbolic' account of liturgy over against the more dominant 'metaphysical' approach inherited from Aquinas. A symbolic account, he says, while never entirely escaping its metaphysical determinations, may nevertheless stand as a constant reminder that such determinations are in operation. As such, the symbolic represents a being 'on the way' towards an escape from metaphysical thinking.[86] The way is opened because symbolic analysis is aware of the way in which human subjectivity is constituted *in* and *by* language, as opposed to having or being a series of pre-linguistic properties which are simply expressed *through* language. For the metaphysical mind, language is purely instrumental in that it becomes the means of communication between two separate realities: being in general (as object) and the individual human consciousness (as subject).[87] Symbolic analysis, on the other hand, conceives of reality as linguistic through and through, erasing the gap between subject and object through the specifically *illocutionary* practise of 'reinserting' human subjectivity into the 'language-game' of which it is always already part.[88] This means that the project of human subjectivity must be conceived as an *event* much like language itself. Chauvet is very close to Ricoeur and Derrida here, conceiving of interlocutionary language as that which both precedes and exceeds us, thus structuring our thinking absolutely. As event, human subjectivity therefore possesses (as self-presenting knowledge) no final

---

Baptism, Confirmation, Eucharist (New York/Mahweh, New Jersey: Paulist Press, 1998), Kenan B. Osborne, *Christian Sacraments in a Postmodern World: A Theology for the Third Millenium* (New York/Mahweh, New Jersey: Paulist Press, 1999), Louis-Marie Chauvet, *The Sacraments: The Word of God at the Mercy of the Body* (Collegeville, Minnesota: The Liturgical Press, 2001), Louis-Marie Chauvet, *Symbol and Sacrament: A Sacramental Reinterpretation of Christian Existence*, trans. Patrick Madigan and Madeleine Beaumont (Collegeville, Minnesota: The Liturgical Press, 1995).

[85] Chauvet, *Symbol and Sacrament*, p. 2.
[86] Chauvet, *Symbol and Sacrament*, pp. 8-9, 46.
[87] Chauvet, *Symbol and Sacrament*, pp. 32-3.
[88] Chauvet, *Symbol and Sacrament*, p. 42.

If It Be Your Will

meaning apart from that accomplished in its performance.[89]

But how does this 'symbolic' approach work itself out as a specifically *theological* method? Chauvet claims that theologians are witnesses to a language of relationship in which they know themselves to be already held. They are *themselves* this language already, specifically as that language is instituted in the Scriptures, teaching, and liturgy of the Church. Thus, the question 'who is God?' can never be answered apart from the question 'who is speaking of God?' This is to understand the task of theology as thoroughly hermemeutical in Ricoeur's sense: not the retrieval of some kind of 'original meaning', but the negotiation of new meanings and new practices in an ever-creative repetition of the tradition to which theology is heir.[90] That presumes, of course, that the tradition has to be read and interpreted, that it has to be engaged seriously in all its historical materiality and eventfulness. Why? Because, as Derrida says, both phonemes and graphemes are already given us in our cultural inheritance. They are the material stumbling-blocks against the metaphysical ambition for an ahistorically conceived presence-to-self of total meaning. 'Language *resists* in the same way that *matter* resists'.[91] It is in this sense that Chauvet can say that the key theologal symbol of grace, the pure and unconditional gift of the possibility of life and freedom, is given us in the tradition as a reality that cannot be 'stocked and stored', or otherwise 'objectified' in any way. In the final analysis, while grace may be given in the tradition, it cannot be finally understood by the mind which seeks to totalise that tradition according to some kind of system or economy. Yet (and here is the paradox of Christian faith), grace as a force of resistance has the effect, not of totalising meaning from the side of God, but rather opening a space for human selves to be *agents* in free and innovative action. Chauvet calls this phenomenon the 'gratuitousness' of grace.[92] Innovations in meaning occur, then, because of the movement of ineffable grace in the language of the tradition to which theology is heir. In theological parlance, one might say that it is grace as a redoubling of Derridean *différance* that gives rise to the possibility of interpretive innovation. To interpret, theologically, is to take *responsibility*, to posit a self in favour of the other through an engagement with the tradition.[93] Thus, neither the living self nor the Christian tradition may speak independently of each other. The tradition constantly refigures itself in the

---

[89] Chauvet, *Symbol and Sacrament*, pp. 87-8, 99.
[90] Chauvet, *Symbol and Sacrament*, pp. 65-9.
[91] Chauvet, *Symbol and Sacrament*, p. 141.
[92] Chauvet, *Symbol and Sacrament*, p. 108.
[93] Chauvet, *Symbol and Sacrament*, p. 145. It is important to underline here that while grace, for Chauvet, is only 'comprehensible' within an anthropo-linguistic framework, this should not be taken to imply that there is no extra-linguistic *origin* for grace. Rather, the anthropo-linguistic structure is said to be constituted, by grace, from '*outside of us (extra nos), in Christ*' (p. 140).

performance of new Christian selves, selves that come to be what they are by an interpretive engagement with the many 'others' embodied in that tradition.

An important corollary of this last point, and one that Chauvet emphasises many times over, has to do with the place of the body in theological thinking. Following Merleau-Ponty in *The Phenomenology of Perception*, Chauvet says that the body is a 'speaking body' that communicates in the double-tongue of oneself and another. This is because the body is at once my own, as well as being part of the embodied, material world in general. We have noted this already in Ricoeur. But Chauvet introduces a related insight from the thought of Dubarle: that the body is therefore an 'arch-symbol' of the whole symbolic order. Everything is conjoined and negotiated in the liminal space of the body: 'no word escapes the necessity of laborious inscription in a body, a history, a language, a system of signs, a discursive network. Such in the law. The law of mediation. The law of the body'.[94] In theological perspective, this means that the tradition should be seen as a 'body' of symbols, the corporeal nature of the *humanum* as such, forming a kind of *palimpsest* on which, and by which, the sacred comes to be. '*The anthropological is the place for every possible theological*' says Chauvet. Now, if Chauvet is right, and I believe he is, then this would call for a veritable revolution in the way the various branches of theology have been conceptualised. No longer would 'fundamental' theology be primary, or 'sacramental' theology simply a 'pastoral' application of 'systematic' theology. Rather, sacramental theology, as a reflection upon the ways in which the faith is lived and practiced in the body, would articulate the fundamental 'dimension' that operates throughout the whole thematics of theology, from beginning to end.[95] In this perspective, the specifically sacramental liturgies of the church would constitute the primary symbolic expression and performance of all that the faith has to say, because here the faith *happens*, is an event, in the bodily speech of gestures, postures, spoken and sung words, colours, smells and silences. In the liturgy, according to Chauvet, one may discern the presence and activity of three different *kinds* of body: (1) the *social* body of the church, that set of relations which exists synchronically amongst the people who gather; (2) the *traditional* body of the church, with its diachronically received history of word and deed; (3) the *cosmic* body of the church—in water, bread and wine, wax, light and ashes, textiles and colours etc.—which is received from the earth and imbued with a particular significance. The sacraments are thus made of 'significant materiality'. The meaning of faith may only be experienced and performed *as* bodily, *by* the bodily, and *within* a body which is the church. Thus, according to Chauvet, there is no room within Christian faith for a gnosticism that aims for knowledge apart from the otherness of 'mediation' in history and materiality:

---

[94] Chauvet, *Symbol and Sacrament*, p. 151.
[95] Chauvet, *Symbol and Sacrament*, pp. 159-60.

> In their significant materiality, the sacraments thus constitute an unavoidable stumbling block which forms a barrier to every imaginary claim to a direct connection, individual and interior, with Christ or to a Gnostic-like illuminist contact with him. They represent the indefeasible mediations, beginning with the Church, outside of which there is no possible Christian faith. They tell us that the faith has a body, that it adheres to a body. More than that, they tell us that to become a believer is to learn to consent, without resentment, to the corporality of faith.[96]

Lest it be said that his thought of the body represents a collapsing of theology into philosophy or anthropology, let it be underlined that Chauvet's starting point on this matter, as on every matter, is the New Testament witness. 'To theologically affirm sacramental grace is to affirm, in faith, that the risen Christ continues to take flesh in the world and in history and that God continues to come into human corporality'.[97] Here Chauvet confirms that the Paschal mystery of Christ—the total event of his incarnation, life, crucifixion and resurrection—is for him both the primary sacrament and the pre-eminent criterion for theological discourse as such.[98] What Chauvet reads in that event is the following: that God chooses not to be God apart from the materiality of human beings in their social, historical and cosmic dimensions; that it is in the very nature of God to become human. Indeed, following Moltmann in *The Crucified God* and Jüngel in *God as the Mystery of the World*,[99] Chauvet also insists that God is nowhere more divine than in the humanity of the Christ. There we see a Trinitarian God who is revealed as Love in the very withdrawal of God from God in the death of the Son, which is also an identification by God with the human existential. Here God cannot be God except by a distancing which is also a proximity.[100] In sacramental terms, this would mean that the ordinary liturgies of baptism and of the Eucharist stand as ever-new performances of the Christ-event in Christian selves who act from the power of the Spirit. There, in water, bread, and wine, the Christ event is both given and taken to the worshipping self as the 'other' who also constitutes that self *as* itself.

---

[96] Chauvet, *Symbol and Sacrament*, pp. 152-53.
[97] Chauvet, *Symbol and Sacrament*, p. 490.
[98] Chauvet, *Symbol and Sacrament*, p. 477.
[99] Jürgen Moltmann, *The Crucified God: The Cross of Christ as the Foundation and Criticism of Christian Theology*, trans. John Bowden and R.A. Wilson (London: SCM Press, 1974), Eberhard Jüngel, *God as the Mystery of the World: On the Foundation of the Theology of the Crucified One in the Dispute between Theism and Atheism*, trans. Darrell L. Guder (Edinburgh: T & T Clark, 1983). I will turn to a detailed analysis of the second of these texts in chapters 2 and 3.
[100] Chauvet, *Symbol and Sacrament*, pp. 493-94.

3.2 The Liturgy as a Vow in Favour of the Christic Other

Saint Paul wrote in the letter to the *Galatians*:

> Through the law I died to the law in order to live for God. I have been crucified with Christ and I no longer live, but Christ lives in me. The life I live in the body I live by faith in the Son of God, who loved me and gave himself for me. I do not set aside the grace of God, for if justice could be gained through the law, Christ died for nothing! (2.19-21).

This passage of Scripture is a key source for the development of my central claim in this book. Here the 'I' of the apostolic self is not only decentered, but actually killed off and resurrected otherwise, in an asymmetrical encounter with the historical Pasch of Christ: a history which, in point of fact, is only available to the apostle in the form of a *sacramental and liturgical tradition*. This is made clear by Paul's subsequent reminder that the Galatians were made children of God by being 'baptized into Christ,' thereby becoming 'heirs according to the promise' (3.27, 29). One may speak here of a Christian self which is performed through a ritual identification with the life, death, and resurrection of Christ in the sacramental liturgy of baptism. One may also say that such a self is performed in the displacement of the self by an 'other' self, a Christic self met in the liturgy, which operates according to the logic of a horizon which Paul refers to simply as 'the promise'. This 'promise' is that delivered to Abraham: blessing and a share in the Abrahamic covenant to all who place their 'faith' in that promise (see 3.6-9, 17-18). Derrida could almost have been exegeting these verses when he described the promise as the inbreaking of a messianic justice which 'inscribes itself in advance in the promise, in the act of faith or in the appeal to faith that inhabits every act of language and every address to the other'.[101] In this Pauline context, the performance of the Christian self in baptismal faith is indeed an inbreaking of the 'other,' who comes from the future to problematise the present through an engagement with the past. Expressed otherwise, when Christ comes to the self in baptism as a new self, a substituted self, everything which may have been stabilized as 'law' for that self up until that present is suddenly called into question with regard to its ultimate justice. Suddenly the self finds that the world has turned and relationships have to be broken and remade according to newly revealed ethical criteria. Of course, even with the 'arrival' of justice, justice does not arrive. If the messianic, for Christians, is personified in Christ, then the promissory structure of the liturgy reminds them that the Church lives in the time between the coming of Christ and an/other coming of Christ. The breaking and remaking of the self in baptism is therefore revealed as the structure of the Christian life as such: life as the baptismal undergoing or suffering of the failure of the law in favour of an/other who is always already

---

[101] Derrida, 'Faith and Knowledge,' p. 56.

arriving as grace within the aporias of the law as it stands. In this perspective, the baptismal vow represents a radical repositioning towards the Christic 'other' who is inscribed in the liturgy as a whole. It is not simply the rite of baptism that accomplishes this stance on its own.

The same can be said of the Eucharist. Chauvet understands the Eucharistic rite to be a radical intensification of what the liturgy as a whole is trying to do: to transform the self of the worshipper into a new corporeal form of the crucified and risen body of Christ. Here he draws upon the Lukan story of the road to Emmaus (Lk 24). This story, like many others in Luke's writings, is about the way in which Christian identity is formed: through a letting go of the need to understand God, and an acceptance of the missional movement of God through the embodiment of Christ in the liturgy. The people met upon the road live in the time of the Church, the time when Jesus of Nazareth is no longer visible. They long to touch, to see, to understand a Jesus who is no longer available to such presentation. 'However, the *Absent One* is present in his 'sacrament' which is the Church: the Church rereading the Scriptures with him in mind, the Church repeating his gestures in memory of him, the Church living the sharing between brothers and sisters in his name. It is in these forms of witness by the Church that Jesus takes on a body and allows himself to be encountered'.[102] Thus, the story speaks of a stranger who encounters them with a Scriptural word which functions to deconstruct their understanding of how God works. The word is symbolic of Christ himself, because the word preached is essentially about Christ. It is Christ witnessing to himself in the memory of the Church. The Scriptural body of Christ then becomes flesh in the breaking of the bread, recalling the moment at the last supper when Jesus said 'This is my body, given for you' (Lk 22.19). At this moment, the disciples recognise the stranger, but he vanishes so that their eyes open only upon an absence that witnesses to the presence they have imbibed as bread. The implication is clear: Christ is embodied *as* the mission of the Church, *through* its sacramental liturgy of story and meal.[103] Again, there is a double movement here. On the one hand, faith requires that we 'renounce our ambition to capture Christ in our ideological nets or in the ruses of our desire'.[104] In the liturgy of the church, says Chauvet, there can be no reducing of faith to a system of religious knowledge by which the otherness of God may be negated or changed into an available object or a dead body.[105] By this, the self as propagation of its same self is displaced by the other. On the other hand, the encounter with such an elusive God, a God who is other, is predicated upon the specifically liturgical repetition of an all too human performance of the self in Jesus of Nazareth. Put like that, it becomes clear that the double-nature of the performative self in

---

[102] Chauvet, *Symbol and Sacrament*, p. 163.
[103] Chauvet, *Symbol and Sacrament*, pp. 168-71.
[104] Chauvet, *Symbol and Sacrament*, p. 173.
[105] Chauvet, *Symbol and Sacrament*, p. 174.

liturgy has its theological foundation in a trinitarian Christology of the 'two natures,' reconciled but not synthesised through the mission of the Spirit. That is why the Eucharistic liturgy, and the selves it forms, might be described as 'iconic' in the same sense in which Christ is iconic (Col 1.15). An icon is neither an idol of the divine nor the 'thing itself'. Rather, it symbolizes the divine by bringing human art or making together with divine inspiration such that the divine resonates in the icon without in any sense becoming the icon itself. Thus, the *Letter to the Philippians* can speak of a God who hollows the divine essence out in the human Christ (2.7) and yet comes into his most splendid divinity by the same movement. Here there is a paradoxical becoming of the Godhood of God through a kenotic procession in the human other: God who becomes God through not being God. Is this not how it is with the liturgical self as well? Here the self becomes its most Christic self by losing (loosing) its own centre, by allowing itself to be hollowed out by the absent presence of the other who is God, neighbour, conscience, materiality. The self becomes itself by responding to the call of the other for love, by becoming itself the broken Love which God already is.

Conclusion

This chapter posits a particular view of the vow and of the human self. A vow, we learned, is like a parasite that depends for its very existence upon the hospitality of a particular self. The vow *takes place* in a space the host provides, even though it can never entirely *take the place* of the host. At the same time, the vow appears to arrive in the self as a consequence of the action or address of another agent or interlocutor. Because of the radical alterity of the vow's origin, the host is prevented from controlling or totalising its meaning. The vow is therefore an event whose import or consequence is never entirely completed, whose meaning could always be otherwise other than what it appears to be. It cannot 'be' apart from a hospitable self, yet it implicates and *changes* that self in ways that the self neither intends nor foresees.

We also learned that while the vowed self is constituted by the force of an agency that exceeds and precedes itself, it also possesses a performative power of initiative, whereby it can reinscribe what it receives in genuinely original ways. A self like this is a 'responsible' self, a self in which vowed constancy appears not as a static repetition of the same, but as a dynamic response/ability towards the other from whom, and towards whom, its performance is oriented. In the 'Here I am' the self responds to the call of another with a sense of resolute *decision*. Yet the decision is primarily about an unconditional *transforming with the other* through the twists and turns of an unforeseeable future rather than about *controlling its future being* by means of a contractual conditionality. Indeed, I argued here that a self is not able to really *be a self* apart from the unconditionality of promising. For the moment of promising is also the moment in which the self is posited or attested—not the adding of another to the self after that self has been established in some kind of monadic unity, but rather the self as that *always already* tension between the other and the same.

I concluded the chapter with a move into Christian liturgy. The worshipping self, with its explicit and eschatological genesis in the action of God in Christ, was presented as a paradigm example of the vowed self because it is performed through a ritual identification with the life, death, and resurrection of Christ. Such a self comes to be itself precisely by its displacement in the excessive, living Christ whom the liturgy presents or re/presents. In worship, I argued, the Christian self is posited not as monadic or auto-produced, but rather as a genuinely interlocutionary and responsible self that lives from the ethical (and therefore ontological) priority of God. Participation in the liturgy of the church, we concluded, was therefore crucial for the formation of Christian identity.

The song of Leonard Cohen (cited at the head of this chapter) captures the paradox of the Christian self well. A self that is able to be 'true,' that is, to be a true voice which also speaks or sings the truth, is only able to be that by virtue of its submission to the truth of another. The reference in Cohen to 'this broken hill' as the site of such performance surely recognises the vow as a corporeal repetition of Christ's avowal at the Last Supper and on the hill of Golgotha: 'This is my body, broken for you. Do this to re/*member* me' (Lk 22.19, my emphasis). The song Cohen sings is therefore both a vow and a liturgy, it is the vow as liturgy. In addressing his speech to the other he asks only for the power to repeat that other's address, and so constitute his own capacity to be, to speak, to sing. The power of the 'I' to be itself is therefore predicated upon the basis of another power, the power of another who *lets* it be.

The 'other who lets be' shall be the subject of our investigations in the next three chapters. How can we know that the divine other is actually interested in relationship? On what basis can we know that God's designs on us are genuinely covenantal and unconditional rather than those of a master towards his or her slaves? I will attempt to answer these questions by developing a doctrine of God which emphasises the dynamism and eventfulness of God's relations with the world, and with human beings in particular. My purpose in doing so is to prepare the ground for a more thorough exploration of Christian worship; for it is there, I contend, that the relationship with God is experienced and performed in its most hermeneutically potent way. In worship God is active as a covenanting God who both *calls* and *empowers* human beings to become all they can be through a spiritual participation in the worship already offered by Christ in his life, death, and resurrection. That God, I will argue, is forever 'more' than human being. Still, in the event of Christ *that worship repeats*, God chooses to become vulnerable to the ideological and technological manipulation by which human beings accomplish themselves. This precisely because God is *not* a master or overlord, but an avowed lover and friend.

CHAPTER 2

Divine Metamorphoses:
Thinking about God in Late Modernity

> *A woman drew her long black hair out tight*
> *And fiddled whisper music on those strings*
> *And bats with baby faces in the violet light*
> *Whistled, and beat their wings*
> *And crawled head downward down a blackened wall*
> *And upside down in air were towers*
> *Tolling reminiscent bells, that kept the hours*
> *And voices singing out of empty cisterns and exhausted wells.*
>
> T.S. Eliot[1]

Introduction

This chapter will outline and evaluate some of the more important metamorphoses 'God' has undergone in the last century within the sphere of Western thought, both philosophical and theological. Beginning with Heidegger's penetrating comments about the *co-dependence* of theology and metaphysics, I will argue that modernity has most often produced a very *human-centred* kind of theological thinking which is, at best, only marginally related to the experience of faith in the covenanting God inscribed and promised within Christian tradition and worship. I will note, however, that more recent trends within what has been called 'postmodern' philosophy and theology may prove capable of imagining a God who is, at once, more Scriptural and more contemporary. My closing remarks will reflect on the strange confluence, in much contemporary thinking, between the newer 'poststructural' epistemologies and the knowledge of God made possible by Christian faith.

1. God and Being

1.1 Heidegger's Critique of Onto-theology

In the contemporary attempt to rethink God, Martin Heidegger looms large as a

---

[1] From the poem 'The Waste Land' (1922).

chief shaker of the foundations. In *Identity and Difference* Heidegger argued that dogmatic theology is inseparable from the tradition of Western metaphysics. As the 'onto-theology' of the earliest Greek fathers, Heidegger charged theology with having departed from its 'existential' origins in the New Testament and taking a rather unhelpful lead from the metaphysical philosophy of the Greeks. Metaphysics, that discipline that tries to think the Being of beings as the self-grounding ground of all things, is said to have so infiltrated theology that even God is imagined primarily in terms of *Being*.[2] The difficulty with that move, as Heidegger famously argued in *The Principle of Reason*, is that Being is not really the ground of anything, not even itself.[3] Positively, as I will note at several points in my later argument, this means that a rehabilitated analysis of being may still be of use to theology. Negatively, and insofar as theology continues to understand being as the self-grounding ground of all things, it may well be true that the doctrine of God is thereby collapsed into a version of Being-itself. It was on the basis of that latter conclusion that Heidegger declared the God of Christianity (i.e. the post-New Testament God) to be *no God at all*. According to Heidegger, the God of the Christian churches is nothing more than Leibniz's *prima causa*, the 'First Cause' which functions in metaphysics to ground every other proposition.[4] As such, the God of Christians is not a truly 'divine' god to whom one might direct prayer or worship.[5] A truly 'divine' god, if 'he' exists, could not be objectified or thematised according to the concerns of the metaphysical tradition, because such thematisation would represent nothing more than an exercise in the human creation of God in our own image.[6] Heidegger therefore claimed that it is not metaphysics or theology that is most capable of thinking God, but the atheistic thinking of someone like Nietzsche: 'The god-less thinking which must abandon the god of philosophy, god as *causa sui*, is perhaps closer to the divine God. Here this means only: god-less thinking is more open to Him than onto-theo-logic would like to admit.'[7] In a final twist, Heidegger quipped that Christian theology would do well to stick more closely to its own origins in New Testament faith. Only then would theology be theology pure and simple, largely free of metaphysical distortions.[8]

---

[2] Martin Heidegger, *Identity and Difference*, trans. Joan Stambaugh (New York: Harper and Row, 1969), pp. 55-60.
[3] Martin Heidegger, *The Principle of Reason*, trans. Reginald Lilly (Bloomington: Indiana University Press, 1991), p. 51.
[4] Heidegger, *The Principle of Reason*, p. 26.
[5] Heidegger, *Identity and Difference*, p. 72.
[6] Martin Heidegger, *Contributions to Philosophy (from Enowning)*, trans. Parvis Emad and Kenneth Maly (Bloomington: Indiana University Press, 1999), p.19.
[7] Heidegger, *Identity and Difference*, p. 72.
[8] Martin Heidegger, *The Piety of Thinking: Essays by Martin Heidegger*, trans. James G. Hart and John C. Maraldo (Bloomington: Indiana University Press, 1976), pp. 13-16.

Divine Metamorphoses 33

To summarise, then, Heidegger's critique of God has three parts. First, because modern theology owes its concept of God to the metaphysical investigation of Being, theology's God stands or falls with the metaphysical concept of Being. Here the God/Being of metaphysics is understood to be a product of the representational thinking of human beings, and therefore not 'divine'. Second, because the thought of Nietzsche offered a damning critique of such a God, its atheistic pathway is also capable of 'making room' for a genuinely *divine* God to appear. Third, in order for theology to think this God, it would do well to return to the 'existential' analytic of faith as it is outlined in the New Testament. Let us now investigate each of these themes in turn, noting the ways in which they have been usefully taken up by our three post-Heideggerian thinkers.

1.2. Lévinas: God is not Being

For Lévinas, the question of God is very much related to how the really 'new' enters human thought and history. 'The desire for the new in us is the desire for *the other*' he says: other, that is, than the old, which is 'the habitual, the well-known, the boring, the familiar'. Western thought has from the beginning, he says, been interested in the reinterpretation of past ideas and events by reorienting that past from the point of view of some apparently 'new' idea or insight. The difficulty here is that the apparently 'new' lasts for only a second before it passes, once more, into the same 'old' thing,[9] so that even where a universal history of ever-increasing knowledge is adopted one must ask whether the apparently 'new' is not simply a reconfiguration of the same,[10] in which case the ever-new imaginings of human consciousness would signify nothing more than re-presentations of the constantly present presence of human beings to themselves. Lévinas says this is the history of *being*, a history in which human beings assimilate everything to themselves as a form of self-knowledge.[11]

In order to escape this ever-vigilant synchrony of consciousness, Lévinas says we need a thought which is absolutely alterior to philosophy's vision of history and, somewhat controversially, he locates exactly that in the thought of the Enlightenment philosopher *par excellence*, René Descartes. Lévinas takes the French master's idea of the 'infinite-in-us' to refer to a thinking which aspires to regions beyond that which the finite consciousness can contain, regions unreachable by the movement of human intentionality, yet made available to consciousness by a 'deposit' from 'God'.[12] This deposit, for Lévinas, causes the breakup of that thinking which merely encloses in a presence, re-presents, brings back to presence, or lets itself be. It is a thinking

---

[9] Lévinas, *Time and the Other*, pp. 121-23.
[10] Lévinas, *Time and the Other*, p. 128.
[11] Lévinas, *Time and the Other*, p. 125.
[12] Lévinas, *Of God Who Comes to Mind*, p. 134.

towards the '*in*-finite,' and in both senses implied by that compound: (1) a *non*-finite thought which is nevertheless (2) found *within* the finite.[13] The thought of infinity is phenomenological evidence, for Lévinas, of a 'passivity more passive than passivity' within human consciousness, a passivity toward the pre-history of consciousness and a radical openness to absolute alterity. Alterity arrives, he says, as an interruption of being-present, an interruption so anterior to being and consciousness that it survives there only as a 'trace' of itself.[14] The thought of the infinite would thus be 'older' than consciousness, from an 'an-archic,' or 'pre-originary' origin which makes consciousness possible.[15] Infinity, for Lévinas, is therefore the wholly Other [*tout Autre*][16] which constitutes and yet overflows human being 'at the same time'.[17]

Lévinas' project may be legitimately characterized as an attempt to think 'God' as one who comes from 'beyond' the categories of being and its manifestation in human consciousness and intentionality. Fundamentally, Lévinas wishes to rehabilitate the notion of transcendence—not, as in Heidegger's *Being and Time*, some kind of immanent movement of ontological difference between Beings and beings—but rather as that which is absolutely 'otherwise than being, or beyond essence'. 'Transcendence,' he says, 'is passing over to being's *other*, otherwise than being.'[18]

1.3 Marion: God is not an Idol

It is precisely this notion of Lévinasian *otherness* that has become so influential in the work of philosopher and theologian Jean-Luc Marion. Marion clearly agrees with Heidegger in his assessment of the received Scholastic wisdom, which dominates much Western theology even today, relying as it does on metaphysical ideas about God as the 'first mover,' 'efficient cause,' 'cause of necessity,' 'cause of perfection,' and the like. By invoking these concepts, Western theology has simply become 'atheistic,' according to Marion, because in doing so it has absorbed the Christian and biblical God into a concern for the philosophical grounding and proof of being. He insists that it is metaphysics, not Christian theology, which requires such strategies. For without a supreme being which 'gives the reason for beings in their Being' the whole metaphysical project collapses. The God of onto-theology, says Marion, is simply an *idol*, the fixing of God in a face which, like a mirror, reflects back nothing other than the Being of beings.[19] This notion of the idol as a projective representation of humanity's *desire for grounding* is the key component of Marion's critique of

---

[13] Lévinas, *Of God Who Comes to Mind*, p. 63.
[14] Lévinas, *Of God Who Comes to Mind*, p. 64.
[15] Lévinas, *Of God Who Comes to Mind*, p. 65.
[16] Lévinas, *Time and the Other*, p. 31.
[17] Lévinas, *Otherwise Than Being*, p. 19.
[18] Lévinas, *Otherwise Than Being*, p. 3.
[19] Marion, *The Idol and Distance*, pp. 10-16.

Divine Metamorphoses

onto-theology:

> The idol presents itself to man's gaze in order that representation, and hence knowledge, can seize hold of it . . . The idol depends on the gaze it satisfies, since if the gaze did not desire to satisfy itself in the idol, the idol would have no dignity for it . . . The gaze makes the idol, not the idol the gaze.[20]

This idol-god is therefore a mirror rather than a portrait, but it is a mirror which does not show itself as a mirror, and that is why the power of the idol is so great. 'If the idolatrous gaze exercises no criticism of its idol, this is because it no longer has the means to do so: its aim culminates in a position that the idol immediately occupies, and where every aim is exhausted'. In this way, the idolatrous concept of 'God' consigns the divine to the measure of a purely human gaze and intentionality.[21]

So how might one think God beyond such idolatry? In an echo of Lévinas' idea of the 'Infinite' as a thought which comes to mind from some place 'other' than human intention, Marion claims that Christian theology begins not with the experience of being, but with the God who makes Godself graspable to the extent that God has 'revealed himself.'[22] This is where that radical notion of transcendent otherness comes in. 'God,' says Marion, 'can meet no theoretical space to his measure [*mesure*], because his measure exerts itself in our eyes as an excessiveness [*dé-mesure*].'[23] This should not be taken to mean that there is *nothing* of God in human or created being. Both Ricoeur and Kearney are worried about that tendency in Marion, but I think it is overstated.[24] As we shall see in chapter three, Marion is not really arguing for a radical apophaticism with regard to God, but rather for 'way of eminence' in which a God from *beyond* being may nevertheless be encountered *within* being.

1.4 Jüngel: God is not the Most Perfect Being

If Lévinas and Marion focus their critique upon a God which has been over-identified with Being-in-general, Eberhard Jüngel reserves his peculiarly Protestant critique for a God who towers *over* being as the 'Supreme Being'. Here Anselm's definition of God as 'that than which nothing greater can be conceived,' is taken to be exemplary. What does such a definition imply? asks Jüngel. Answer: God as 'the most perfect being,' and therefore only thinkable

---

[20] Marion, *God without Being*, pp. 9-10.
[21] Marion, *God without Being*, pp. 12-13.
[22] Marion, *God without Being*, p. 36.
[23] Marion, *God without Being*, p. 45.
[24] Paul Ricoeur, 'From Interpretation to Translation,' trans. David Pellauer, *Thinking Biblically: Exegetical and Hermeneutical Studies*, eds. André LaCocque and Paul Ricoeur (Chicago: Chicago University Press, 1998), p. 359; cf. Richard Kearney, *The God Who May Be: A Hermeneutics of Religion* (Bloomington: Indiana University Press, 2001), p. 32.

as one who is incomprehensible to the human mind. Importantly for what will follow in this chapter, Jüngel notes that Anselm's definition has the effect of dividing God into two parts: first into a 'thing' (*res*), a word-sign which dwells amongst human beings and their temporalities; but also into the 'being' (*esse*) which this sign signifies, a being which is 'absolutely other than and beyond the entire world whose existence is defined by space and time.'[25] This amounts to a schematic distinction between God's 'essence' and 'existence,' which, while intended as a purely methodological strategy in Aquinas, nevertheless became catastrophic for the theology which followed him. For the next logical step was to think of God's essence or being (*esse*) as something static and incapable of change, which then called into question the very possibility that God could *exist* in the world of temporalities at all.[26]

To Jüngel's mind, this situation was strongly reinforced by the Scholastic theory of an analogy of being (*analogia entis*) between human beings and God, which Kant retrieves and repeats in the German Enlightenment. According to Kant, when human beings speak of God, they speak only of points of contact between God and the world, rather than about God in Godself.[27] This conclusion is based upon the coalescence of two Aristotelian definitions of analogy. First, there is an *analogy of proportion*, which is a metaphor or transference in language which expresses 'the perfect similarity of two relationships between quite dissimilar things (a:b=c:d). What matters here is not so much the essence of the things themselves, but the *proportionality of the relations* between them. As long as the proportionality of a:b, on the one hand, and c:d, on the other, is *known*, then one can draw a conclusion of proportional equivalence between the two sets of relations.[28] Second, there is an *analogy of attribution*, where analogy is seen as a middling relation between 'equivocity' (equivalence) and 'univocity' (difference). Here it is recognised that there are similarities between things, and there are differences. But the very possibility of such comparison is predicated upon the notion that each of the terms share a particular essence with the first term, to which each is related in its own way (a=b, a=c, a=d).[29] These doctrines of analogy were used by Dionysius, Aquinas and Kant to claim some kind of relation between God and the world: in the first case by claiming that God is to the world as the soul is to the body; and in the second by claiming that God is the unconditioned condition for everything that exists. Jüngel points out, however, that neither strategy actually *works* unless one is first able to demonstrate either that the God is knowable in Godself, or that the precise proportionality between God and the world is already known. Thus, the traditional doctrines of analogy succeed only to underline and

---

[25] Jüngel, *God as the Mystery of the World*, pp. 7-8.
[26] Jüngel, *God as the Mystery of the World*, pp. 106-8.
[27] Jüngel, *God as the Mystery of the World*, pp. 262-63.
[28] Jüngel, *God as the Mystery of the World*, p. 267.
[29] Jüngel, *God as the Mystery of the World*, pp. 269-70.

reinforce the belief that while we might know something of God's 'effects' in the world, we can know nothing of the essence of God in Godself. Here, 'Talk about God does not transcend the human experience which is supposed to be generally known.'[30]

With the 'essential' God out of the picture, 'God' metamorphosed into a word-thing which came to be understood as a product of human desire. *Contra* Lévinas, Jüngel argues that the philosophy of Descartes ends up simply confirming this conclusion rather than challenging it. For the attempt of Descartes to reintroduce a God from 'beyond' human consciousness is done so in the belief that such a God is '*necessary*' as the ground for a continuing sense of identity in the 'I think' which is discovered through methodological doubt:

> Without the certainty of God there is still the self-certainly which was arrived at through doubt, but there is still no assurance of this self-certainty beyond the present moment. The self-certainty which I owe to my doubt must therefore be guaranteed through the assurance of the existence of God. God is necessary as the back-up insurance against my own doubt.[31]

According to Jüngel, the effect of the Cartesian logic is devastating for the onto-theological understanding of God. By reintroducing the God from 'beyond' Descartes succeeds only in showing that the Infinite, too, is a creation of human need. The 'necessary' God, the highest being who guarantees the human project in its fallibility, is a God 'who is appropriated by man; man only has relation to God on his own terms; man is responsible for God.' The difficulty in the Cartesian logic, as Jüngel notes, is that God may now enter into existence only as a presence which allows God to *be,* that is, to be imagined or *represented* as God the Infinite by human beings.[32] The Scholastic division of God into an essence beyond and an existence in human representation is thereby repeated and confirmed, making it possible for moderns to do away with God altogether.[33] It is to *that* possibility, the possibility of atheism, and to the possibilities such atheism opens for the return of a more *Christian* God, that we now turn.

2. 'God is Dead': On the Possibilities of 'Atheism' for Faith

2.1 Which 'God' is Dead?

In the parable of the madman in *The Gay Science,* Nietzsche famously proclaimed the 'death of God'. But it is an odd death, for the messenger arrives 'too early' with the news, even though the murderers are said to be 'we,' a

---

[30] Jüngel, *God as the Mystery of the World*, pp. 277-79.
[31] Jüngel, *God as the Mystery of the World*, p. 120.
[32] Jüngel, *God as the Mystery of the World*, p. 125.
[33] Jüngel, *God as the Mystery of the World*, p. 126.

nomination which apparently includes both the astonished onlookers and the readers of the parable. Furthermore, there is no evidence of the death, no *habeas corpus*.[34] This leads Marion to conclude that while the madman is seeking for a God who is dead, any such God would be no more than an idol. For an idol is precisely a dead corpse and, in Nietzschean terms, no-one can see God until God dies. On this understanding, the way to kill God would be to do exactly as the madman does by the light of his lamp: to return God's gaze, take God into full view, and thus kill him by the power of this idolatrous gaze.[35] For the light which both produces and destroys God, in the Nietzschean imagination, is the light of Platonic reason in an alliance with Christianity. According to Marion, then, the God that Nietzsche intended to destroy is precisely the God of metaphysics, the God who causes and grounds the human project.[36] In this, adds Jüngel, Nietzsche thinks of God as the Infinite who is no longer plausible as being beyond being. He thinks of the death of God as an overcoming of both Christianity and metaphysics, because now the infinity of the horizon is something which human beings in their finitude can move beyond. The horizon becomes 'our' horizon: the opposition between finitude and infinitude is overcome because the latter is collapsed into the former.[37] What this finally means for Nietzsche, then, is that God is no God at all, because God is no longer Infinite. Nietzsche posits, instead, the human 'super-ego' (*Über-Ich*) which has the power to transcend or expand the limits of its own finitude. Here the metamorphosis is complete. The Infinite is transformed into the becoming or emergence of the Superman from its own ground.[38]

There is a profound aporia, then, in Nietzschean 'atheism'. On the one hand, it represents a powerful critique or *Destruktion* of the metaphysical concept of God as a Super-being who grounds the human project. In the wake of *this* kind of atheism, there are indeed opportunities for the arrival of a new God, even the God of the New Testament. On the other hand, Nietzsche also repeats the metaphysical pattern over again with his reconception of humanity in god-like terms. Here the infinite and moralistic God is succeeded by another God who is also a subject, a subject of the 'will to power.' In this later mode, Nietzschean modernity reduplicates the necessity of powerful gods everywhere, even in the human soul.[39] It is the new advent of paganism and a renewed worship of idols.[40] Nietzsche's Zarathustra figure now takes over the god-role of

---

[34] Friedrich Wilhelm Nietzsche, 'The Gay Science,' trans. Walter Arnold Kaufmann, *The Portable Nietzsche*, ed. Walter Arnold Kaufmann (New York: Penguin Books, 1982), pp. 95-6.
[35] Marion, *The Idol and Distance*, pp. 28-30.
[36] Marion, *The Idol and Distance*, pp. 32-5.
[37] Jüngel, *God as the Mystery of the World*, p. 147.
[38] Jüngel, *God as the Mystery of the World*, pp. 149-50.
[39] Marion, *God without Being*, p. 38.
[40] Marion, *The Idol and Distance*, p. 36.

Divine Metamorphoses

'evaluation' or establishing beings in their Being. Such valuation can never countenance a term or reality which comes from elsewhere than its own will to power. This is what is meant by the 'eternal return' of synchrony that we identified earlier in relation to Lévinas: 'The future has nothing better to do than to give again what passes, because nothing passes that the will to power cannot read in its Being as a being to be valued.'[41]

2.2 The Promise of Nietzschean Atheism

If we are to rediscover a genuinely Christian God we must therefore follow the promise of that first part of the Nietzschean paradox. 'The death of the idol frees up a space—an empty space.'[42] This is the space wherein a non-idolatrous kind of divinity may be discerned, a divinity which coincides, in an enigmatic redoubling, with the 'death of God' as it is understood by Paul. For in his essay 'The Anti-Christ,' Nietzsche recognised something that many theologians have still not recognised, even today: that 'God, as Paul created him, is the negation of God.'[43] Here the great thinker recognises that Paul made a new conception of God possible. Unfortunately, Nietzsche then rejects Paul's God as no more than his own creation, for he cannot stomach Paul's talk of a God who dies, whose power is perfected in weakness. Nietzsche's commentary reverberates with disgust: '*God on the cross*—are the horrible secret thoughts behind this symbol not understood yet? All that suffers, all that is nailed to the cross is *divine* . . .'[44] Of this potentially earth-shattering text Jüngel writes: 'how precisely Nietzsche grasped the incompatibility of the Christian understanding of God with the metaphysical concept of God.'[45] In a similar commentary, Marion argues that it is the anteriority of the 'Christian event' that structures 'The Anti-Christ' in spite of itself, by imposing upon it the terms of the debate. Hence, the figure of the 'Anti-Christ' becomes a pastiche on Christ himself, only Nietzsche's christology ends up being a hollowed-out adoptionism in which the Johannine incarnation is only half-complete. The Word, in Nietzsche's astonishing text, never entirely becomes flesh because it is the ghost of metaphysics that finally prevails.[46]

---

[41] Marion, *The Idol and Distance*, pp. 41-2.
[42] Marion, *The Idol and Distance*, p. 36.
[43] Friedrich Wilhelm Nietzsche, 'The Anti-Christ,' trans. Walter Arnold Kaufmann, *The Portable Nietzsche*, ed. Walter Arnold Kaufmann (New York: Penguin Books, 1982), p. 627.
[44] Nietzsche, 'The Anti-Christ,' p. 634.
[45] Jüngel, *God as the Mystery of the World*, p. 206.
[46] Marion, *The Idol and Distance*, pp. 59-60.

3. (Re)turn to the Self-revealing God?

3.1 Heidegger and Luther

When Heidegger argued that Christian theology ought to return to its source in New Testament faith, he assumed that the primary data of theology were not metaphysical at all, but rather revelational. Here the 'already given disclosure' of Christian theology is not simply the historical and cultural forms of the church, but a knowledge of 'Christianness,' which is nothing less than 'faith in the crucified God'. In Christianity, he says, one *knows* this fact by *believing*, which means submitting to the data of the cross 'existentially'.[47] For Heidegger, it is this specifically Christian *Dasein,* or mode of human being, which theology must take as its positive datum, because 'Insofar as theology is enjoined upon faith, it can find sufficient motivation for itself only through faith . . . Theology has a meaning and a value only if it functions as an ingredient of faith.'[48] Thus, while theology is certainly a positive or 'ontic' science in that it reflects on data given historically, it is not a science which may pretend to found or secure the legitimacy of its source after the manner of metaphysics. On the contrary, Heidegger says that theology has no other task or competency than to 'place' believers within the orbit or conceptual world of the New Testament, for it is in the existential of New Testament faith alone that theology has its source and legitimacy.[49]

What are we to make of this analysis? Is Heidegger advocating some kind of naïve Pascalian return to the 'God of Abraham, Isaac and Jacob' over against the 'God of the philosophers'? And wouldn't such a return, even if it were possible, condemn Christian thinkers to a new kind of sectarianism in which the thinking of church and world would be seen as necessarily separate and impermeable? The second question can be answered, I think, only by attending to the first. Is it either possible or desirable that theology know nothing but a Scriptural God, a God revealed in the foundational experiences of Covenant, Exodus, and Pasch?

The first difficulty with Heidegger's schema is that it is historically naïve about the sheer complexity of theology's thinking about being:

> Heidegger ignores the constant pressure exercised on ontology by the thought of a One beyond Being, and by Dionysius's apophatism, which . . . runs through medieval ontology. Even more important, Heidegger completely overlooks the care Thomas takes to situate the Act of Being above every being, making impossible any confusion between this Act of Being and the *ens commune*, that is, the general fact that every being has to be. Also overlooked is the fact that the divine name drawn from Exodus 3.14—*qui est*—remains inadequate for Thomas Aquinas to the sacred Tetragrammaton. In this sense, we ought not to speak of a

---

[47] Heidegger, *The Piety of Thinking*, pp. 9-10.
[48] Heidegger, *The Piety of Thinking*, p. 11.
[49] Heidegger, *The Piety of Thinking*, pp. 6, 12-13.

fusion, much less of a confusion, between God and Being, but of a convergence that *respects the misalignment between the philosophical and the biblical names*.[50]

This proves, at least negatively, that even the Thomist ontology which has been so influential for theology cannot be taken to simply *correspond* to onto-theology in the Heideggerian sense. In the end, Heidegger seeks to expel the revelational God of Judeo-Christianity to a first-century region of historical enquiry, thus ignoring the continuing influence of that revelation beyond its origins.

Clearly Heidegger *did* intend to distinguish between philosophy as an adherence to the manifestation [*Offenbarkeit*] of Being, and (primitive) theology as the adherence to the revelation [*Offenbarung*] of God. For him, the God of philosophy would be some kind of highest being, while the God of an authentic Christian theology is the crucified God.[51] Ironically, Heidegger learned this from the post-New Testament 'region' of the Reformation. Caputo has written of the profound influence of Luther on Heidegger, especially in the reformer's critical distinction between the *theologia crucis* and the *theologia gloriae*. Luther taught that in the cross of Christ God reveals Godself not by metaphysical analogy or by 'approximate ascent through similitudes,' but rather through his opposite, through his back or 'rearward' parts (Exod 33.23). Thus, God is revealed not through the order of the natural world, but through Christ, through the 'perversity and disorder' of his death [*per passiones et crucem*], not through the glory of natural manifestations but rather in the concealment of death and ignominy. Caputo comments that, for Luther, 'The defining feature of Christianity, that which sets it apart from paganism and a merely natural knowledge of God, is the cross, something that is neither visible to the senses nor understandable to reason but that is accessible only to faith.'[52]

3.2 Theology and Philosophy

Yet, despite this Lutheran influence, it should ultimately be recognised that Heidegger saw the data of faith, even New Testament faith, as a modification of pre-Christian *Dasein*, which he declared philosophy more competent to investigate than theology. Philosophy is said to have a 'corrective' function for theology, because theology's 'ontic' concepts are seen to have arisen from a

---

[50] Ricoeur, 'From Interpretation to Translation,' p. 356 [italics mine]. See also the detailed discussion of the relationship between being and theology in David Bentley Hart, *The Beauty of the Infinite: The Aesthetics of Christian Truth* (Grand Rapids, Michigan: William Eerdmans, 2003), pp. 242-48.

[51] Marion, *God without Being*, pp. 62-4.

[52] John D. Caputo, 'Toward a Postmodern Theology of the Cross: Augustine, Heidegger, Derrida,' *Postmodern Philosophy and Christian Thought*, ed. Merold Westphal (Bloomington: Indiana University Press, 1999), pp. 210-13.

pre-Christian 'ontology' of human 'being'.[53] Heidegger appears, then, to place his bets both ways, but the bigger bet is on philosophy. On the one hand he sees theology as a legitimate field of enquiry into a real and privileged experience of God in the Christ event, with the crucified Jesus as its centrepiece. On the other hand, he clearly believes that the Christian experience only becomes *thinkable* with the assistance of philosophy. I am inclined to conclude, as Marion appears to, that Heidegger thereby fails to think either philosophy *or* theology beyond the confines of metaphysics, opting finally for a theology within the limits of being alone: 'Being offers in advance the screen on which any 'God' that would be constituted would be projected and would appear.'[54] And so the question of theology's relation to philosophy remains. What if philosophy were able, somehow, as a consequence of its own history and effort, to transcend or overcome the weight of the metaphysical tradition? Could it then, from its own powers and volition, think a post-metaphysical God? And were this possible, would such a God have any relation to the God of Christian faith, revealed in the event of the crucified Jesus?

3.3 God and the Thought of God

Lévinas, for his part, does not believe it helpful to simply oppose a God of 'faith' and a God of 'philosophy',[55] and this because he conceives post-metaphysical philosophy as, itself, a faith-full kind of thinking. There is a certain identity, he says, between the 'demand, search and desire' of philosophy and the 'bursting of the 'more' in the 'less'' which he does not hesitate to call 'God'. For while the metaphysical tradition conceives the human project in terms of self-identity and self-grounded being, *even here* there is a recognition that with the passing of time and of aging, 'which no-one can either make or prevent,' there is a gradual leaving of this ground, 'a dis-interest which is an *adieu* to the world.' The *adieu* is a crucial concept in Lévinasian thought, for the *adieu* of farewell is also an *à-Dieu*, a thinking 'unto-God'.[56] Here the action of God and the human thought of God meet: 'The *in-* of the Infinite is not a simple negation, but rather time and humanity. Man is not a 'fallen angel who remembers the heavens'; he belongs to the very meaning of the Infinite.'[57] The Infinite, Lévinas' God, is therefore understood as a reality that both 'is' human consciousness and yet bursts out into the 'beyond' of human consciousness as the utterly transcendent. It affects human thought by 'simultaneously devastating it and calling it; through a 'putting it in its place,' the Infinite puts thought in place. It wakes thought up.'[58] We have the beginnings here, I think,

---

[53] Heidegger, *The Piety of Thinking*, pp. 17-20.
[54] Marion, *God without Being*, pp. 69-70.
[55] Lévinas, *Of God Who Comes to Mind*, p. 57.
[56] Lévinas, *Of God Who Comes to Mind*, p. 50.
[57] Lévinas, *Of God Who Comes to Mind*, p. 51.
[58] Lévinas, *Of God Who Comes to Mind*, p. 66.

Divine Metamorphoses

of a genuinely covenantal or sacramental understanding of God, a God who addresses human beings even before they are able to think, and who is constantly arriving at Godself by way of a specifically human passage. 'The difference between the Infinite and the finite is a non-indifference of the Infinite with regard to the finite.'[59]

We note, at this point, that the Protestant theology of the Word speaks in startlingly similar terms concerning the relationship between God and the thought of God, whether that thought be primarily philosophical or theological:

> When thinking endeavours to think God, then the God who is thought has already laid claim on it. What constitutes it as thinking is that it cannot reduce itself to a zero point with regard to God, in order then 'apart from God' (*remoto deo*) to construct a thought of God. It can arrive at something like a thought of God only because thought is already addressed by God.[60]

For this theology, God becomes thinkable because God has *already spoken* in a language we can understand. God has addressed and continues to address human beings in and through a particular human consciousness and experience, the *human* Jesus Christ. Therefore, 'a genuinely Christian theology may only proceed on the basis of the God who is human. While God is indeed free, his freedom determines that God not be God apart from human beings . . . God does not want to perfect himself apart from man.'[61] That would be to move beyond the dead-end of the *analogia entis* into an *analogia fidei* where it is understood that human speech about God is *enabled* by God, *from* God. The coming of God (x) would then be seen as an analogy of advent in the form x:a=b:c, with the understanding that the world relationship (b:c), which of itself can give no reference to God, is now enabled to speak of God as that reality which is more obvious even than itself. This is because God has *really* come to the world in Jesus (x→a), thus 'making use of what is obvious in the world in such a way that he proves himself to be that which is even more obvious over against it.'[62] 'The difference between God and man, which is constitutive of the essence of the Christian faith, is thus not the difference of a still greater dissimilarity, but rather, conversely, the difference of a still greater similarity between God and man in the midst of a great dissimilarity.'[63] It turns out, then, that the thought of God is not something that either philosophy *or* theology can produce in and of themselves. The thought of God is always already made possible by God's address.[64]

---

[59] Lévinas, *Of God Who Comes to Mind*, p. 65.
[60] Jüngel, *God as the Mystery of the World*, p. 158.
[61] Jüngel, *God as the Mystery of the World*, pp. 37-8.
[62] Jüngel, *God as the Mystery of the World*, p. 285.
[63] Jüngel, *God as the Mystery of the World*, p. 288.
[64] DeHart notes that while Jüngel freely uses philosophical language to elucidate the meaning of God, such language is fundamentally refigured by faith in God's address.

Not that this produces any simple identity between the word of God and human words. Let us be clear about that. On the contrary, the address to human beings comes in a fundamentally *interruptive* mode, to which the thought of neither philosophy *nor* theology is entirely adequate. The divine 'Word' confirms us in neither what we already think nor in our illusions of self-presence or mastery. In that sense, the Word of God is our adversary.[65] Paradoxically, though, that interruptive Word is carried into consciousness as a hidden deposit in what *we ourselves* say, experience and think. Ebeling says it well: 'Only by means of a spoken language is it possible to listen to a language which transcends spoken language', and this because 'language is itself dependent upon the fact that the range of the phenomenon of language goes further than it does itself.'[66] The Catholic Marion agrees. In the words of human beings concerning God, there is a redoubling or repeating of the Word already spoken by God. But this is only possible because the Word himself traverses the distance between sign and referent,[67] so dispossessing the human speaker of what they intend in speaking that their words are enabled to return to them as the address of the Other who is Christ. And so we find ourselves returning, again, to the Lutheran theology which influenced, but never finally converted, Heidegger. 'The revelation of God is a revelation in concealment, and indeed in a concealment under its contrary, *absconditus sub contrario*. Consequently, theology cannot be a *theologia gloriae,* but must be a *theologia crucis,* that is, if it is to persevere in the attribution of understanding which is in accordance with the language of faith.'[68]

3.4 The Thought of God as a Faithful Response to Mystery

It therefore seems clear to me that while a post-metaphysical philosophy is certainly not a post-metaphysical Christian theology, or *vise versa*, yet each has profoundly influenced the other's re-definition of human thought as a *faith* response to the concealed-revealed *mystery* of the *other*. This is nowhere more evident, I think, than in the later writings of Jacques Derrida. In an extraordinary passage from his lecture 'How to Avoid Speaking,' Derrida writes about something he calls the 'God effect,' in which all human discourse is said to tend toward the theological. Whenever we refer to an 'other' which is completely heterogenous to, or incommensurable with, the subject of which we speak, then we begin to speak of 'God,' says Derrida, whether God is called by this name or another: 'God's name would then be the hyperbolic effect of that

---

See Paul DeHart, *Beyond the Necessary God: Trinitarian Faith and Philosophy in the Thought of Eberhard Jüngel* (Atlanta: Scholars Press, 1999), p. 3.

[65] Gerhard Ebeling, *Introduction to a Theological Theory of Language*, trans. R.A. Wilson (London: Collins, 1973), pp. 17-18.

[66] Ebeling, *Introduction to a Theological Theory of Language*, p. 87.

[67] Marion, *God without Being*, p. 140.

[68] Ebeling, *Introduction to a Theological Theory of Language*, p. 210.

negativity or all negativity that is consistent in its discourse ... Every negative sentence would already be haunted by God or by the name of God, the distinction between God and God's name opening up the very space of this enigma.' Such discourse, says Derrida, could then be understood to be productive of God, but perhaps also the very *product of God*. One would thus arrive at a kind of proof of God, 'not a proof of the *existence* of God, but a proof of God *by His effects,* or more precisely a proof of what one calls God, or of the name of God, by effects without cause, by the *without cause.*'[69] The God of which Derrida speaks is certainly a post-metaphysical God, because here the divine has been evacuated of the classical properties of ground and causation. Derrida understands God to be an *event* which announces itself *within* human language as that which both proceeds and exceeds human language, and this as 'neither an alternative nor a contradiction.'[70] Thus, he concedes that 'theological' language speaks of a language before language and a history before history. Furthermore, the archaic language of God is also an 'injunction' or 'call' 'which commits (me), in a rigorously asymmetrical manner, even before I have been able to say *I*, to sign such a *provocation* in order to reappropriate it for myself and restore the symmetry.'[71]

But is this Derridean God also a theological God in the sense in which a *Christian* theologian would use that term? Is Derrida's God the God of Jewish and Christian revelation? Yes and no. For, on the one hand, one might interpret such other-centred philosophy as a repetition of the Christian *kenosis* of God, or the baptismal decentring of self in favour of the Christic other who is, at once, God and neighbour. On the other hand, as Derrida makes clear, one might also read here a figuration of the Platonic 'no-place' or *khora*, an empty vessel in which things are promised as the possibility of nomination or address.[72] In the end, according to Derrida, it is perhaps impossible to have the one without the other. For as he believes that Heidegger never ceased to write a very Christian 'God' under the figure of a rehabilitated notion of *'Being'* (Being as that which withdraws from the totalising gaze of beings), so it is impossible to decide which is ontologically prior in the Western tradition—a Greek thinking of the *khora* or the Christian story of God.[73] Indeed, Derrida seems genuinely unsure about the status of his *own* discourse in this regard. Does it concern the non-religious 'transcendental conditions of all discourse'?[74] Or is it religiously

---

[69] Derrida, 'How to Avoid Speaking,' p. 6.
[70] Derrida, 'How to Avoid Speaking,' p. 28.
[71] Derrida, 'How to Avoid Speaking,' p. 30.
[72] Derrida, 'How to Avoid Speaking,' pp. 37-8.
[73] Derrida, 'How to Avoid Speaking,' pp. 59-62.
[74] Jacques Derrida, 'On a Newly Arisen Apocalyptic Tone in Philosophy,' trans. J.P. Jr. Leavy, *Raising the Tone of Philosophy: Late Essays by Emmanuel Kant, Transformative Critique by Jacques Derrida*, ed. Peter Fenves (Baltimore: John Hopkins University Press, 1993), p. 156.

eschatological through and through, continually reaching toward a non-presentable origin and end in the figure of the other?[75] De Vries concludes that, for Derrida, there can be no simple distinction between the general conditions of revelation and its singular instances. Here, 'The singular conditions the general as much as it is conditioned by it. One is the 'element' and the 'effect' of the other.' This serves to resist any simple binary or dialectical logic between revelation as history, and revelation as some kind of transcendent ideality.[76]

This amounts to a 'doubling' of deconstructive philosophy with Jewish and Christian religion. As de Vries says, neither is the source of the other and yet both are the source of the other.[77] That is to confess and decide that Christian theology is sourced and inspired by its own unique experience of God in the Crucified. But it is also to confess and decide, as a matter of faith, that the deconstructive thought of the other, in the work of Lévinas and Derrida, may be uniquely placed to both *critique* and *help* theology as it seeks to articulate that revelation in a post-metaphysical age. For there has *always* been something of God in God's other, as Luther says, even if that sense of God is only able to come to speech in an interpretive language of faith. Obviously, that is to confess and decide that the thought of *khora* ultimately serves the thought of God, even if it does so in the most critical mode possible.[78]

Conclusion

So, where have we come to? Perhaps to this: that the knowledge of *faith* is indeed different from the *epistemological* knowledge proffered by metaphysics. While metaphysics pretends towards the creation of God in the image of an entirely self-referential human consciousness, faith claims a knowledge that, in all its dimensions, is *always already* constituted and possibilised by the address of an/other, God. Thus, even that post-metaphysician who 'rightly passes as an atheist'[79] must decide and confess that some other has constituted and possibilised their thinking even before they intend to think at all. Of course, the precise identity of that other is a matter for ongoing discussion. Whatever one's conclusions, it is nevertheless striking to the present commentator that both philosophers and theologians of the 'post-modern' ilk seem to draw upon a language which is clearly Jewish and Christian in its origin and structure. That could mean, of course, that the self-emptying language of faith witnesses only

---

[75] Derrida, 'On a Newly Arisen Apocalyptic Tone in Philosophy,' pp. 162-68.
[76] De Vries, *Philosophy and the Turn to Religion*, pp. 325-26.
[77] De Vries, *Philosophy and the Turn to Religion*, p. 335.
[78] Richard Kearney, *Strangers, Gods and Monsters: Interpreting Otherness* (London/New York: Routledge, 2003), pp. 200-06.
[79] Jacques Derrida and Geoffrey Bennington, *Circumfession/Derridabase*, trans. Geoffrey Bennington (Chicago: University of Chicago Press, 1993), p. 155.

Divine Metamorphoses

to a transcendental *nothing*. On the other hand, it could witness to a God who has already nominated Godself within the stories of faith. Either way, each discourse is clearly implicated in the other. Each references the other, as in a conversation.

That leads me to conclude that Heidegger was probably right about theology, but in a way he did not, perhaps, anticipate. Theology and philosophy have indeed been entangled with one another from the beginning. Even in the Hebrew Bible, it is clear that Babylonian and Hellenistic thinking provided categories by which faithful Jews could both tell and interrogate their stories in ways rather different from those they had received. However, one may not conclude, on that basis, that the indigenous Jewish faith was thereby subsumed into the structure and agenda of a discourse that was somehow *foreign* to itself. What is more likely is that Jewish faith read and interpreted each new concept encountered in such a way that these ideas actually became *revelatory* in the specifically Jewish sense. That history of reception has, I think, an immense relevance to the discussion at hand. Could it be that theologians and philosophers, whatever their intentions in reading the Western traditions 'otherwise' than they have usually been read, are, in fact, themselves *being read* by the stories of faith which are at the core of those traditions? Could it be that their readings and interpretations, self-consciously *different from* those offered before, are nevertheless the very means by which that anarchic language of faith incarnates itself anew in the world?

If that hypothesis is correct, then the recent 'return' of a Judeo-Christian God to philosophical discourse is not so very surprising as it might appear to be at first. It would also account for the continuing difference *by which* that God returns. As I see it, there are at least three versions of a post-metaphysical God on offer at present. One is the 'ethical' God of deconstructive philosophy, particularly as it shows itself in the Lévinas-Derrida stream of thinking. This is a 'messianic' God who never finally arrives in being or human experience, except as the 'trace' of an immemorial past or an 'impossible' future ethics, because this God is completely and utterly otherwise than being. Here God becomes the name of humanity's desire for, and faith in, an 'other' who constantly escapes our nomination, and yet, rather paradoxically, addresses us in the face of another human being. A second version is that of Jean-Luc Marion who, while affirming the Lévinasian thesis that God is 'otherwise than being,' says that God has nevertheless revealed the divine self to human beings through the 'gift' or 'foreclosed event' of Christ. Thus, while God may never be finally 'thought' in a definitive way, God can indeed be known through the experience and practise of another kind of knowledge, Christ-like love. A third version is articulated by both Richard Kearney and Eberhard Jüngel. For them, God is an incomplete 'event' of love which, while coming from a place beyond being, freely chooses to come to Godself through the humanity of Christ, thus joining the fortunes of human beings to the fortunes of God forever. Crucially, with this last theology, the event of God is said to be a loving unity of life and death in the service of life. The chapter to follow will examine each of these options in more detail.

CHAPTER 3

The Beyond in the Midst:
The God Who is Love

As kingfishers catch fire, dragonflies dráw fláme;
As tumbled over rim in roundy wells
Stones ring; like each tucked string tells, each hung bell's
Bow swung finds tongue to fling out broad its name;
Each mortal thing does one thing and the same:
Deals out that being indoors each one dwells;
Selves—goes itself; myself it speaks and spells,
Crying Whát I do is me: for that I came.

Í say móre: the just man justices;
Kéeps gráce: thát keeps all his goings graces;
Acts in God's eye what in God's eye he is—
Chríst—for Christ plays in ten thousand places,
Lovely in limbs, and lovely in eyes not his
To the Father through the features of men's faces.

Gerard Manley Hopkins[1]

Introduction

In this chapter I will analyse, at length, a number of more recent proposals concerning God, as they appear in what has been called a 'postmodern' theology or philosophy of religion. Three different versions of God emerge from this school of thought, each retaining a critical reference to the witness of the Jewish and Christian Scriptures. First there is the 'ethical' God of deconstructive philosophy, particularly as it percolates through the writings of Lévinas and Derrida. Here the word 'God' refers, in radical undecidability, to both the Infinite who precedes us and to the mysteriousness of another human person. Then there is the God who presents Godself as a gift of love in Christ. Jean-Luc Marion, while affirming the Lévinasian thesis that God may never be finally 'thought' in a metaphysical way, nevertheless argues that God may be known through the conscious imitation of Christ's love. A third version is articulated by both Richard Kearney and Eberhard Jüngel. For them, God is an

---
[1] From the poem 'As kingfishers catch fire' (1888).

incomplete 'event' of love who, while coming from a place beyond being, freely chooses to come to Godself through the humanity of Christ, thus joining the fortunes of human beings to the fortunes of God forever. Crucially, with this last theology, the event of God is said to be a loving unity of life and death in the service of life. God reveals Godself in a *new kind of human experience,* inaugurated and made possible by the crucified and risen Jesus. Having explored these positions at length, the chapter will close with a positive discussion of their theological usefulness for my own proposals concerning the covenant between God and Christian selves.

1. A God Who (Never Entirely) Arrives in the 'Other'

1.1 Lévinas: God is the Infinite

The basic contours of Derrida's 'messianic' God did not emerge out of nowhere. They are already present in Lévinas' great work, *Totality and Infinity*. In keeping with his philosophical vocation, Lévinas there begins his search for God not from a biblical hermeneutics of faith, but from a phenomenology of human desire. Desire, he argues, is a fault line in the totalising vision of being. For desire, even 'metaphysical' desire, is oriented toward the elsewhere, the otherwise and the other. It moves from the familiar, the at-home [*chez soi*], to the unfamiliar outside-of-oneself [*hors-de-soi*].[2] Crucially for Lévinas, desire for the other is never satiated in the sense that bread satiates physical hunger. For desire 'desires beyond anything that can simply complete it.' It is a hunger without term or aim, a hunger nourished only by a greater hunger. Desire is therefore absolute in the sense that it never ceases to be a longing for the 'Desired invisible', which is 'invisible' because it never presents itself to intentional consciousness. So while there *is* a relationship here between desire and the Desired, it is not one in which there can be any adequation of desire to the Desired. 'Desire is desire for the absolutely other', for the alterity of the 'Other' and of the 'Most-High.'[3] Lévinas therefore insists that the relationship with the other cannot be represented, because that which is representable is a repetition of the ontological dominance of being, which never escapes itself, but simply returns to itself over and over.[4] By contrast, 'the absolutely other is the Other' [*L'absolument Autre, c'est Autrui*], someone with whom the 'I' has absolutely *nothing* in common. This other is also the Stranger [*l'Estranger*], one who is free in the sense that the 'I' has no power over him or her. While the 'I' and the other are related, the relation is not one of correlation, but rather of mutual otherness.[5]

---

[2] Lévinas, *Totality and Infinity*, p. 33.
[3] Lévinas, *Totality and Infinity*, p. 34.
[4] Lévinas, *Totality and Infinity*, p. 38.
[5] Lévinas, *Totality and Infinity*, p. 39.

The Beyond in the Midst

It is in connection with the 'absolutely other' that Lévinas introduces the notion of Infinity, adapted, as we noted earlier, from Descartes' third *Meditation*. 'Infinity is characteristic of a transcendent being as transcendent; the infinite is the absolutely other. The transcendent is the sole *ideatum* of which there can be only an idea in us; it is absolutely removed from its idea, that is, exterior, because it is infinite'.[6] The idea of the Infinite is attractive to Lévinas because it excludes the possibility of a relationship in which the other can be thought as a term or object of representation. Lévinas says that the encounter with the Infinite is like Plato's '*delerium*', where a god overwhelms and possesses human thinking so that it is released from custom and convention. 'Possession by a god,' says Lévinas, 'is not the irrational, but the end of the solitary . . . or inward thought, the beginning of a true experience of the *new* and of the noumenon'. The idea of Infinity therefore invokes in the self a desire not for that which can be possessed, but for the *noumenon* which can never be possessed. Only this kind of desire, a desire empty of the need to know or possess, can be truly called 'goodness' in Lévinas' lexicon.[7]

Thus we see the essential reasoning behind the radical Lévinasian refusal of a knowable, thinkable God. If God were known, then God would not be God. God would rather be an idol of our own making, built from the materials of being. It is not for us to know God, but for God to know us. That logic is exemplified in Lévinas' distinction between desire and need. Need is generated by the human being as a drive towards the completion of its own being. Desire, by contrast, is actually generated *by the Infinite* as an aspiration in the human soul.[8]

The relationship of human beings to God must therefore, somewhat paradoxically, be understood as a radical form of philosophical 'atheism'. Why? Because, for Lévinas, the participatory mysticism, or the transportation outside oneself characteristic of positive religious mythology, is hostile to the integrity of both the 'I' and the Infinite. Thus he wants to distinguish the idea of the Infinite from the God of positive religious myth. 'The idea of infinity, the metaphysical relation, is the dawn of a humanity without myths. But faith purged of myths, the monotheist faith, itself implies a metaphysical atheism'.[9] There is a profound irony here, for, according to Lévinas, it is the Judeo-Christian 'Creator' that makes atheism possible.[10] What Lévinas sees in the Judeo-Christian doctrine of *creatio ex nihilo* is the affirmation of a reality in which God contracts into Godself in order to make the world possible as a completely separate and autonomous world, a world that is completely without

---

[6] Lévinas, *Totality and Infinity*, p. 49.
[7] Lévinas, *Totality and Infinity*, pp. 49-50.
[8] Lévinas, *Totality and Infinity*, p. 62.
[9] Lévinas, *Totality and Infinity*, p. 77.
[10] Lévinas, *Totality and Infinity*, p. 58.

need of God.[11]

This is to break radically from the ontology of Parmenides, Leibniz and Hegel, an ontology which sees the ultimate structure of being as that of oneness or unity in being. For that tradition, God and the world began in oneness. Because of a fault or illusion, however, we now see ourselves as fragments which are nevertheless destined to be rejoined in a whole. Lévinas, for his part, refuses to situate the finitude of creaturely life within this teleology of the 'Odyssey'.[12] Instead, reality is conceived as essentially dualistic. The finite is free of the Infinite, though it is the Infinite that makes this very freedom and independence possible.[13] In this consists the essential difference between life conceived as a *dependence* on what is given in being, and life as 'grace'—a 'living from' [*vivre de*] what is given in happy independence.[14] Happiness, Lévinas insists, is not simply a psychological state, but the 'pulsation' of an 'I' in its independence from the totality of being's plenitude.[15]

The relationship of human beings to God is therefore more properly a non-relation, a non-relation that is revealed, paradoxically, in that social encounter which Lévinas famously called the 'face to face'. The face to face with other human beings—particularly with those destitutes the Bible calls 'stranger', 'widow' and 'orphan'—is here understood as the unique means by which the Infinite addresses, calls, and solicits us. This is such an important idea, for both Lévinas *and* Derrida, that I must quote at length:

> The atheism of the metaphysician means, positively, that our relation with the Metaphysical is an ethical behaviour and not theology, not a thematisation, be it a knowledge by analogy, of the attributes of God. God rises to his supreme and ultimate presence as correlative to the justice rendered unto men. . . . The comprehension of God taken as a participation in his sacred life, an allegedly direct comprehension, is impossible, because participation is a denial of the divine, and because nothing is more direct than the face to face, which is straightforwardness itself. A God invisible means not only a God unimaginable, but a God accessible in justice.[16]

Here the Other is not an incarnation or a mediator of God. On the contrary, the face 'signifies' God by being disincarnate, by encountering the 'I' even before it can clothe the face with a form and beauty derived from the unconscious archetypes of being. Thus, the face is actually 'naked' according to Lévinas, naked in a nakedness which eludes the object-cognition of the intentional gaze. Nakedness is also transcendence, a strange destitution [*étrangeté misère*] that

---

[11] Lévinas, *Totality and Infinity*, p. 104.
[12] Lévinas, *Totality and Infinity*, p. 102.
[13] Lévinas, *Totality and Infinity*, pp. 104-05.
[14] Lévinas, *Totality and Infinity*, p. 110.
[15] Lévinas, *Totality and Infinity*, p. 113.
[16] Lévinas, *Totality and Infinity*, p. 78.

interrupts the familiar forms of enlightened knowing with a call to give.[17] This is the birth of ethics, then. In the face of the other, the Infinite measures the 'I' with a gaze which grasps me before I can grasp the other. The Other thus 'imposes himself as an exigency that dominates [my] freedom' and hence is 'more primordial than everything that takes place in me.' 'The Other, whose exceptional presence is inscribed in the ethical impossibility of killing him . . . marks the end of my powers. If I can no longer have power over him it is because he overflows absolutely every *idea* I can have of him.'[18]

It should be noted that Lévinas associates *ideas* with the essentially Greek priority of light and form. That is why he prefers to say that the Infinite is 'signified' in the face, rather than 'incarnated'. The advantage of signification is that the Signifier (here the Infinite or the face) can be said to initiate an interlocution concerning the signified (the world) without thereby proposing itself as a theme *in* that world. Here the Other 'manifests himself in speech by speaking of the world and not of himself,' by *thematising* a world which he can nevertheless remain free of himself.[19] In this perspective, language can be seen as an essentially accusative mode of questioning that issues from the interruptive facing of the other, and thus as a phenomenon that both precedes and interrupts the constitution of the 'I' as a call to obligation and justice.[20] 'The face signifies by itself . . . every explanation begins with it.'[21] I will have occasion to return to this idea in chapter four, particularly as I turn to the idea of liturgical language as some kind of mediator or metaphor of God's action in human action.

One may perhaps summarise Lévinas' approach to the question of God by invoking the idea of messianic time. Messianic time is 'eschatological' time: it comes from a place 'beyond' not only a past or a present, but beyond historical time taken as a whole.[22] Messianic time comes to submit history as a whole ('totality') to the judgement of the Infinite. One must be careful, here, not to mistake the eschatological judgement for some kind of teleological destiny towards which all being is inexorably moving, as in the philosophy of Spinoza or Hegel. That would imply that the eschatological was still part of history, and also, perhaps, that part of history which is yet to happen. In fact, Lévinas reaches for a much more radical idea: the eschatological as that which is certainly *not* history, and yet is the transcendental condition for history's very possibility.[23] Infinity comes to history or the finite, but not as something which the finite can contain or know according to its own unfolding; Infinity comes in

---

[17] Lévinas, *Totality and Infinity*, pp. 74-5.
[18] Lévinas, *Totality and Infinity*, p. 86.
[19] Lévinas, *Totality and Infinity*, p. 96. cf. pp. 195-97.
[20] Lévinas, *Totality and Infinity*, pp. 204-06.
[21] Lévinas, *Totality and Infinity*, p. 261.
[22] Lévinas, *Totality and Infinity*, p. 22.
[23] Lévinas, *Totality and Infinity*, pp. 23-4.

every possible moment as the possibility of that moment being other than it is. Infinity therefore comes to condition subjectivity for hospitality, hospitality for that event which is other than itself.[24] At one point, Lévinas calls that event a 'possible' which history, as history, deems to be impossible.[25] Here the eschatological is *fecund,* and not only as an alternative future. For memory, too, is able to refigure the past for the sake of a present. This demonstrates a power in subjectivity which is other than the power of history to totalise itself, a power which comes from 'beyond' the bifurcation of the possible and the impossible: the secret.[26] God, then, might be called an eschatological 'secret' which gives itself as the possibility of alternative pasts and futures, but never as God's own or essential self.

1.2 Derrida: God is the Secret (or, the Secret is God)

When Derrida talks of God he speaks, in the same breath, of a 'secret' which remains secret even as it is disseminated and repeated in performative testimony. There is a language that faith and belief cannot master, he says, a language that speaks *through* us as testimony [*témoignage,* 'bearing witness'] and yet is not *from* us. 'We testify [*témoignons*] to a secret that is without content, without a content that is separable from its performative experience, from its performative tracing. This would not be a secret that one might detect and demystify.'[27] The secret, he says, is neither sacred nor profane, because it is beyond all such reductions as the condition of their possibility.[28] Because it exceeds the play of disclosure or concealment, the secret can be spoken about *ad infinitum*. But for all that, the secret will *remain* secret, 'mute impassive as the *khora.*'[29] At times, Derrida seems to identify the secret with Plato's thought of the *khora,* that receptacle of nothingness which gives a place for every narrative, and yet does not, itself, become the *object* of any narrative.[30] The *khora* is understood, here, to be some kind of pre-originary spacing or condition of possibility which renders all truth—whether philosophical, religious or scientific—a place to become.[31] At other times, however, Derrida seems convinced that the 'negative theology' of the Christian tradition is equally uncompromising in its respect for the secret. 'Negative theology,' according to Derrida, is a language which names God only to destroy the possibility of the name ever taking 'place,' or gathering to itself any definitive meaning. As such, it signals the *kenosis* of discourse, the impossibility of our

---

[24] Lévinas, *Totality and Infinity*, pp. 27, 23.
[25] Lévinas, *Totality and Infinity*, p. 55.
[26] Lévinas, *Totality and Infinity*, pp. 55-8.
[27] Derrida, *On the Name*, pp. 23-4.
[28] Derrida, *On the Name*, pp. 25-6.
[29] Derrida, *On the Name*, pp. 26-7.
[30] Derrida, *On the Name*, p. 117.
[31] Derrida, *On the Name*, pp. 124-25.

faith-full iterations ever having anything to say about God whatsoever.[32] Derrida argues that while 'negative' theology is inextricably tied to the Christian tradition and its historical language, it is at the same time ever seeking to cast off these 'shackles' in order to render a truth 'independent of revelation.'[33]

Is God, then, the 'secret,' some kind of transcendental condition of possibility? Or is God a story told (amongst others) to give place or expression to that which the 'secret' makes possible without, at the same time, giving up the alterity of the secret? We noted earlier that Derrida reserves judgement on this question. Whatever the answer might be, it is clear that Derrida is unable to speak of God without reference to the Judeo-Christian tradition, in which he sees the 'secret' being figured as the 'otherness' of God or of neighbour in their arrival as from an interminable or eschatological future. These themes are discussed at length in *The Gift of Death*, where Derrida asks why it is that we tremble with fear or dread or panic sometimes. Citing Philippians 2.12, he answers that we tremble without knowing why. We tremble, but as before the 'mystery' or 'secret' of the other: the *mysterium tremendum*. 'Hence I tremble because I am still afraid of what already makes me afraid, of what I can neither see nor foresee. I tremble at what exceeds my seeing and my knowing although it concerns the innermost parts of me, right down to my soul, down to the bone, as we say.'[34] We *work out* our salvation because we are in the hands of, and under the gaze of, a God who asks us to be responsible to God, even though we cannot know God's specific will. 'We fear and tremble before the inaccessible secret of a God who decides for us although we remain responsible, that is, free to decide, to work, to assume our life and death.'[35] If Paul says *adieu* to his own readers and disciples in this manner, argues Derrida, it is because he knows that all people of faith must work and pray in the presence of an 'absent, hidden and silent' God, who asks for obedience nevertheless.[36]

For Derrida, as for Kierkegaard (whose *Fear and Trembling* he is reading at this point), this situation creates an aporia or double-bind with regard to the operation of ethical responsibility. On the one hand, one is called by God to obey God absolutely, singularly, uniquely, and without knowing why. On the other, one is called to account for one's actions before other people. But it is impossible, as Kierkegaard said, to do both. For in the moment that one speaks to another person regarding the meaning or justification of one's actions, one immediately *loses* and *sublimates* the absolute singularity of the divine command. How can one represent the unknown and unrepresentable in terms of

---

[32] Derrida, *On the Name*, pp. 51-6.
[33] Derrida, *On the Name*, p. 71.
[34] Derrida, *The Gift of Death*, p. 54.
[35] Derrida, *The Gift of Death*, p. 56.
[36] Derrida, *The Gift of Death*, p. 57.

the known and speakable?[37] Only, says Derrida, by the sacrifice of that which one loves. The divine command can only be honoured if one is prepared to lose, entirely, the ethical credibility which comes from socially inscribed acts of duty. And that is to sacrifice what one loves in the *name of love*, to sacrifice the legitimate and just demands of some others for the sake of the claims and demands of another 'other'. 'I cannot respond to the call, the request, the obligation, or even the love of another without sacrificing the other other, the other others.'[38] Paradoxically, by being prepared to make a decision, by choosing to obey the divine injunction silently and without explanation, the legitimate debt or duty towards other others is absolved.[39] The God of Derrida is therefore a God who both commands and absolves, and God does so, as we shall see, in and through the figure of the neighbour who faces me.

What is implicit in Lévinas' discussion of the face is made explicit in Derrida's phrase *tout autre est tout autre,* which means 'every other (one) is every (bit) other.'[40] Here there is a play which introduces God as the 'infinite other' into the field of the other as any human other:

> God, as the wholly other, is to be found everywhere there is something of the wholly other. And since each of us, everyone else, each other is infinitely other in its absolute singularity, inaccessible, solitary, transcendent, nonmanifest, originally nonpresent to my ego (as Husserl would say of the alter ego that can never be originarily present to my consciousness and that I can apprehend only through what he calls appresentation and analogy), then what can be said about Abraham's relation to God can be said about my relation without relation to every other (one) as every (bit) other, in particular my relation to my neighbour or my loved ones who are as inaccessible to me, as secret and transcendent as Jahweh.[41]

That is to say that Kierkegaard, with his emphasis on absolute obedience to God, and Lévinas, with his accusative facing of the neighbour, are ultimately united. Both accounts witness to an aporia without foundation, which constantly threatens the surface of ethics and politics, as well as philosophy and theology. Here there is a play of undecidability between God as the infinitely other and God as the neighbour, a play which figures the 'secret' as a God who faces me in the neighbour, and yet is not revealed as God. Here God holds me in the divine gaze, even as I am unable to hold the divine face in my own gaze. Even if I listen for God, God's voice may be heard only in God's other: prophet, postman, angel.[42] But there is another implication, perhaps more radical than even this. If I reverse the self-neighbour bilateral, so that I, myself,

---

[37] Derrida, *The Gift of Death*, pp. 59-60.
[38] Derrida, *The Gift of Death*, pp. 67-8.
[39] Derrida, *The Gift of Death*, pp. 72-3.
[40] Derrida, *The Gift of Death*, pp. 77-8.
[41] Derrida, *The Gift of Death*, p. 78.
[42] Derrida, *The Gift of Death*, pp. 89, 91.

am the face of God for another, then it follows that I, myself, may be the keeper of the divine word or secret. Then we might say, with Derrida, that the name of God is the name of the possibility I have for keeping a secret which is visible for the interior, but not for the exterior:

> Once such a structure of conscience exists, of being-with-oneself, of speaking, that is, of producing invisible sense, once I have within me, thanks to the invisible word as such, a witness that others cannot see, and who is therefore at the same time other than me and more intimate with me than myself, once I can have a relationship with myself and not tell everything, once there is secrecy and secret witnessing within me, then what I call God exists, (there is) what I call God in me, (it happens that) I call myself God—a phrase that is difficult to distinguish from 'God calls me,' for it is on that condition that I can call myself or that I am called in secret. God is in me, he is the absolute 'me' or 'self,' he is that structure of invisible interiority that is called, in Kierkegaard's sense, subjectivity.[43]

Is this to collapse God into the human, after the manner of Feuerbach or Nietzsche? Not likely, for what Derrida crucially retains here is a sense of God as the mysterious other, an other who comes to displace, even dispossess, the self. We discover here an affinity, oft noted in recent times, between Derrida and Augustine. In the *Circumfessions* Derrida speaks about his inability to finally constitute himself as himself, and this because he is the 'last of the eschatologists,' who knows that his suffering arrives as from somewhere else, from another who suffers already.[44] Having suffered a facial paralysis which he associates with the dual trauma of his childhood circumcision and the suffering of his mother before her death, Derrida declares that his is no longer the 'face, the *persona*' that it was before. He has been disfigured, even converted.[45] This testimony of one who has been converted is no longer simply one's own, but that of another in the self,[46] perhaps in the sense of Ricoeur's 'oneself *as another.*' Perhaps Caputo is right to locate a Derridean *theologia crucis* here, repeating as Derrida does the Augustinian grief at the loss of both mother and self to a God who is barely visible.[47] Certainly, Derrida describes this mourning as 'the terror of an endless crucifixion, a thought for all my well-beloved Catherines of Siena'.[48] But is this confession or literary artifice? Is there a difference?

In some senses, Derrida has been making a career out of the claim that there *is no difference* between truth and fiction. The truth *is* fiction in the sense that fiction displaces or takes the place of the secret. Here the secret continually

---

[43] Derrida, *The Gift of Death*, p. 109.
[44] Derrida and Bennington, *Circumfession/Derridabase*, pp. 75-6.
[45] Derrida and Bennington, *Circumfession/Derridabase*, p. 123-24.
[46] Derrida and Bennington, *Circumfession/Derridabase*, p. 147.
[47] Caputo, 'Toward a Postmodern Theology of the Cross,' p. 216.
[48] Derrida and Bennington, *Circumfession/Derridabase*, p. 239.

differs and defers itself in a 'supplement' which is literature itself.[49] Thus the writing of God in theology is, for Derrida, both a making and an unmaking of God. Theology speaks in many voices because no voice manages to capture the God who is 'beyond' the categories of being which language is able to draw upon.[50] Does that mean that theological talk is doomed to failure, that theology is really anthropology, the expression of a desire entirely human but failing to come to its term in God? Not exactly. In keeping with that sense of the other in the self that is so *crucial* to both Lévinas and Derrida, Derrida speaks, finally, of a 'death' of desire in 'absolute desire.' Here the phrase 'desire of God' marks a possibility impossible for merely human desire, the possibility that our desire for God is really the trace of the *desire of God for* us, *in* us, and *toward* us.[51] Of course, there is no way of being certain, one way or the other. Still, Derrida wants to keep open this possibility, the possibility that an eschatological 'tone' might always arrive, 'to come at no matter what moment to interrupt a familiar music.'[52] He notes that the voice of Christ in *The Book of Revelation* promises to 'come' not in the common sense of 'coming to be,' but in the sense that 'I am in the process of coming.' That sense of *process* and of incompleteness is inscribed in the fact that Christ's voice is emitted and sent, in this text, through a myriad of different messengers and scribes, and that it is precisely that process which makes the text an *apocalypse*, an unveiling of truth in its other![53] In religious testimony, then, it is not easy to separate out the 'self' of the speaker, from the 'self' which speaks as another from beyond. We shall make much of this insight in the next chapter.

2. Marion: The God Who Arrives in the Gift of Christ

A second approach to a God after metaphysics is that of Jean-Luc Marion. Marion is a committed Christian thinker who has been profoundly influenced by the work of Lévinas and Derrida. According to Marion, God gives Godself to be known not according to the horizon of being, but according to the horizon of the gift, a gift that provides both the mode and body of the revelation itself.[54] There is only one way in which God gives Godself, argues Marion, and that is by way of the event we know as Christ. For in Christ, God gives himself as from a 'distance,' beyond being, and yet 'crosses' being as an 'excess' of love (*agape*).[55] But the gift does not end with Christ, for Christ speaks and sends himself in two other bodies of givenness: the Eucharist and the Word. Here we

---

[49] Derrida, *On the Name*, p. 28.
[50] Derrida, *On the Name*, p. 35.
[51] Derrida, *On the Name*, p. 37.
[52] Derrida, 'On a Newly Arisen Apocalyptic Tone in Philosophy,' p. 150.
[53] Derrida, 'On a Newly Arisen Apocalyptic Tone in Philosophy,' pp. 156-57.
[54] Marion, *God without Being*, p. xxiv.
[55] Marion, *God without Being*, p. 108.

learn that Christ becomes both a human body and its speech, thus making it possible for human beings to speak of God, and even know God.[56] Marion teaches that the godliness of such speech and knowledge is by no means guaranteed, however, because of the continuing persistence of human beings in their impulse toward idolatry.[57] Let us now trace these ideas in more detail.

2.1 God and the Icon

Crucial to Marion's entire project is the emblematic distinction drawn between the idol and the icon. We have heard about the idol already, noting that in the onto-theology of being human desire projects itself, as a gaze, upon a surface or idea which is made to function like a mirror, so that the surface or object throws back or returns only that light that has been put there by a human intention or need. The icon, says Marion, is identical to the idol in that it is also a material 'object,' and yet it is crucially different because the icon is not the *result* of human vision, but its *provocation*. 'Whereas the idol results from the gaze that aims at it, the icon summons sight in letting the visible . . . be saturated little by little with the invisible.' That is not to say that the invisible comes into visibility by way of some kind of reproduction, but rather that the visible icon is made to 'refer' to something 'other' than itself, namely the invisible *as* invisible. Thus, the icon in fact 'corrects and teaches' the idolatrous gaze so that it is converted towards an infinity.[58]

In Marion's schema, this is precisely the mode in which Christ is said to refer to God by Paul, in Colossians 1.15: '*eikon tou theou tou aoratou*'. The *hypostasis* or *persona* of Christ is not a mere presence, for presence in the sense of being-present is produced by a human gaze. Rather, in the face of Christ, the invisible God gazes upon the faces of human beings, such that their own gazes are 'summoned' into the depths of its invisibility. Thus, the truly iconic face of Christ is a face not so much 'seen' as 'venerated'.[59] In *this* encounter it is the divine that measures humanity, rather than humanity that measures the divine. The result is this: *our* faces become mirrors for the divine gaze, saturated by divinity, such that we reflect the glory of God in the face of Christ (cf. 2 Cor 3.18).[60] Marion adds that the same kind of encounter may occur with regard to ideas and concepts as well. In this mode, 'The only concept that can serve as an intelligible medium for the icon is one that lets itself be measured by the excessiveness of the invisible that enters into visibility through infinite depth, hence that itself speaks or promises to speak this infinite depth, where the visible and the invisible become acquainted.' Here the icon only functions as a genuine revelation of the *divine* if it is able to respect and welcome the *distance*

---

[56] Marion, *God without Being*, p. 4.
[57] Marion, *God without Being*, p. 14.
[58] Marion, *God without Being*, pp. 17-18.
[59] Marion, *God without Being*, pp. 17-19.
[60] Marion, *God without Being*, pp. 21-2.

of the divine from being so that 'union increases in the measure of distinction, and reciprocally.'[61]

2.2 God is Distance

Marion, like Lévinas and Derrida, thinks God at a great 'distance' from being in order to protect God from the idolatrous gaze that would make God into Being or the Supreme Being. Like Heidegger, Marion admires Hölderlin's poetry because, in his view, it writes a kenotic 'withdrawal' of God from being that human beings are called to imitate in order to imagine the truly divine *poetically*.[62] We discussed earlier the withdrawal of *creatio ex nihilo* in Lévinas. Heidegger, for his part, demythologised the doctrine as the ontological difference between Being and beings. In my view, Marion's 'distance' owes more to Lévinas than to Heidegger because he agrees that even in the ontological difference thought cannot free itself from the return or folding of Being. The breakthrough from ontic to ontological is not, therefore, an escape from being's synchrony, but rather the repetition of the truth of being in another mode.[63] Marion emphasises the distance of God from Being by crossing out the word 'God' in his text *God Without Being*. This move expresses, he says, the *freedom* of the biblical God of Exodus 3.14 from variations on the verb 'to be' which might aim to determine God in some way. For that text speaks more of a God who will be as *God* will be. The crossing out thus 'demonstrates the limit of the temptation, conscious or naïve, to blaspheme the unthinkable in an idol'. Importantly, for my own purposes, the crossing-out should not be taken to mean that God has disappeared altogether, that God is unthinkable without remainder. *Au contraire*, God *enters* our thinking as that which exceeds or criticizes our thinking. God crosses out our thought not by a simple absence or difference, but by 'saturation'.[64]

2.3 The Eminent, Excessive God

'Saturation' and 'excess' are cardinal terms in Marion's work. They are what best express his conviction that God gives Godself according to the horizon of the 'gift' rather than the horizon of 'being'. They are also his answer to the question 'How does incomprehension [of God] remain knowledge and not just the failure of knowledge?'

Traditionally, in spiritual theology, there have been two 'ways' or 'paths' to know God. Marion says that each of them has a corresponding phenomenological description. The *kataphatic* (affirmative) way assumes that

---

[61] Marion, *God without Being*, p. 23.
[62] Marion, *The Idol and Distance*, pp. 88-9, 94, 99.
[63] Jean-Luc Marion, *Reduction and Givenness: Investigations of Husserl, Heidegger, and Phenomenology*, trans. Thomas A. Carlson (Evanston, Illinois: Northwestern University Press, 1998), pp. 109, 112.
[64] Marion, *God without Being*, pp. 45-6.

The Beyond in the Midst

the intention to know God is confirmed by a real, worldly, intuition of God.[65] Marion is not convinced, however, judging that the kataphatic way idolatrously repeats Husserl's mistake of making intuition that faculty which actually *supplies* what is lacking in the worldly evidence.[66] The *apophatic* (unknowing) way, on the other hand, assumes that the intention to know God necessarily exceeds all the intuitive evidence one might supply.[67] But that would be an even more naked form of idolatry, according to Marion, for there the thinker would seem to *knowingly* invent a God over and beyond the evidence of intuition. A third way, the way which Marion himself holds to, is what might be called the 'way of eminence'.[68] For the *via eminentiae*, the impossibility of constituting God 'does not come from a deficiency in the giving intuition, but from its surplus, which neither concept, signification, nor intention can foresee, organise, or contain.' The way of eminence would thus be a reversal of the way of unknowing, because now God comes not because of a lack of intuition, but because of an abundance or 'excess' which it receives from the 'outside'. God now comes to 'saturate' intuition with a presence not its own, such that God remains incomprehensible, certainly, but not imperceptible.[69]

There is a call, writes Marion, that comes from a place 'beyond' the call of Being. This call would oblige human beings to 'stand there in favour of another—another favour.' Such a call might even have the power to 'dismiss or submerge the first call issued by the claim of Being'. Indeed, Marion writes of a call within all calls, the call 'as such,' 'the call to render oneself to the call itself, with the sole intention of holding on to it by exposing oneself to it.'[70] How then does one know or experience God? Marion answers in a manner reminiscent of our examination of Ricoeur in chapter 1: *by thinking or being in a mode that is interlocutionary*. For only an interlocutor [*interloqué*] can be a subjectivity which is forever in a state of becoming as from *another* origin. Here the self hears, suffers, and is judged by the claim of the other, and comes to its 'true' self only by way of the responsive 'Here I Am!'[71] Later, in chapter 7, I will argue that this is precisely the position of the one who makes a baptismal vow, whether the avower be human or divine.

Marion's God is one who saturates human intuition as the sheer gift of love, or *agapé* (1 Jn 4.8). For him, that is the only God human beings may think without reducing God to an idol. What is peculiar to love, he says, is that it

---

[65] Jean-Luc Marion, 'In the Name: How to Avoid Speaking Of "Negative Theology",' *God, the Gift, and Postmodernism*, eds. John C. Caputo and Michael J. Scanlon (Bloomington: Indiana University Press, 1999), p. 39.
[66] Marion, *Reduction and Givenness*, p. 16.
[67] Marion, 'In the Name,' p. 39.
[68] Marion, 'In the Name,' p. 24.
[69] Marion, 'In the Name,' p. 40.
[70] Marion, *Reduction and Givenness*, pp. 196-97.
[71] Marion, *Reduction and Givenness*, pp. 200-02.

gives itself unconditionally, that is, without *requiring* that there be either an interlocutor to receive it or an abode of being to accommodate it. Only a gift that transcends *those* conditions is capable of outwitting or dismissing the determinations of being, for 'God can give himself to be thought without idolatry only starting from himself alone: to give himself to be thought as love, hence as gift; to give himself to be thought as a thought of the gift.'[72] Here Marion appears to agree with Derrida. The gift escapes the conditions of being because it cannot be appropriated into an economy of exchange.[73] Where he apparently disagrees with Derrida is on the question of whether such a gift can be described either phenomenologically or theologically, that is, in terms of presence.[74] Derrida says it is impossible to do so, because the moment a gift is described as such it re-enters the economy of exchange, and is therefore no longer unconditional, no longer a gift. Marion, on the other hand, says that the gift can indeed be described as gift, because not all description is at the mercy of the predeterminations of being. Eschatological discourse, for example, escapes such determinations because there neither the giver nor the receiver is entirely present as other things are said to be present.[75] I am in essential agreement with Marion at this point. One might argue, as I will in the next chapter, that with a thoroughly *eschatological* theology neither God nor the self can be said to be 'all there' because they are still coming to themselves through the interlocutionary difference of the other. In that way, the gift-nature of love is preserved. Neither God nor self is able to totalise the meaning-in-being of either self or other. In some sense yet to be determined, each remains, literally, at the other's covenantal *mercy*.

2.4 Outwitting Being by the Gift

Such mercy does not destroy being and its categories, Marion might say, but rather 'outwits' them so that the authority of Being over human thinking is ultimately broken. To achieve that outcome, according to Marion, one needs to 'trick' Being into playing its own game by different rules. And what is Being's game? The game of 'ontic' or 'ontological' difference that Heidegger identified between Being (also called non-being) and beings in their folding and withdrawal. Marion proposes that the way to change the rules of this game is to find another rule which allows the game to be played otherwise, but does not

---

[72] Marion, *God without Being*, p. 47.
[73] Jacques Derrida and Jean-Luc Marion, 'On the Gift: A Discussion between Jacques Derrida and Jean-Luc Marion, Moderated by Richard Kearney,' *God, the Gift, and Postmodernism*, eds. John C. Caputo and Michael J. Scanlon (Bloomington: Indiana University Press, 1999), pp. 59, 62.
[74] For more on this, the reader is advised to consult Robyn L. Horner, *Rethinking God as Gift: Marion, Derrida and the Limits of Phenomenology* (New York: Fordham University Press, 2001), especially chapter 6.
[75] Derrida and Marion, 'On the Gift,' p. 62.

cancel the game altogether.[76] But how does one perform such a thing? He cites the outstanding example in 1 Corinthians 1.26-29. Marion translates the text like this:

> For consider your call, brethren (*ten klesin humon*), namely, that there are not [among you] many wise according to the flesh, not many powerful, nor many well born. But God chose the foolish things of the world, God chose them to confound the wise, and the weak things of the world God chose to confound the strong, God chose the ignoble things of the world [*agene, ignoblia* says the Vulgate] and the contemptible things, and also the non-beings, in order to annul the beings (*kai ta me onta, hina ta onta katargese*)—in order that no flesh should glorify itself before God.[77]

What Marion sees in this text is a 'divine indifference' to the ontological difference. God regards non-beings as beings, and beings as non-beings. That is not to say that God destroys this difference altogether. It is rather 'annulled' [*kartagese*] in the sense of 'distracting' the philosophical orientation towards Being. 'In other words; annulling the fold that bends being to Being, removing being from that through which it is, Being, spreading or unfolding being outside of its unique or universal meaning, that it *is*.'[78] In more concrete terms, while the Corinthian Christians are non-beings in the sense of being 'nobodies' in the eyes of Corinthian society, the apostle asks them to consider their standing not according to that determination, but according to the call of God. Paul's difficulty with the philosophical orientation towards Being is not ultimately, according to Marion, a difficulty with some kind of ontological difference in Being, but rather with the pretension that Being creates its own glory. God responds, according to Paul, by proclaiming that salvation comes not from the self-production of Being in difference, but from the free gift of God in Christ.[79] Here the ontological difference is possibilised by God rather than created in the folding of Being. Beings are no longer seen to be funded and founded on Being, but rather they are called by Christ into a new kind of Being, a being-otherwise which depends not on self-funding, but on God.[80]

This is to understand even Being as a gift from God, following the kenotic pattern given in Christ. 'Through the giving, Being befalls being as the abandonment or the letting that abandons or gives to itself. In this very withdrawal, it manifests its donation.'[81] The gift therefore 'delivers' Being in the sense of putting being into play; but it also 'delivers' being *from* Being or the ontological difference by 'distracting' Being/being from the ontological

---

[76] Marion, *God without Being*, pp. 83-5.
[77] Marion, *God without Being*, p. 89.
[78] Marion, *God without Being*, pp. 89-91.
[79] Marion, *God without Being*, pp. 92-4.
[80] Marion, *God without Being*, p. 95.
[81] Marion, *The Idol and Distance*, p. 235.

difference.[82] This differs from the Heideggerian scheme absolutely. Heidegger always maintained that what gave Being to being was Being.[83] Here the distance between giver, gift and recipient is ultimately erased, and the 'clearing' becomes a place of appropriation without distance. If, however, one insists on the distance between giver, gift and recipient, the giver cannot be so easily appropriated into the fold of Being's clearing. According to Marion, the gift, as a middle term, could then be read as the revelation of infinite distance between recipient and giver. 'Distance lays out the intimate gap between the giver and the gift, so that the self-withdrawal of the giver in the gift may be read on the gift, in the very fact that it refers back absolutely to the giver.'[84] By the gift, the giver is given to be seen, but without losing the sense of distance between the giver and giving.

God, then, is best understood as neither Being nor the highest essence. God is distance, and the gift of distance which is inscribed in the disappearance of God in the crucifixion and resurrection of Christ.[85] In that disappearance, God names Godself *agape,* and declares that all who would know God must root themselves in the same love that was in Christ, as the apostle teaches (Eph 3.18-19). Such love is at once a digging out of personal foundations in Being and a making of room for the gift of divine love which is definitively storied in the distance, and in the Spirited traversing of that distance between the Father and the Son.[86] For Marion, then, it is precisely this analysis of giving which suggests the appropriateness of a specifically *relational* language of Trinity.

2.5 God is Trinitarian Filiation

Marion insists that God is a Trinity of persons who—in their relations to one another across the distance that he calls, in this theological context, 'filiation'— write the meaning of love beyond the determinations of Being. Christ, for Marion, is 'the one who receives in his humanity the divine overabundance and who, so to speak, absorbs its shock in his flesh, to the point where the human and the divine are translated one into the other with neither confusion nor separation.'[87] Christ is the measure of what *human beings* can know or experience of God. In Christ, then, the measure of God becomes a human body which is specifically and strictly 'filial'. Here the distance between the divine and the human is measured as the proximity of a son and a father in their filiation.[88] In Christ, the strange coincidence of the closeness and the distance of God is made known as a filial relationship of love between a father and a son.

---

[82] Marion, *God without Being*, p. 101.
[83] Heidegger, *The Principle of Reason*, p. 86; cf. Marion, *God without Being*, p. 103.
[84] Marion, *God without Being*, p. 104.
[85] Marion, *God without Being*, pp. 104-05.
[86] Marion, *The Idol and Distance*, p. 248.
[87] Marion, *The Idol and Distance*, p. 107.
[88] Marion, *The Idol and Distance*, pp. 108-09.

The glory of the Father befalls human beings only 'obliquely,' says Marion, in the poverty and nakedness of the Son. This shows us that there is 'nothing more properly divine than masked glory and the absence of immediate appearance.' In the poverty of the Son, Jesus is the Father's other. But it is only in the form of his most 'other' other that a God who takes his distance from Being may be fully revealed.[89] The withdrawal and the proximity of God in Christ are revealed in the Pasch of cross and resurrection. 'The cross manifests the withdrawal as distinction, and the Resurrection, the same withdrawal as union.'[90]

2.6 Theology as a logos of the Logos

All of this begs a question, however. Can God become one with human beings without human beings, at the same time, becoming gods themselves, masters of the world and of meaning in a self-present present? Yes, says Marion, because in the Pasch of Christ God traverses the distance from *God's* side, without, at the same time, enabling human beings to traverse the distance from *their* side. This is spelled out most clearly in a comment upon Christ as the Johannine Word:

> The Word, as Said of God, no man can hear or understand adequately, so that the more men hear him speak in their own words, the less their understanding grasps what the words nevertheless say as clear as day. In return, men cannot render to the Word the homage of an adequate denomination; if they can—by exceptional grace—sometimes confess him as 'Son of God,' they do not manage (nor ever will manage) to say him as he says himself.[91]

Here Marion appears to take up Barth's theology of the Word, albeit through the prism of Hans Urs von Balthasar. Christ is figured as the unique Word of God who also says *himself* in human speech in order to make God known and vulnerable. But that is no guarantee that human beings, even as their own speech becomes the speech of God, will necessarily understand all that is being communicated.

Theology, then, must understand itself as a *logos* spoken by the *Logos*. Every theory of meaning generated by theology must be willing to submit itself to a 'redoubling in a capital, intimate, and anterior distance' which recognises that theologians may not pretend to master the meanings that they nevertheless utter.[92] 'In short,' says Marion, 'it is a question of learning to speak our language with the accents—with the accents of the Word speaking it.'[93] In that sense, the Word of God, the Christ event, is like a nuclear explosion in human

---

[89] Marion, *The Idol and Distance*, p. 113.
[90] Marion, *The Idol and Distance*, p. 118.
[91] Marion, *God without Being*, pp. 140-41.
[92] Marion, *God without Being*, p. 143.
[93] Marion, *God without Being*, p. 144.

consciousness which is too bright for us to bear. Yet this explosion leaves 'traces,' in our sacred texts and on our bodies, which are like a 'negative' of the event itself.[94] We cannot guarantee that our signs refer to God from our side. Christ, however, as Word of God, traverses the gap between sign and referent from his side. He speaks himself as a human word which is also God's Word.[95]

2.7 The Gift in Sacramental Form

From there, Marion develops a hermeneutics of liturgy, in Word *and* sacrament, which privileges the action of that which escapes and transforms human consciousness from 'beyond'. In reading Luke's 'Road to Emmaus' story (24.13-49), he concludes that it is finally the breaking of the bread which allows the words of the text to pass to their referent, Christ, who is then recognised by the disciples as the nontextual Word who speaks himself in human words.[96] Here the word and the sacrament appear as each other's condition of possibility: the Word appears in the non-verbal action of the Eucharist as he who has spoken the words of the text. At the Eucharistic moment, the Word does not so much disappear as cause the worshipper to disappear into the Word. Here communicants are 'assimilated by the one they are assimilating'.[97] At this point Marion offers a fresh interpretation of the traditional Catholic doctrine of transubstantiation. The singular advantage of the doctrine, he argues, is its insistence that in the concrete phenomena of the bread and the wine the *ex*/istence of Christ is underlined, that is, the reality of Christ apart from and beyond the intentional consciousness of human beings. In this way, the worshipping community is forced to come to terms with a reality which is entirely 'other' than its own imagination. 'What the consecrated host imposes, or rather permits, is the irreducible exteriority of the present that Christ makes us of himself in this thing that to him becomes the sacramental body . . . Only distance, in maintaining a distinct separation of terms (of persons), renders communion possible, and immediately mediates the relation.'[98]

Furthermore, if the Eucharistic presence is first understood as a *gift* which comes from beyond us, then it may not be understood as some kind of permanently available presence which guarantees all that we do in Christ's name.[99] Eucharistic time, says Marion, is messianic time. The presence of Christ in the Eucharist comes from a covenantal past which, itself, 'bends' the present towards a future which has not yet arrived (see Phil 3.13). Thus, Christ becomes present as a thoroughly incomplete history: a critique and a

---

[94] Marion, *God without Being*, p. 145.
[95] Marion, *God without Being*, pp. 147-48.
[96] Marion, *God without Being*, p. 150.
[97] Marion, *God without Being*, pp. 151-52.
[98] Marion, *God without Being*, pp. 168-69.
[99] Marion, *God without Being*, p. 172.

transformation of the present in favour of its other, a *figura nostra* which is the action of God alone.[100] That is not to say that Christ is not 'real' in the sense that he takes no being to himself in either incarnation or liturgy. On the contrary, in these events Christ shows himself to be 'more than real,' or 'more real than real.' In the Eucharist he is a 'mystical' presence which both possibilises the being of the present, and yet resists the tendencies of that present towards domestication or idolatry.[101]

In this schema, it is participation in the liturgy of word and sacrament that becomes both the guarantee and the contestation of theological hermeneutics. 'The Eucharist requires of whoever approaches it a radical conceptual self-critique and charges him with renewing his norms of thought.'[102] The confession of faith therefore comes from Christ, passes through the believer, and then returns to Christ.[103] Faith is a refusal to master its own self, in favour of the Self who comes from beyond. It is a redoubling in the self of the kenotic movement of divine love which has already made room for our becoming.[104]

2.8 Is Marion's God too Domineering to Enter into Covenant?

We noted, in the last chapter, Richard Kearney's concern regarding Marion's theology. For all God's traversing of distances in order to 'saturate' human being, is this not done so in a way that there is little possibility that human beings might produce a genuine *response* or *responsibility,* as from a free and uncoerced centre of personhood? Despite Marion's protestations to the contrary, Kearney believes that he has done little more than repeat the mistakes of the negative or 'apophatic' tradition, whose God is far too 'transcendent' to enter into a covenantal relationship with human beings. The God of pure gift, he says, does not actually *need* human beings in order to be fulfilled, because once the Word has been given in the saturated phenomena of a burning bush or the Eucharist, there is nothing further that human beings can say or do to make that Word more fully alive in the world. To Marion's idea of mystical bedazzlement Kearney responds with Pauline sobriety. While the Word may come as a thief in the night, we are not entirely in the dark at this coming. There are ways in which we can prepare ourselves so as to be awake, sober and ready. The difficulty with a bedazzling gift is that it is extremely difficult, in the unconditionality of that vision, to discern the difference between *God* and the 'monstrous sublime' of which Slavoj Žižek writes.[105]

---

[100] Marion, *God without Being*, pp. 172-76.
[101] Marion, *God without Being*, p. 180.
[102] Marion, *God without Being*, p. 163.
[103] Marion, *God without Being*, p. 196.
[104] Marion, *God without Being*, p. 197.
[105] Kearney, *The God Who May Be*, pp. 31-4. See also the critique of the unpresentable subject in Slavoj Žižek, *On Belief* (London: Routledge, 2001), especially chapter 2.

While I agree that Marion might well be read that way, especially on the basis of his *God Without Being*, I do think that Kearney has overstated the case somewhat. Even in the text cited, there is evidence to the contrary. Remember, first, Marion's insistence that God does not cancel or wipe out human being by the arrival of the gift. Rather, it is the gift that puts being into play, and this in a way which transgresses the tendency of being, as being, to arbitrarily cancel out the dignity of *some* people in the process of its differential unfolding. A second point is christological. Remember that Marion's Christ is the measure human beings may have of God, and this measure is a 'translation' of the divine into the human and the human into the divine, yet without either confusion or separation. Although it is true that Marion concentrates very much on the divine in Christ, especially as he comes to us in the Eucharistic word of address, it must be remembered that Christ is also, for Marion, the paradigmatic human being. He is what human beings may become, the measure of our possible dignity. The Eucharistic displacement of the communicant self by the self that is Christ should not be read, therefore, as a myth about the enslavement of human beings by God. What is given in Christ is precisely the *withdrawal* of God's power in order to make room for a human offering or *sacrificium* that is both free and spontaneous. It is the Father's *withdrawal* at the point of crucifixion that allows Christ's offering to be both human and free. The gift of the Eucharist, precisely as Christ's body, must therefore be understood as nothing other than a radical act of invitational hospitality by God towards all that human beings may choose to offer by way of response.

Elsewhere, Marion insists that the offering of human beings is simply the free and uncoerced decision to abandon the condition of solitude for the sake of a distance in which a genuine *relation* comes into being. Here the grace of God does not intervene as a 'surplus, illegitimate and incomprehensible, but as a new modality (*tropos*, says Maximus Confessor) of this same will. Thus grace constitutes the most proper depth of the will—*interior intimo meo*—as well as its most intimate stranger'.[106] Thus, there is *plenty* of room in Marion's theology for a free choosing of covenant with God. Grace makes only for a greater human freedom. To return to the example of the liturgy, there the worshippers perform the role of Christ not as an exact replica whose lines are set in stone from on high, but as a *free improvisation* on a given theme. The Spirit is there, says Marion, to help the worshipper like a prompter helps an actor, giving them confidence that they are playing the role aright despite the vast difference between Christ and themselves. 'Distance allows the disciples to become not servants but *friends*, not spectators but *actors* of the redemptive and revelatory action of Christ . . . Thus, as much by the Eucharist as by the gift of the Spirit, the *withdrawal* of the Ascension makes the disciples come unto a perfect, though paradoxical presence in Christ'. 'Presence: not to find oneself in

---

[106] Jean-Luc Marion, *Prolegomena to Charity*, trans. Stephen Lewis (New York: Fordham University Press, 2002), p. 65.

the presence of Christ, but to become present to him (to *declare* oneself present, available) in order to receive from him the present (the gift) of the Spirit who makes us, here and now (in the present), bless him like he blesses the Father—until and in order that he return'.[107] The language Marion utilizes in this passage is unmistakably covenantal. God empowers and makes possible. Yet it is still necessary that human beings both choose and act in order for the blessing of Christ to become their own blessing.

3. Jüngel: God in Becoming

3.1 Theology Thinks after Faith

Like Marion, Jüngel insists that God must be thought from the evidence of the Christ-event alone, for that event is normatively the self-revelation of God. According to Jüngel, it is nonsense to suppose that one can think the Christian God through some kind of philosophical theology which brackets out the specifically Christian evidence of the biblical texts and of faith. Theology must think God from the experiences of God which these texts preserve and promise.[108] That means that theology, as a thinking 'after' faith, assumes a number of hermeneutical 'decisions' or 'presuppositions' even before it begins. First, it believes that the meaning and structure of thought itself may only be arrived at by first thinking God as the Christian God. Second, the task of thinking God is guided by a possibility given in a 'very special experience of God,' an experience that claims a more general validity. Third, the possibility for thinking God is guided by the biblical texts which proclaim that the place of God's conceivability is a Word of address which precedes all human thinking.[109] The 'special experience of God' of which Jüngel speaks is that of Jesus of Nazareth:

> To believe in Jesus means to understand him as that person through whom and in whom God has become definitively accessible. Our access to God is thus understood as God bringing us to himself. Therefore, that event in which one comes to the thinking of God is also to be understood as an event in which God brings us to himself, 'retrieves us.' The thought of God results from this event, and is not therefore its presupposition.[110]

Jüngel therefore disputes the claim of philosophy that one needs to determine the anthropological 'conditions' for access to God before one may discover if it is really *God* who is made known in Jesus. He would rather decide what human beings are, and what they are capable of knowing, on the basis of the revelation

---

[107] Marion, *Prolegomena to Charity*, p. 145 [italics mine].
[108] Jüngel, *God as the Mystery of the World*, p. 154.
[109] Jüngel, *God as the Mystery of the World*, pp. 154-55.
[110] Jüngel, *God as the Mystery of the World*, p. 155.

in Jesus. As God clearly *addresses* human beings in that revelation, human beings may then be defined as fundamentally *addressable beings*, beings set free by God to be addressed not only by God, but also by 'everything and everyone,' even the powers which make for evil.[111] Theologians must proceed on this path, says Jüngel, because of Paul's statement in 1 Corinthians 1.18ff that the word of the cross is foolishness to both Jews and Greeks. This word implies, he says, 'a radical break with the thought of God which appears to be presupposed as generally valid.'[112]

3.2 Thinking God from God

This does not prevent Jüngel from engaging with philosophy in sophisticated ways, for what the Christ-event reveals, amongst other things, is that God has finally chosen for *being* over non-being. That God is not only 'above' the contradiction between being and non-being, but also '*in the midst of*' this contradiction is, he says, the whole point of Christian god-talk.[113] Amongst the many consequences of this claim is a new definition of what is reasonable, a definition that contradicts the thought of onto-theology entirely. Reason is rational, he says, when it comprehends that it cannot construct God out of itself, when it comprehends that God is thought as *God* only on the basis of what God has revealed about Godself.[114] The idea of God's self-revelation implies, of course, that God is 'going on ways to himself' which travel into regions at some distance from God, regions which include the region of human beings, and which the Bible calls *creation*. The thinkability of God is therefore predicated upon a God who takes human beings along with God on God's 'ways'.[115] Of course, if human language were seen as merely informational, referring to God as to some substance entirely absent from human speech about God, then thought of God would indeed be impossible. But Jüngel sees human language as essentially *sacramental*, that is, performative and relational, which means that human words about God can also be the presence and activity of God's own self. In the *event* of language, he argues,

> the being of some content is expressed in language in such a way that it addresses the being of a person and summons that person out of himself through the word that addresses him, and in the word which addresses him that person is brought to himself or perhaps divorced from himself. In the language event what happens is that a person is drawn together into the word, and there, 'outside himself' (*extra se*), he comes to himself in the other word.[116]

---

[111] Jüngel, *God as the Mystery of the World*, p. 155.
[112] Jüngel, *God as the Mystery of the World*, p. 156.
[113] Jüngel, *God as the Mystery of the World*, p. 35.
[114] Jüngel, *God as the Mystery of the World*, p. 158.
[115] Jüngel, *God as the Mystery of the World*, p. 159.
[116] Jüngel, *God as the Mystery of the World*, p. 11.

This reading again suggests that speech about God may be understood as an interlocutionary event that brings God and human beings together 'lingually and thus really.' If God is not, as for philosophical theology, a substance somehow entirely beyond us, then it is indeed possible that God could be amongst us in the word-event of address. Now, that is precisely what the Gospel of John claims when it says that Jesus is the Word of God become human flesh. This is no communication from a God whose essence is somehow elsewhere. Rather, God's own subjectivity becomes present and active in Jesus. Here God tells us not *about* Godself, but rather enfolds and implicates human beings into God's own becoming (see Rom 4.17, Jn 1.14). In this way, Christian theology ties itself to a listening to Jesus as the very self-revelation of God, a word in which God goes out from Godself in and as the *humanity* of Jesus.[117] Theologically, then, the Christian is not free to understand God except on the basis of Christ's humanity.[118]

3.3 Beyond the Necessary God

This *humanity* of God has profound implications for any doctrine or theory of God.[119] Perhaps the most surprising of these, given Jüngel's insistence on a theology from revelation, is the *theological* discovery that God is *not necessary*. As we noted in the last chapter, Jüngel is amongst those who characterise modernity as a thought concerning human beings as the centre and measure of all things, beings who are able to secure themselves apart from God as the necessary ground or first cause. In this perspective, human beings can be human apart from God, who then becomes, at best, the product of legitimately human needs or desires. Now, while that conclusion is clearly the result of a long *philosophical* process, Jüngel claims it is a legitimate *theological* conclusion to draw as well.[120] He cites Bonhoeffer, who asserted in his *Letters and Papers from Prison* that the existence or non-existence of God is irrelevant to the way human beings must now live their lives. God as the ground and reason for human existence and endeavour is no longer *necessary* in this strictly metaphysical sense.[121] Jüngel, for his part, sees that conclusion as eminently positive for theology, because now theology can think a more biblical God, a God who is *more than necessary*.

The opposite of metaphysical necessity is not some kind of accidence, argues Jüngel, for the idea of accidence still depends upon the idea of necessity

---

[117] Jüngel, *God as the Mystery of the World*, pp. 12-13.
[118] Jüngel, *God as the Mystery of the World*, p. 14.
[119] Jüngel's reflections on God's humanity of course owe a great debt to the later Karl Barth. See, for example, Karl Barth, *The Humanity of God*, trans. John Newton Thomas and Thomas Wieser (Richmond, Virginia: John Knox Press, 1960), pp. 37-65. Compare DeHart, *Beyond the Necessary God*, pp. 5, 6.
[120] Jüngel, *God as the Mystery of the World*, p. 18.
[121] Jüngel, *God as the Mystery of the World*, pp. 19-20.

in order to be meaningful. Neither should the phrase 'more than necessary' be understood quantitatively as 'necessary and more than necessary.' Instead Jüngel argues that God is 'not necessary *because* more than necessary.'[122] A more-than-necessary God would be a God without metaphysical grounds, a God who disposes over being and non-being alike, rather than being derived or posited from them. Thus, while the possibility of non-being in late-modern philosophy may indeed raise the question of God, it cannot, as a matter of necessity, lead to God's existence. If God exists, then such existence may be affirmed on the basis of God's self-revelation alone, not on the basis of metaphysical necessity. God, if God exists, comes from God alone.[123]

This phrase, 'God comes from God' is a more positive, motivated and determined form of the traditional idea of God as the unconditioned *mysterium tremendum*, which we have already met in Derrida.[124] It is to imagine God not as an *arbitrary* otherness, but as a free personal centre who *decides* to come to Godself through the concrete human history of Jesus of Nazareth. Jüngel argues that God, far from being a foreign and indifferent other, freely determines Godself for no other 'place' than 'the human existence of the man Jesus, in order to be *God* in and with this man . . . While God is indeed free, his freedom determines that God not be God apart from human beings.'[125] But this means that God cannot be thought apart from the perishability implied by the *cross* of Jesus. Citing Hegel, Jüngel insists that the crucifixion of Jesus effected not only his human, but also his divine nature.[126] For Hegel had argued, in his *Lectures on the Philosophy of Religion*, that Christ's death was also the death of God. There the human event of death is understood to be a moment in God's own becoming, so that the relation of God to God's other may also be seen to be a relation to *Godself*-as-other. From this insight, Hegel developed a doctrine of the Trinity, a doctrine clearly grounded in the biblical story of the passion.[127]

It is important to note at this point that in spite of his admiration for Hegel's achievement, Jüngel is nevertheless uncomfortable with that oft-cited tendency in Hegel to absorb human beings into the history of God as a universal Spirit. Here human beings ultimately become divine; they lose their identity and dignity as human beings who may choose to be *fully human*, but certainly not divine.[128] 'To say that God does not desire to come to himself without man posits a permanent difference between the human God and the human man . . .

---

[122] Jüngel, *God as the Mystery of the World*, p. 24.
[123] Jüngel, *God as the Mystery of the World*, pp. 33-4.
[124] Jüngel, *God as the Mystery of the World*, pp. 35-6.
[125] Jüngel, *God as the Mystery of the World*, p. 37.
[126] Jüngel, *God as the Mystery of the World*, p. 77.
[127] Georg Wilhelm Friedrich Hegel, *Lectures on the Philosophy of Religion: The Lectures of 1827*, trans. R.F. Brown, Peter C. Hodgson, J.M. Stewart and H.S. Harris, One Volume ed. (Berkeley: University of California Press, 1988), pp. 468-70; cf. Jüngel, *God as the Mystery of the World*, p. 93.
[128] Jüngel, *God as the Mystery of the World*, p. 95.

The dignity of the subject consists of the fact that he is nothing more than man, to whom nothing human but everything divine is alien. By contrast, God, as the subject who in his love is always free, bears in his own being the fatal godlessness of man and is thus in his deity also human.'[129] The more promising possibility of the Hegel lectures, according to Jüngel, is the thinkability of a God who comes to Godself in perishability and temporality.[130] Let us look carefully at the relationship between these two terms.

3.4 The Cross of Christ: God's Perishability and Possibility

What Marion leaves in the margins of his work, Jüngel brings to the centre: the cross of Christ as a place of mutual vulnerability between God and human beings. The best place to think the *perishability* of God, according to Jüngel, is in Paul's 'word of the cross,' because there God addresses human beings under the thoroughly 'ontic' conditions of a Here and Now without finally submitting to the logic of their identity.[131]

If one understands the divinity of God out of its unity with the poverty and of the existence of the Crucified One, then God's being can no longer be thought as infinite in contrast with every finitude, and certainly not as independence in contrast with every dependence, and obviously not as eternity which excludes time, nor as a highest essence which does not know nothingness. The God who is in heaven *because* he cannot be on earth is replaced by the Father who is in heaven in such a way that this heavenly kingdom can come *into the world*, that is, a God who is in heaven *in such a way* that he can *identify himself* with the poverty of the man Jesus, with the existence of a man brought from life to death on the cross.[132]

Here the metaphysical God is confronted absolutely. Against the privileging of presence in an eternal Now, constructed by metaphysics as a buffer against the threat of non-being, the word of the cross posits a temporality in which the certainty of death signifies not the threat of nothingness, but the 'limitation of the real'. The more positive meaning of perishability, for Jüngel, is the *possibility* of a new kind of being *beyond* the limits of the real, a possibility which is actually hidden in the real already. This possibility makes the present take on a new meaning. 'Disclosed presentness insists not only on that which is real, but also exists out of the possible, and toward the possible.'[133] While metaphysics privileges actuality (*energeia*) over potency (*dynamis*), the word of the cross insists, says Jüngel, on the priority of potency or possibility over actuality. History could then be read as a story of possible pasts, presents, and

---

[129] Jüngel, *God as the Mystery of the World*, p. 97.
[130] Jüngel, *God as the Mystery of the World*, p. 187.
[131] Jüngel, *God as the Mystery of the World*, p. 191.
[132] Jüngel, *God as the Mystery of the World*, p. 209.
[133] Jüngel, *God as the Mystery of the World*, pp. 212-13.

futures which does not permit what is past to become nothing.[134] It is possibility, according to Jüngel, that permits both non-being and being at the same time. Possibility might therefore be called, in the language of the Bible, a *promise* which addresses the present from a place which is ontologically prior to both being and non-being.[135] There are clear resonances, here, with both Derrida and Marion.

On the basis of the word of the cross and the resurrection, one might then say that God's being is that which possibilises both being and non-being, but this in order to struggle against the final victory of non-being by the way of love. By suffering in Godself the full effects of non-being, God reveals that, despite appearances to the contrary, non-being is finally unable to overcome the power of possibility. In this manner, the nihilating designs of nothingness are annihilated. In the paschal events, Jüngel discovers a God who is forever beyond Godself in being *for* human beings; and who is therefore self-differentiating in God's identification with the human struggle. The shorthand term for the former is *love,* and for the latter *Trinity*. 'As the one who is different from nothingness, God is also the one who is related to it . . . The being of love unites love and death in that in the event of love life goes beyond itself.' [136] In the addressing word a God who comes from elsewhere actually summons the human self to an outside-itself which is also the outside-itself of God. The crucified is here understood as the *extra nos* of God in which we experience our own *extra nos*.[137] In the crucified, temporality as an absolute present is re-experienced as a future which has already come, a distance which paradoxically de-secures self-certainty and self-grounding in favour of a new kind of certainty from God.[138]

3.5 The Cross of Christ: Creating New Human Selves

The advent of God therefore explodes the metaphysical determinations of both space and time. While the addressing word *is* 'Here' and 'Now,' says Jüngel, it places the Here and the Now in a new relation with each other so that they can no longer simply be identified with each other. 'It gives the Now, so to speak, space beyond the point of Here and it gives the Here time beyond the point of Now.' This is because of the capacity of an addressing word to refer the 'ego-now-here' to a place and time *beyond* the ego-now-here such that the person addressed is carried elsewhere. 'Thus the dimension of an existential distance is asserted through which the ego is set in its relationship to its own 'Here and Now' in such a way that together with the spatial difference of Here and Now,

---

[134] Jüngel, *God as the Mystery of the World*, pp. 213-15.
[135] Jüngel, *God as the Mystery of the World*, pp. 216-17.
[136] Jüngel, *God as the Mystery of the World*, pp. 218-21.
[137] Jüngel, *God as the Mystery of the World*, p. 183.
[138] Jüngel, *God as the Mystery of the World*, p. 184.

the Now is encountered by the past and the future.'[139] That is not to take the ego *entirely* out of its here and now, but rather to place within its very identity a difference which is revealed in the phrase 'the Here *in* the Now,' a difference which reveals that the present is always already a temporal space in which the ego approaches itself from *elsewhere*. Thus, the word of address from God makes the present possible as a precisely *temporal* present, a present which comes to itself out of a past and toward a future, a present which is therefore grounded not in itself but in the word of address.[140]

The address of God therefore problematises the metaphysical notion of the human self as a self-grounding presence in the 'I think'. The address distances the ego from itself, taking it into what Jüngel calls an *'eschatological spiritual presence,'* which amounts to a new way to be present in the world. 'The old has passed away; behold, the new has come.' (2 Cor 5.17). This has the effect of 'destroying or negating' every dimension of the here and now which is focused on itself, and for itself, alone.[141] From now on, the ego can have a 'new experience with experience' in which experience, as the product of representation and a tendency towards non-being, is experienced anew or transfigured from its beginning to its end.[142] The movement one makes from anxiety to gratitude is therefore not of one's own making. Rather, it is a *miracle* which comes from God.[143] Faith, though a thoroughly human phenomenon (which may be studied phenomenologically), should be understood as an experience and knowledge that ultimately comes from God. It is God's gift towards the possibilisation of a new self-definition for the subject who chooses to receive it.[144] In this is the substance of the covenant between God's call and the response of human faith.

3.6 Humanity Becomes Itself in God's Becoming

So what kind of God is this God who addresses us? According to Jüngel God is here-and-now, but not in such a way that God is collapsed into the self-presence of the representing ego. Rather, God goes out of Godself in order to address us; and that address has the consequence of taking us out of ourselves as well, such that we meet with God in a distance which is also closer to us than we are to ourselves.[145] Thus, for faith, there can be no 'God with us' (*deus pro*

---

[139] Jüngel, *God as the Mystery of the World*, p. 172.
[140] Jüngel, *God as the Mystery of the World*, pp. 173-4. The influence of Heidegger's reflections on time is unmistakable at this point.
[141] Jüngel, *God as the Mystery of the World*, p. 175.
[142] Jüngel, *God as the Mystery of the World*, p. 32.
[143] Jüngel, *God as the Mystery of the World*, p. 33.
[144] In this, Jüngel follows Bultmann's essentially Pauline understanding of faith over and against the Platonic view that faith is mere opinion. For Bultmann, and Jüngel, faith is a genuinely human knowledge which nevertheless has its genesis in God's address. See DeHart, *Beyond the Necessary God*, pp. 22-4.
[145] Jüngel, *God as the Mystery of the World*, p. 182. There is an echo here of

nobis) or 'God in us' (*deus in nobis*) without a more fundamental distancing of the human self from itself. It is the person who lives outside of his or herself who is identical with the nearness of God, a nearness defined most specifically in the event of the cross.[146]

In the Paschal event of crucifixion and resurrection, God shows Godself to be an infinite abundance: an overflowing of non-being by being, an overflowing of actuality by possibility. In this abundance, God shows Godself to be ex/istent in God's very essence. God constantly comes to Godself by going out from Godself into God's other. One must say then, with Karl Rahner, that the economic Trinity *is* the immanent Trinity.[147] The designation of God as 'mystery' should not therefore be attached to any seeming aporia between 'natural' and 'revealed' knowledge of God, as is the case for onto-theology in its severing of God's existence and essence.[148] Rather, as in the New Testament usage of the term, mystery should be understood as a secret which remains secret even as it discloses itself: 'A true mystery draws us to itself and into its confidence. It allows itself to be known in confidence *as* a mystery. The mystery is therefore the subject of the process of letting itself be grasped: it *reveals* itself *as* mystery.' In the New Testament, the mystery is Christ, and Christ is made known as the speech of God which is also human speech.[149] Not that this speech leaves human speech as it was. It is 'parabolic speech,' a paradigmatic form of address in which common understanding is interrupted and transformed by the playfulness of a naming which is far from necessary. It was not necessary to call Jesus 'God's Son,' says Jüngel. And yet 'In such talk, a certain reality is expressed through *possibilities* in such a way that this possibility leads forcefully to the discovery of a new dimension of reality and to greater precision in talk about what is real. Metaphors and parables thus express more in language than was real until now.'[150] Here I note another clear parallel between Jüngel and Marion. Recall that Marion, also, imagines God as an excess of divinity over being, an excess which reveals itself, within the humanity of Christ, to be 'more real than the real.'

The parable of Christ is also, therefore, a *sacrament* in that it allows the hearer to find an eschatological refiguration of his or her own life in the story of another.[151] By participating in the eschatological story of Christ, a human person comes to participate in the power of becoming in God's own possibility. Paul speaks of the word of the cross as the 'power of God' (*dunamis theou*)

Augustine's *Confessions*.

[146] Jüngel, *God as the Mystery of the World*, pp. 182-84.

[147] Karl Rahner, *The Trinity*, trans. Joseph Donceel (Tunbridge Wells, Kent: Burns and Oates, 1970), Jüngel, *God as the Mystery of the World*, pp. 223-24.

[148] Jüngel, *God as the Mystery of the World*, pp. 249-50.

[149] Jüngel, *God as the Mystery of the World*, pp. 252-54.

[150] Jüngel, *God as the Mystery of the World*, pp. 290-91.

[151] Jüngel, *God as the Mystery of the World*, p. 309.

which *surpasses* reality *within* reality (1 Cor 1.18).[152] Crucially for my thesis concerning the covenant, this power of God is, for Jüngel, not a power-*over*, but a power-*with* and a power-*for*. It is the power of *love*, which Jüngel defines in a densely meaningful phrase as 'the event of a still greater selflessness within a great, and justifiably very-great self-relatedness . . . the event of the unity of life and death for the sake of life.'[153] Let us finish, then, with an exploration of what this statement might mean.

3.7 The Trinity: Covenant Love Embodied

Jüngel notes that the Johannine nomination of God as 'love' occurs in a context which insists that the specific character of this God, and this love, is made known in the coming of Jesus *in the flesh*. The opponents of this claim apparently argue that there is a fundamental difference between the heavenly Christ who belongs to the Father and the earthly, fleshly Jesus (1 Jn 2.22). But the Johannine author claims, on the contrary, that it is those who deny the earthly Jesus who also deny God (4.3). The main purpose of this polemic, according to Jüngel, is to establish *the being of God as love* on the basis of God's identity with the earthly Jesus.

That is not to say that God and love are somehow distinguishable from each other, that God *expresses* a love. No, John claims that God *is* love, which is possible only if God can be both lover and beloved at the same time. God's *being* as love is therefore revealed, according to John, in the sending of Jesus into the world as the beloved 'other' who is also at one with the Father. This is not the self-love of a solitary ego, but the differentiated love of a Father and a Son. The Father can only be love in that he subjects himself to all that is not love in his beloved Son, a Son who has become closer to the Father than the Father is to himself. Thus, God is not 'in love,' but the 'radiated event' of love itself. This means that 'God has himself only in giving himself away . . . That is how he *is*. His self-having is the event, is the history of giving himself away and thus is the end of all self-having'. God's own self *is* this history, says Jüngel. The historical love of the Father and the Son is not a symbol of the essence of a God who is hidden somewhere 'beyond' history, but the very essence of Godself.[154]

From here Jüngel moves towards a doctrine of the *Trinity* as an explication of the being of God as covenant love. For it is the Spirit, according to Jüngel, who enables the Father and the Son to participate in mutual love, even at the moment of their most radical separation. Because God is Spirit, God can remain God even as the Father gives up his Son to death, thus *turning toward all who are human*, all who suffer and die. Because God is Spirit, the Father can remain in relationship with his Son even in the distance of death; and by

---

[152] Jüngel, *God as the Mystery of the World*, p. 310.
[153] Jüngel, *God as the Mystery of the World*, p. 317.
[154] Jüngel, *God as the Mystery of the World*, pp. 326-28.

that connection also *draws human beings into the life of God.*[155] The doctrine of the Trinity might therefore be understood as the vitality of God through and beyond death, and this not in contradistinction from the history of human beings. The Trinity is, rather, God's history *with* humankind as well as being God's own historicity. It is the story of the *becoming of God.*[156] As such, the greatest mystery of God is that God does not yet *have* Godself any more than the world has itself. Both are waiting for the eschatological coming of God which the world cannot see because that coming is a surpassing and critique of the world's desire for self-possession. God is a mystery for the world because the world is not yet empty enough to become full of God.[157]

4. Kearney: The God of Passage

The correspondences between Jüngel's *God as the Mystery of the World* and Kearney's *The God Who May Be* are astonishingly plentiful given that the latter book does not refer to the former even once.[158] Kearney shares Jüngel's concerns absolutely, writing passionately about a post-metaphysical God who has not yet arrived, a God of the possible rather than the actual, a God who has tied the divine destiny to human beings in irrevocable ways. Both see the biblical accounts of Jesus as somehow revelatory of the way that God *is,* in Godself, rather than as merely symbolic of the way that God acts upon or affects the world. They also share a preference for story and metaphorical surplus as more promising vehicles for the divine-human encounter than talk about a God either 'beyond' or 'otherwise' than being. Finally, and most importantly, they agree that *love* is the primary metaphor or parable for God, not because human beings make their own experience of love into God, but because in Christ God has shown us the way of love in such a way that we read there the very nature of Godself.

4.1 The God Who May Be

Kearney begins with a definition of God as that which 'neither is nor is not but may be.' What he intends with this definition is to confront the onto-theological notion of God as being or actuality with a God of eschatological possibility.[159] Not that such a God has nothing to do with being at all. Rather 'The divine possible takes its leave of being having passed through it, not into the pure

---

[155] Jüngel, *God as the Mystery of the World*, pp. 328-29.
[156] Jüngel, *God as the Mystery of the World*, pp. 344-47.
[157] Jüngel, *God as the Mystery of the World*, pp. 377-78.
[158] A connection does exist, however. Paul Ricoeur, who supervised Kearney's doctoral work in Paris, has written that Jüngel's *God as the Mystery of the World* represents a theology that successfully avoids the temptations of a new foundationalism of the self. See Ricoeur, *Oneself as Another*, p. 25.
[159] Kearney, *The God Who May Be*, p. 1.

ether of non-being, but into the future which awaits us as the surplus of *posse* over *esse*—as that which is more than being, beyond being, desiring always to come into being again, and again, until the kingdom comes.'[160]

As a poet, as well as a philosopher, Kearney chooses to make his case by reading the story of the encounter between Moses and God in Exodus 3. There, when Moses asks the divine voice what its name is, the reply comes in Hebrew: *'ehyer 'asher 'eyyeh* (Exod 3.15). This reply has, of course, fascinated philosophers down through the centuries, particularly in its dominant translations as *ego eimi ho on* (Greek), *ego sum qui sum* (Latin), and, in English, *I am who I am* or *I am he who is*. In each of these cases, the Tetragrammaton appears to partake in the semantic field of the verb 'to be,' in either its constative or conditional mood. The usual interpretation has been either that God is here reducing Godself to a metaphysics of being or presence, or is refusing to do so absolutely.[161] Thus, the dominant reading is ontological to the core. According to Kearney, Augustine and the Latins argued that there was no fundamental difference between the *ego sum qui sum* and the *esse* (being) of metaphysics, while the medieval scholastics saw the formula as a way of speaking about the *vere esse, ipsum esse* (Being-itself). Indeed, in the hands of the two influential schools, God was divided into two. Echoing Jüngel's analysis, Kearney notes that God became first an essence (*nomen substantiae*, who God is for Godself), and then an existence (*nomen misericordiae*, who God is for us). The first, pure *ousia* or *essentia*, is hidden behind the second, and it is the first that the Exodus account is said to be about. Augustine said that the essential, hidden God cannot and does not change. Aquinas took this further, turning the immutable Being into the first cause and reason for every creature. Such a being necessarily cannot have either a past or a future, says Kearney, and thus is without movement, change, desire or possibility. Such a being is of course a long way removed from the fluctuations of history and perspective that human beings inhabit. Thus, according to this metaphysical school of thought, we cannot know what God is, in Godself; we can only know *that* God exists. The Exodus name is here said to guarantee both the singularity and the incommunicability of God. In this way, Kearney concludes, scholasticism conflates its own God with the biblical God absolutely. Of course, it is only a short step from that conflation to the '*mystical ontologism*' in which the divine and human are also conflated. For if God is the Being of all beings, then we are all One.[162]

To this ontological interpretation Kearney opposes what he calls an 'eschatological' notion of God, which issues from a more exegetically sensitive reading strategy. Here it is noted that the divine self-naming occurs within the horizon of a 'call,' a summoning of Moses to a divinely ordained mission.

---
[160] Kearney, *The God Who May Be*, p. 4.
[161] Kearney, *The God Who May Be*, p. 22.
[162] Kearney, *The God Who May Be*, pp. 22-4.

Moses is therefore summoned as towards an eschatological horizon. Kearney cites Rabbi Solomon ben Isaac (1040-1105), often called Rashi, who rendered the Exodus name as 'I shall be what I shall be.' Rashi apparently read the name as a promise to Moses that God would be 'with' both him and all the Hebrew people as they went about their future mission of liberation, a mission entrusted to them by God. This God is not a 'once-off' deity, but one who promises to *remain* and *become* with God's people, whatever the future may bring. Rashi claimed that the promissory nature of the name also helped to ensure the fidelity of the people toward God, just as God had promised fidelity toward them.

There is a sense here of the vulnerability of the God who covenants, for the success of the covenant appears to depend as much on the people themselves as on God. Here God's 'I shall be' calls for and requires Moses' 'Here I am' if it is to enter history and blaze a path toward the kingdom. Kearney has great sympathy with this reading, noting that its more dynamic sense of context pushes aside the dominant syllogistic and substantialist interpretations of the verb 'to be' in favour of function and narrative.[163]

Another insight from exegesis supports this conclusion. It seems likely that the quest for a divine name was, at the time when this text was written, a quest for that secret name of power by which one's enemies would be defeated. The refusal of a stable, proper name could then be read as a refusal on the part of God to be co-opted and used for magical purposes. In God's refusal to become an idol, God guarantees for himself a future agency. In this past century, both Buber and Rosensweig thought as much.[164] Kearney concludes that the name is therefore '*both* an I that is identical with itself in its past *and* a Thou that goes forth into the future.' It reveals God but also commits God to a future which is historical and human. 'This is why the name is both theophanic and performative. It serves as the pre-name and the sur-name of that which cannot be objectively nominated. And it is that excess or surplus that saves God from being reduced to a mere signified—transcendental or otherwise.' Henceforth, God is a 'saving-enabling-promising God' who is neither too close nor too distant. God gives the promise unconditionally as a gift; but that means that it can only be received as an *unconditional* gift. This makes God's being in the world very vulnerable.[165]

4.2 God Becomes God With and For Us

Kearney has a strong sense of the God who is vulnerable, who is with us, who shares our human history. The Exodus story, he says, is the inauguration of this shared history. From that point onwards, God is one who '*becomes with us.*' The becoming takes the form of a *covenant*, whereby each party of the

---

[163] Kearney, *The God Who May Be*, pp. 25-6.
[164] Kearney, *The God Who May Be*, p. 27.
[165] Kearney, *The God Who May Be*, pp. 28-9.

relationship is dependent upon the other to become. Kearney argues that if the unaccomplished nature of the verb *'ehyer* is taken seriously, then God should be understood as one whose own being is not yet accomplished, and will not be accomplished until God's historical coming in the kingdom of which the Scriptures speaks (cf. Is 11.9; Ps 110.1; Zech 14.9; 1 Cor 15.24-28). The relative pronoun *'asher* may then be read as a question addressed to human beings—what? who? This implies that the quality of God's coming is intimately tied to the *decisions* of God's people. Indeed, the Scriptures are a record of precisely that kind of God, a God who is affected and vulnerable, who wrestles with Godself in lament, regret, seduction, and forgiveness. This is a God who persuades rather than coerces, invites instead of imposing, and asks rather than impels. The biblical God cannot be Godself except by relating to God's other, humanity. Thus, the coming of God promised in Exodus 3.14 is performative rather than constative, performative in the sense of an *address* which calls forth a *response* in the direction of co-creativity. Kearney comments that, for Christianity, it is precisely *this* God who comes in Jesus, and is coming again.[166]

4.3 God as Pure Passage

In a move (ironically) similar to Marion's *via eminentia*, Kearney therefore proposes his own *via tertia* between the polar oppositions of onto-theology and negative theology, a way which opens up in the 'chiasmus' where God puts being into question even as being gives flesh to God. Unless God can take on a voice or a form, there can be no witness, and nothing remembered concerning the promise. But if God is reduced and collapsed into these forms, then God becomes an idol.[167] So, in a clear reference to Marion, Kearney says: 'There's more to God than being. Granted. But to pass *beyond* being you have to pass *through* it.' God is pure gift, but also pure *passage*. While God gives Godself in the promise, God never stays put. Citing Eckhart, Kearney argues that God only ever takes leave of being having payed it homage. 'Transiting through and beyond metaphysics, God reveals himself, in keeping with his promissory note in Exodus, as a God that neither is nor is not but *may be.*' God, says Kearney, is an absolute possibility which transcends, certainly, but also *includes* the actual. Only *that* kind of God could possibly enter into a covenant which promises justice and love for all who will wait.[168] I am inclined to agree.

4.4 The Face: Where Spirit and Flesh Meet

To explore the nature of this human-divine encounter more fully, Kearney turns to another biblical story, that of Luke's 'transfiguration' of Christ. In the Transfiguration, he says, the divine *persona* of Christ shines forth in the

---

[166] Kearney, *The God Who May Be*, pp. 29-31.
[167] Kearney, *The God Who May Be*, pp. 34-5.
[168] Kearney, *The God Who May Be*, pp. 36-8.

humanity of Jesus of Nazareth, and this signifies Christ's 'coming into his own, fully assuming his messianic calling announced by the prophetic tradition from Moses to Elijah.'[169] The idea of the *persona* is taken from the Latin fathers. In Kearney's phenomenological hands it becomes an 'eschatological aura of 'possibility' which eludes but informs a person's actual presence here and now.' It is the name for the *other* as singular and elusive, escaping into a past or future that cannot be finally recovered or predicted. It is the reality that inspires us to figure the flesh-and-blood person before us as an 'absence in presence'. We see them but we do not see them. Something escapes; something remains strange, even in the familiar.[170]

The *persona* is that dimension of the other that is able to surprise us, and therefore limit our power over him or her. Following the analyses of the 'other' in Lévinas, Ricoeur and Derrida, Kearney says that one's ego is relatively powerless until another empowers it by saying 'Even though you are powerless, I believe you can do this.' In this encounter, the ego also confronts the limitation of its capacities for present/ation, for the *persona* comes from an immemorial past as well as an unexpected future.[171] For Kearney, that idea is an echo of the Pauline God who chooses non-beings in order to annul or cancel beings (1 Cor 1.28). *Persona* takes the place of a no-place but not to the extent that it takes place itself. 'It is the non-presence that allows presence to happen in the here and now *as* a human person appearing to me in flesh and blood.' It is intricately tied to flesh and blood, such that it could not *be* without them; and yet the *persona* is always more than flesh and blood, as the torturer discovers when his victim is dead but unrepentant.[172] The *persona* is therefore different from the other as an alter-ego or fetishised object in that the *persona* gives, calls, solicits and even forbids murder, while the fetishised object simply does not care because it does not exist.[173] Finally, it is the *persona* which, in the trinitarian language of the Greek fathers, cedes its place to the ego (*cedere*), so that the ego can come to be as a being-in-relationship (*sedere*). It *transfigures* the ego before the ego can *configure* it. This has the effect of disrupting the sense of ego in the self. In responding to the call of the *persona*, the self 'outdistances' itself in the direction of the other, moving into immemorial or not-yet-arrived time.[174]

What therefore happens in the Transfiguration of Christ, says Kearney, is that Jesus gives place to the divine other or *persona* so radically that he becomes the human *prosopon* or face *par excellence*. Luke says that while Jesus was praying on the mountain, 'the aspect of his face (*prosopon*) was

---

[169] Kearney, *The God Who May Be*, p. 39.
[170] Kearney, *The God Who May Be*, pp. 10-11.
[171] Kearney, *The God Who May Be*, p. 12.
[172] Kearney, *The God Who May Be*, p. 13.
[173] Kearney, *The God Who May Be*, p. 14; cf. Žižek, *On Belief*, pp. 13-15.
[174] Kearney, *The God Who May Be*, pp. 15-16.

changed (*heteron*) and his clothing became sparkling white.' (Lk 9.29). This means, literally, that his face was 'othered,' that the divine other shone through this man's face, without at the same time making him into someone else.[175] The Greek *prosopon* was a theatrical term which referred to the present figuration of an absent personage through a speaking and an acting. In its most literal form, it means 'in front of' or 'toward' (*pros*) an eye or countenance (*opos*). To be a *prosopon*, then, is to 'be-a-face-toward-a-face, to be proximate toward the face of the other.' The term, then, is radically intersubjective. It is the *prosopon* that gives a concrete place to the irreducible transcendence of the *persona*. The pair *prosopon-persona* therefore, in Kearney's estimation, 'perfectly captures the double sense of someone both proximate to me in the immediacy of connection and yet somehow ineluctably distant, at once incarnate and otherwise, inscribing the trace of an irreducible alterity in and through the face before me.' *Transfiguration* can then be understood as the name of that which Jesus allows God to do to him, in the suffering or summons which the *persona-prosopon* actually is. In transfiguration, the good of the *persona* takes precedence over the ego's drive to be (*conatus essendi*) and holds it to account.[176]

Citing the *Homily on the Transfiguration* of John of Damascus, Kearney says that the Transfiguration is an encounter between the human and divine natures of Christ in which the human receives the divine other as an 'investment' rather than a 'fusion,' which is exactly the point of the Chalcedonian dogma. The Transfiguration 'signals a surplus or incommensurability between *persona* and person even as it inscribes the one in and through the other.' The God of transfiguration is therefore far in God's nearness, 'but not so far as not to be (or be read) at all.'[177] Such a God cannot be fetishised. God can, however, be conversed with. That is the essential difference between the responses of the disciples and of Moses and Elijah in the Lukan narrative.[178] The transfigured Christ is therefore to be regarded as a '*way* not a terminus, an *eikon* not a fundamentalist fact, a *figure* of the end, but not the end itself.' He is an annulment of the God of pure and permanent presence in favour of the biblical God of exodus and passage: neither, as Tertullian said, a *hypostasis* without *ekstasis* (idolatry of God as merely human), nor an *ekstasis* without *hypostasis* (mysticism of God as inhuman).[179]

4.5 God is Pure Possibility

Like Jüngel, Kearney wants to talk about a God who *possibilises* the apparently impossible. In Mark 10.27, in response to a question about who may be saved,

---

[175] Kearney, *The God Who May Be*, p. 40.
[176] Kearney, *The God Who May Be*, pp. 18-19.
[177] Kearney, *The God Who May Be*, pp. 40-1.
[178] Kearney, *The God Who May Be*, p. 42.
[179] Kearney, *The God Who May Be*, pp. 43-4.

Jesus responds 'For humans it is impossible, but not for God; because for God everything is possible.' (*panta gar dunata para to theo*). This suggests an 'eschatological possible,' a *dunamis* that takes over when our human powers of doing, thinking and saying reach their ultimate limit, thus transfiguring our very incapacity into a new kind of capacity. Kearney notes that this entire passage in Luke draws its sense of transcendence from the power of the Spirit in and through the paschal events of the death and resurrection of Christ, which is for him the possibilisation of the impossible *par excellence*. A similar understanding may be discovered in the prologue to John's gospel, where it says that 'to all who received him, to those who believed in his name, he gave the power (*dunamis*) to become children of God—children born not of human descent or a father's will, but born of God.' (1.14). Here the possibilisation relates to a new kind of *filiation*, a filiation which transcends the limits of biology or will. 'No longer mere offspring of archaic gods and ancestors, we are now invited to become descendents of a future still to come, strangers reborn as neighbours in the Word, adopted children of the *deus adventurus*—the God of the Possible.'[180]

Finally, Kearney cites the story of the Annunciation, where the angel declares that the child to be born 'will be called the Son of God . . . for nothing is impossible (*a-dunaton*) with God.' (Lk 1.34-37). Tellingly, in some ancient traditions, Mary is called the 'container of the uncontainable' (*khora tou akhoretou*), a transfiguration of the Greek philosophical tradition by the Word of God, if ever there was one.[181] Philosophically, these stories speak of a God whose possibility holds a priority over Gods being. The divinity chooses to come to Godself via a passage through being in order to open being itself to a beyond or an other-than-itself. Nicholas of Cusa wrote of the *posse est* (or, in his own coinage *possest*) as neither prior to nor posterior to actuality, but rather *co-existent* with actuality.[182] Kearney is concerned to read this idea not as a collapsing of the finite into the infinite, or the other way around, but rather as the possibility of a covenant or *communion* of others which is known, in the Greek tradition, as the *perichoresis* of the Trinity.

4.6 The Trinity: God as Giving Place

For Kearney, as much as for Jüngel and Marion, it is the trinitarian dogma that most clearly exegetes the becoming of God as covenant. For the Greek fathers, the Trinity was a *perichoresis,* a dancing around of the three divine *personae*. In Latin, the same idea is conveyed with the term *circumincessio*, which seems to refer to a circular dancing whereby the Father, the Son, and the Spirit give

---

[180] Kearney, *The God Who May Be*, p. 81.
[181] Kearney, *The God Who May Be*, pp. 82-3.
[182] Kearney, *The God Who May Be*, p. 103. cf. Nicholas of Cusa, 'Trialogus De Possest,' *A Concise Introduction to the Philosophy of Nicholas of Cusa*, ed. Jasper Hopkins (Minneapolis: University of Minnesota Press, 1980), p. 69ff.

place to each other in a reciprocal movement of dispossession which is the very opposite of a monarchical fusion into one. The Latin etymology is most significant. It puns on the dual phonic possibility of circum-in-*cessio* (from *cedo*, to cede, give way, or dis-position) and circum-in-*sessio* (from *sedo*, to sit or assume a position). So here the three persons move *toward* each other in a gesture of proximity or immanence, but also *away* from each other in a movement of distance or transcendence. Human beings are included in this dance because of the decision of God to become a human being in Jesus Christ. Thus, we ourselves are players or dancers in an 'eschatological game of which we are neither the initiators nor the culminators, a game which we cannot master since its possibles are always beyond our possibles, refiguring the play of genesis, prefiguring the play of eschaton, a game that knows no end-game, no stalemate, whose ultimate move is still to come.'[183]

Kearney contrasts the dance-play of God with the mirror-play (*Spiegel-Spiel*) of being in the late Heidegger. Unlike the play of the Same, which folds back on itself in an eternal recurrence, the eschatological play is essentially about the summoning power of the other. Where the destiny of being unfolds from a gathering, the eschatological God invites human beings to freely realise (or not) its prophecies and promises.[184] The play is therefore possibilising but not destining: human beings are free to actualise what is possible or not. The motif of play is, for Kearney, the eschatological *posse* of both 'promise and powerlessness, fecundity and fragility.' For by choosing to be a player in creation rather than an emperor, God chooses the path of powerlessness which is beautifully expressed in the Pauline hymn of *kenosis* (Phil 2.5-11):

> God thus empowers our human powerlessness by giving away his power, by possibilizing us and our good actions—so that we may supplement and co-establish creation ... It is then the dis-possessed self, emptied of ego and naked as a child, that becomes a 'lodging' for the 'in-dwelling' of God ... Abandoning ego, I allow the infinite to beget itself in my persona.[185]

Human beings participate in the game by virtue of the gift or grace which summons us beyond ourselves and into a being *for* the other and *on behalf of* the other. To play this game is to be willing to lose oneself in order to find oneself, to become a no-body (*personne* in French) in order to become oneself again, but this time *as another* (also *personne* in French). For even the eschatological God is closer, in such movements of grace, than we are to our selves.[186] Kearney stresses the covenantal nature of the game until the last, insisting that if such play can save us, it is only by virtue of our willingness to let God bring about God's promise of a kingdom of justice and peace within

---

[183] Kearney, *The God Who May Be*, pp. 109-10.
[184] Kearney, *The God Who May Be*, p. 106.
[185] Kearney, *The God Who May Be*, p. 108.
[186] Kearney, *The God Who May Be*, p. 17.

our lives and relationships.[187]

Conclusion

It has perhaps become obvious by now that my own convictions concerning a post-metaphysical God are very close to that proposed by Jüngel and Kearney. That is not to imply, however, that I see nothing of value in the accounts of Lévinas, Derrida and Marion. Jüngel has been decisively influenced by the post-metaphysical thought of Heidegger, Bultmann and Barth,[188] while Kearney is currently engaged in sympathetic dialogue with Lévinas, Derrida and Marion.[189] Thus, there is much agreement between all the thinkers I have engaged here, agreements which may be presented thematically. By way of concluding this discussion, I should therefore like to summarise those themes which shall be of particular importance for the second half of the book.

God comes to human beings as a mystery. If there is anything that all of our thinkers agree on, it is this. God is never entirely what human beings think God to be. God resists every attempt to wrap the divine in intuitions or ideologies which spring from the human desire to secure our existence against nothingness. Therefore, the covenant between ourselves and God can never be about securing God's blessing for all that we plan to do on our own, from our own.

God reveals or gives Godself under the species of the material and human. While there is a persistent mysteriousness about God, all of our thinkers also agree that whatever is known of God can only be known because God, in God's freedom, chooses to reveal Godself under the conditions of human and historical existence. In this movement, God displays a certain vulnerability: an intention to come to Godself by way of the temporal, the spatial, and the human. This makes God, in a certain sense, 'subject' or vulnerable to the machinations of the human enterprise, whether that is expressed in philosophy, theology, art, science, politics or technology.

God approaches human beings in the form of an interlocutionary address or call. This call, it is agreed, comes from a time and space 'beyond' ordinary time and space, and yet is encountered within ordinary time and space as that which interrupts or fractures the supposed totality of the same. The inbreaking of this 'messianic' or 'eschatological' voice is differently located by each of our thinkers, and yet there is a recognition in all of them that such inbreaking is real, that it actually 'happens' in the form of an event, a trace, an incarnation, an ethical injunction, or a resurrection. Importantly, that trace or incarnation has its effects. Parable-like, it has the power to displace and refigure the dominance of both our self-monologues and cultural homogeneities in favour

---

[187] Kearney, *The God Who May Be*, p. 110.
[188] See DeHart, *Beyond the Necessary God*, especially the Introduction.
[189] The latest example is Kearney, *Strangers, Gods and Monsters*.

of that reality that is 'more than real': God.

It is the call or address of God from 'beyond' which makes human beings what they are: intersubjective and responsible. Because God addresses us from a time before and after Now and a place beyond Here, we can never constitute ourselves in the Here and Now except in the form of that quintessentially prayerful reply or response: 'Here I Am'. That means that the most important reality in our constitution as human beings is from elsewhere, from God. We are interlocutionary beings, who produce and perform ourselves in cooperation with another. Furthermore, because the call precedes the formation of an ego absolutely, because we experience the call 'asymmetrically' as it were, we are ethically responsible from the very beginning. There is no escaping the plea or address of the other, any other, for just and truthful recognition.

The call or address of God from 'beyond' may well be most vividly narrated in the life, death and resurrection of Jesus. Lévinas aside, I think that even Derrida could assent to this proposition in its current form. It is certainly the position of Marion, Jüngel and Kearney. For what is encountered in Jesus is the address of God in a language which, at least, *sounds and feels* like human language. There is a certain symmetry in the fact that Derrida discerns the trace of the 'other' in human language as such, while Jüngel speculates that human language is interlocutionary to the core because God has addressed us in the human life of Jesus. That is not to claim that Derrida asks a question to which Jüngel gives an answer, the only answer, but rather that Jüngel and Derrida at least agree that there is something genuinely *revelatory* about the Christian dialectic of the God-man. In Kearney's terms, Christ is that human person in which the *persona* of God shines forth as the promise of cosmic salvation—justice and peace for all.

Finally, and this is the most Christian of the themes, it would appear that even God is unwilling to constitute the divine self apart from a radical involvement and conversation with human beings. Following on from (2) above, God is not one who sits 'above it all,' high and mighty in monadic otherness, although God could. Because God is *love,* God not only makes human freedom possible in creation, but also subjects Godself to an historical struggle with the worst excesses of that freedom. As Jüngel says, in Christ God takes the form of a slave so that God might become a unity of life and death in the cause of life. In trinitarian terms, this means that it is of the nature of God to cede the divine self for the sake of another in the form of an irrevocable vow or covenant of love, such that God only comes to God's own future via the treacherous route of suffering and death in the human Christ.

CHAPTER 4

The Desire of God[1]

My heart says of you, 'Seek God's face!'
Your face, Lord, I will seek.
Do not turn me over to the desire of my foes,
For false witnesses rise up against me.,
Breathing out violence.

I am confident of this:
I will see the goodness of the Lord
In the land of the living.

Wait for the Lord;
Be strong and take heart
And wait for the Lord.

from Psalm 27

Introduction

Having investigated at length the character of God's being in the world, I will now follow the implications of that investigation through with regard to the specific encounter, in *Christian experience*, between God and human beings. As a Christian theologian, I will of course make no specific claims about extra-Christian experience. That is not to say that some of my remarks would not be of interest to scholars from other traditions (indeed, I suspect there is much here of value for the study of humanity as such). It is simply to state and acknowledge that my primary interest is theological in the Christian sense. Therefore, when I read the philosophical poststructuralists, I am mining them for their potentially theological import; I am not reading them, necessarily, according to some version of their stated or unstated 'intentions.' In this I am simply imitating their own reading strategies. John Caputo argues, for example, that contemporary philosophy must read Heidegger *against the grain* of his own apparent intentions, and necessarily so if philosophy is to recover

---

[1] An earlier version of this chapter was published as Garry J. Deverell, 'The Desire of God,' *The Heythrop Journal* 48.3 (2007): 343-70.

something of Heidegger's value for a non-Nazi mythology of being.[2] In a similar manner, I will sometimes read Derrida, and especially Lévinas, against the grain of their apparent intentions. In doing so I seek to identify in them what Ricoeur has called a 'surplus of meaning,' a fruitfulness possibly unintended by the author (if an author can be identified), but nevertheless available to be plucked by any who have the eyes, or the *faith*, to see it is there.[3]

The chapter will begin in a phenomenological fashion. By exploring the contours of human longing and desire, particularly in its complex relationship with the body and material reality, I will show that it is in the very nature of the *humanum* to seek after and promise the presence of a divinity whose arrival cannot be guaranteed (not from the human side, at least). In the second part of the chapter, Biblical poetry from the *Psalms* and the *Song of Songs* will be invoked and explored as exemplars of exactly that psychic landscape. There we shall discover that while human desire is not enough to guarantee God's arrival, it perseveres on the basis of a mysterious sense of call or promise which, while experienced and apprehended *within* the self, nevertheless appears to emanate or broadcast as from *another place*.

This mapping of human desire raises a question. If one cannot guarantee the arrival into presence of that which one longs for, how can one claim some kind of reality or substantiality for the object of desire? In attempting to answer that question, I will revisit the intriguing suggestion, from Derrida, that a self's desire for some kind of non-yet-arrived 'other' may well be read as the sign or promise of that other's desire or love for the self. In a theological sense, the phrase 'desire of God' could then be read in two distinct and yet interrelated senses: our desire for God, but also God's desire for us. Could our desire for God *already* be God's desire for us? I will answer, 'yes,' and argue further that the human body is the privileged site for the confluence or negotiation of these two kinds of desire. The self, as I argued in chapter 1, is not at one with itself. It is present and identifiable in the body, and yet is still arriving, as from some other 'place' or 'time', in what has been called *persona* or *spirit*. But neither is God at one with Godself, as I argued in chapter 3. God, who is *spirit*, has nevertheless chosen to arrive at Godself via the material and human history of Christ and the church.

---

[2] John D. Caputo, *Demythologising Heidegger* (Bloomington: Indiana University Press, 1993), pp. 5-6.
[3] See for example Paul Ricoeur, *Figuring the Sacred: Religion, Narrative, and Imagination*, trans. David Pellauer, ed. Mark I. Wallace (Minneapolis: Fortress Press, 1995), p. 85.

1. Desire and the Body

1.1 The Body: The Desirable before Desire

According to Lévinas' early reflections in *Existence and Existents*, it is the phenomenon of desire that shows us that there is both a world and a relation that precedes the action of the intentional ego as it moves out from itself, from the interior to the exterior. Philosophy, he says, has always assumed that 'the world' was that which the *intending consciousness* produces as its field or horizon of perception. '*Existing*, in the whole of Western idealism, refers to the intentional movement from inwardness to the exterior. A being is what is thought about, seen, acted upon, willed, felt—an object.' Here the centre of the world is the ego, and the world itself a function of that ego. The discovery of the unconscious, however, implies that there is an event in some way prior to this world, an event that Lévinas names 'the desirable'. Here there is a forgetting of personal intentions in favour of a reality that does not come about by the objectifying movement of the ego, but is rather 'given'.[4]

> The world is what is given to us. This expression is admirably precise: the given does not to be sure come from us, but we do receive it. It already has a side by which it is the terminus of an intention . . . Desire as a relationship with the world involves both a distance between me and the desirable, and consequently a time ahead of me, and also a possession of the desirable which is prior to the desire. This position of the desirable, before and after the desire, is the fact that is given. And the fact of being given is the world.[5]

That the desirable is not simply an idea, projection, or object of intention is underlined in what Lévinas says about the nude or naked body. The nude signifies, for him, that which is desirable, the genuinely 'other'. This because the nude retreats or hides from society into a place where it is no longer inscribed or 'dressed' with the forms or markings of social and cultural life.[6] The nude can therefore be said to both proceed and exceed the intentionality of philosophical consciousness.

Desire such as this, directed towards a mystery that is able to resist objectification, is what Lévinas does not hesitate to call 'love.' Love, he says, is an insatiable hunger: insatiable because it cannot be fulfilled within the circumscribing orbit of economic exchange, which is the world of the subject. In the phenomenon of a lover's caress he locates an absolute limit to such designs:

---

[4] Emmanuel Lévinas, *Existence and Existents*, trans. Alphonso Lingis (The Hague: Martinus Nijhoff, 1978), pp. 37-9.
[5] Lévinas, *Existence and Existents*, p. 39.
[6] Lévinas, *Existence and Existents*, pp. 40-1.

The trouble one feels before the beloved does not only precede what we call, in economic terms, possession, but is felt in the possession too. In the random agitation of caresses there is the admission that access is impossible, violence fails, possession is refused . . . The other is precisely this objectless dimension. The hunger of love pulls away from every being.[7]

According to Lévinas, the solitary subject is not able to transcend itself, to save itself, from the bondage of self-enclosure. The possibility of salvation comes through an encounter with absolute *alterity* in the figure of the body, and especially the *face* of another.[8] The naked face, then, is the precise location of otherness for Lévinas. It is the persistence of particularity over the universalising tendencies of Being. 'The body is a permanent contestation of the prerogative attributed to consciousness of 'giving meaning' to each thing; it lives as this contestation.'[9]

Furthermore, it is from the specific locatedness of the body in space and time that the very possibility of unique and conscious identity arises. 'Consciousness comes out of rest, out of position, out of this unique relationship with place. Position is not added to consciousness like an act that it decides on; it is out of position, out of immobility, that consciousness comes to itself.'[10] The *spirituality* of the body is therefore described by Lévinas as a certain non-coincidence between the locality of one's body and the transcending consciousness it makes possible.[11] We met with something similar in Jüngel's analysis of the Here and the Now, phenomena which do not correspond with each other because of the distanciation of eschatological time and space. The ego becomes *spirit* or consciousness precisely as it comes to itself from a space beyond the Now, and a time beyond the Here.[12] For Lévinas therefore, as much as for Jüngel and Kearney, the selfhood of the self is a correlation without correlation, a product of this difficult non-coincidence of body and the temporality of consciousness the body makes possible.

To summarise Lévinas' early work, then, the self is constituted by a twofold encounter with alterity. First, there is the encounter with the otherness of one's own body, an encounter which is 'immemorial' in the sense that it occurs even before I become conscious of myself. Indeed, it can be said to *possibilise* such consciousness, for consciousness is precisely a desire towards that which precedes and exceeds consciousness. Second, there is the encounter with the body, and particularly the face, of another, a particularity that resists inscription or possession even as my own body does. In the face one encounters not an *alter ego* or *Miteinandersein*, as with Heidegger, but an *other* who claims an

---

[7] Lévinas, *Existence and Existents*, p. 43.
[8] Lévinas, *Existence and Existents*, p. 93.
[9] Lévinas, *Totality and Infinity*, p. 129.
[10] Lévinas, *Existence and Existents*, p. 70.
[11] Lévinas, *Existence and Existents*, p. 72.
[12] Jüngel, *God as the Mystery of the World*, pp. 173-74.

asymmetrical power of desire even over my own desire, a certain 'distance' even in proximity.[13]

1.2 The Face to Face: Desire as a Pre-lingual Ethics

In the later text, *Totality and Infinity*, Lévinas draws an explicit connection between desire, the face, speech, and 'religion.' Because desire comes into being as from the bodily 'isness' of another, desire is that which lives from the persistence of *mystery* in the other. Paradoxically, it is therefore in the interests of subjectivity to make room for the other within its own self-definition. Without such 'hospitality', desire would cease to be desire, for the other would be vanquished as other.[14] There is a certain 'madness' to desire, then. It is able to put aside self-interest in order to attend to the interests of another. Desire is a madness that is able, if you like, to transmute itself into goodness, goodness defined by Lévinas as the preoccupation of the self not with itself, but with another being. Desire, he says, is 'Religion.' While Platonic love longs for the immortality of the self in communion with some kind of demiurgic divinity, religion is a self being able to surpass itself in 'glorious humility, responsibility, and sacrifice'.[15] The truth of ethics in Lévinasian religion should not be understood, therefore, as some kind of culturally constructed moralism or social contract by which the truth of other beings comes to light in the manifesting glow of one's own being. Against the Heidegger of *Being and Time*, Lévinas argues that ethical truth comes not as a matter of manifesting 'disclosure' but of 'revelation'. Here the being of the other 'tells' itself before any such manifestation even becomes possible, 'revealing' itself not according to a thematising gaze or form, but according to its own pre-eminent will and authority.

The revealing other reveals itself, as we now understand, in the *face*. But we must emphasise that in Lévinas the face cannot be simply identified with 'form,' if form is understood as some kind of cultural 'dressing' which we provide for nakedness.[16] For the self-expression of the face exceeds whatever forms we may place upon it, and it does so by a kind of 'speaking' or 'signifying' which comes directly from the eyes.[17] What Lévinas means by this metaphor is somewhat difficult to discern. On the language side, he clearly regards the signifying movement of language as essentially interlocutionary in character. One can picture two people facing each other in a mutual gaze, such that the interlocutionary, as a language event, arises from facing.[18] Signification (the face to face) makes the sign (language) possible. 'Meaning is the face of

---

[13] Lévinas, *Existence and Existents*, pp. 95-6.
[14] Lévinas, *Totality and Infinity*, p. 24.
[15] Lévinas, *Totality and Infinity*, pp. 62-4.
[16] Lévinas, *Totality and Infinity*, pp. 65-6.
[17] Lévinas, *Totality and Infinity*, p. 66.
[18] Lévinas, *Totality and Infinity*, p. 69.

the Other, and all recourse to words takes place already within the primordial face to face of language.'[19] There is reference, here, to a language somehow *before* language, somewhat in the mode of Kierkegaard's ethics before ethics. In the case of Lévinas, ethical conversation arises first from an encounter with the *eyes* of the other which, he says, speak more frankly even than the face, which is capable of being either a mask or a mirror. The eyes speak a truth for the face that is 'impossible to dissemble.' In the language of the eyes is 'the coinciding of the revealer and the revealed in the face.'[20]

Marion's exegesis of these rather dense metaphors is helpful, I think. In *Prolegomena to Charity* he reflects upon the nature of love. What makes the other necessarily invisible to my objectifying gaze is not some special quality that the other possesses but I do not. It is simply that the other can do what I do—intend objects which are unable to first intend or see me. If the other can do this also, then he or she can render himself or herself invisible to every object he or she intends, including myself! 'The other, as other, irreducible to my intention, but origin of another intention, can never be seen, by definition.' This is borne out, as it happens, in the phenomenon of the mutual gaze. When I want to fix my intention exclusively on another, I focus on the eyes, and the pupils in particular. But the pupil appears to me as an emptiness, a black hole, so that even here in the midst of a visible face 'there is nothing to see, except as an invisible and untargetable [*invisable*] void.'[21]

Marion develops these ideas further in his text *In Excess*. Friendship, he says, is the paradigm example of the face-to-face as an *event*. In friendship, I first 'take for myself [the other's] point of view on me, without reducing it to my point of view on him; and thus he comes to me.' This looking to position oneself in the place of being seen is termed *anamorphosis*: literally, allowing oneself to be morphed or figured according to the gaze of another. Whence, secondly, 'the event of this friendship is accomplished all at once, without warning or anticipation, according to an *arrival* without expectation and without rhythm'. One cannot produce the event from oneself alone. The other gives itself before I am ready to receive it. Third, the phenomenon given in this way 'gives nothing other than itself. Its ultimate meaning remains inaccessible, because it is reduced to its *fait accompli*, to its *occurrence* [*incidence*].' Thus, for Marion, the meaning of the other is surplus to its appearance: 'we cannot assign to it a single cause or any reason, or rather, none other than itself, in the pure energy of its unquestionable happening'. This suggests that what shows *itself* in the face 'only manages to do so by virtue of a *self*, strictly and eidetically phenomenological, that assures to it the sole fact that it gives *itself*

---

[19] Lévinas, *Totality and Infinity*, p. 206.
[20] Lévinas, *Totality and Infinity*, pp. 66-7.
[21] Marion, *Prolegomena to Charity*, p. 81; cf. Jean-Luc Marion, *In Excess: Studies of Saturated Phenomena*, trans. Robyn Horner and Vincent Berraud (New York: Fordham University Press, 2002), p. 115.

and which, in return, proves that its phenomenalization presupposes its givenness as such and starting from itself.'[22]

1.3 Asymmetry and Covenant: Friends or Antagonists?

This begs the question, of course, as to whether there can be any really mutual *partnership* or covenant in the face-to-face. If the very *selfhood* of the other perseveres in darkest mystery, even as I constitute myself in response to his or her 'isness', wouldn't this mean that my relationship with the other is not so much a partnership as an *antagonism*? Antagonism: 'The mutual resistance or active opposition of two opposing forces, physical or mental; active opposition to a force.'[23] It is not difficult, certainly, to find evidence for that claim. *Totality and Infinity* is shot through with the language of radical asymmetry—the other's 'mastery' over the I.[24] The freedom of the other is often said to be a freedom which is 'superior' to my own freedom in that it 'dominates' my own.[25] If one imagines that sense of superiority cutting two ways, as Marion would have it, it is indeed difficult to picture the relation as anything other than a mutual *resistance*. Lévinas, as we saw in chapter 1, has often been accused of disqualifying the possibility of a perception of the other that could lead to partnership. In his enthusiasm for protecting the otherness of the other from manipulation and objectification, does he not also make that other unreachable, even in the mode of invocation?

I agree that Lévinas certainly does err towards that outcome. Yet, it is difficult to conclude that the door is closed entirely. In a key passage of *Totality and Infinity*, Lévinas hypostasizes the Other as a 'Beloved' who, in a 'paroxysm of materiality' (i.e. the nakedness of a body, face and eyes), indeed *appears*, yet without appearing, and *signifies*, yet without speaking. That paradoxical mode of speech is necessary, according to Lévinas, not because relationship is entirely impossible but because it is an *event*, a process of becoming which correlates with the becoming of the subjectivities it enfolds. The self, he says, is not always the same. It is identical with the changes it undergoes through the encounter with its other.[26] What appears and is manifest in a present is in fact the 'not yet' of eschatological time.[27] That is not simply to say that the present implies a future, but that the 'Eternal' or the 'Infinite' has a priority over temporality such that even those things which seem temporally impossible might turn out to be possible after all[28]—relationships of love included.

---

[22] Marion, *In Excess*, pp. 37-8.
[23] From the *Oxford English Dictionary* online: http://dictionary.oed.com.
[24] Lévinas, *Totality and Infinity*, pp. 69, 75.
[25] Lévinas, *Totality and Infinity*, p. 86.
[26] Lévinas, *Totality and Infinity*, pp. 36-7.
[27] Lévinas, *Totality and Infinity*, p. 256.
[28] Lévinas, *Totality and Infinity*, p. 55.

Lévinas speaks about the eventfulness of relationships in time when he says that the impossible is also the infinitely 'fecund'. *Fecundity is the self ever in search of itself in the other.* It is a relationship with 'infinite time' in which a kind of 'eternal youth' is made possible because every moment is a recommencement towards an infinitely open future.[29] In order to explain what is meant here, Lévinas introduces a metaphor that is uncannily *relational* and even *trinitarian* in its patterning and force. The embodied encounter with the mystery of the Beloved other, while remaining a mystery, also creates the possibility for a new kind of relationship: paternity. 'By a total transcendence, the transcendence of trans-substantiation, the I is, in the child, an other. Paternity remains a self-identification, but also a distinction within identification—a structure unforseen in formal logic.'[30] My child is at once me, but also a stranger: myself, but not of my own making.

Surely Lévinas is reaching here for a way in which desire for the other can return to a habitation in the self as *a genuine experience of intimacy*. If my child is myself as a stranger, she is also myself as myself. This means that the stranger can also be, literally, familiar. If it is the stranger that I desire, without prospect of absorption into the self, it is nevertheless a familiar stranger: the self *as* another. What Lévinas prefigures here is the possibility that self and other actually constitute each other in such a way that they may come even to *know each other* in and as that mode of *self*-knowledge which I am calling 'covenant', or the performance of the self as from another. Additional support for this perspective may be garnered from what Lévinas says (albeit in a very masculine way), about 'Woman'. 'Woman' is the name of that intimate someone who is at once a presence and an absence, the very meaning of hospitality. For hospitality is the 'secret' welcome made by a *present* Intimate, an empty space or habitation carved out *within* the self—in/habitation, a recollection in interiority. The Woman, says Lévinas (and one may surely add 'the Man' as well), is a welcoming before all welcoming because she is a welcoming that has always already occurred from the deepest and most interior sanctum of interiority.[31] Surely this suggests that the 'Other' is already closer to me than I am to myself, already producing the distance of relationship within the proximity of intimacy. If that is so, then Lévinas cannot finally be read, even in *Totality and Infinity*, as a denier of covenant. For covenant is exactly this: the self that is unable to produce itself apart from this distance-in-proximity with another.

Marion tweaks the famous Lévinasian asymmetry by saying that it is only in the crossing of *two* asymmetrical gazes that a genuinely ethical injunction towards love may be discerned.[32] What I see in the other's eyes is an invisible

---

[29] Lévinas, *Totality and Infinity*, p. 268.
[30] Lévinas, *Totality and Infinity*, p. 267.
[31] Lévinas, *Totality and Infinity*, pp. 155-58.
[32] Marion, *Prolegomena to Charity*, p. 88.

The Desire of God 97

gaze that already sees me.[33] Such a gaze is able to dismiss the priority of the nominative 'I' in favour of an accusative 'me', so that while I may never know precisely who or what this other is, I may know that she or he faces *me* and aims at *me*. This has the effect of stripping away the *I* so that the decentred *me* of the other's injunction is all that remains.[34] Yet the asymmetry of this experience cuts both ways, leading Marion to make this proposal for a phenomenological definition of love: 'two definitively invisible gazes (intentionality and the injunction) cross one another, and thus together trace a cross that is invisible to every gaze other than theirs alone.'[35] In this kind of love, the other remains untamed and undomesticated, and yet the 'I' comes to see this fact as deeply desirable. 'If to love is to love the love the Beloved bears me, to love is also to love oneself in love, and thus to return to oneself.'[36] I may not know everything about the Beloved, in other words, but I sure love 'the look of love' within his or her eyes!

It is not yet clear, however, that the relationship established in 'secret' is in any way *communicable*. How, in other words, does the more-or-less invisible and wordless relation of the face-to-face come into visible, communicable reality? Marion has something to say about this. With regard to visibility, he imagines the invisible *self* of the other projecting itself on *l'adonné* (I, myself) as onto a screen; all the power of what is given comes 'crashing down' on this screen, provoking a 'double visibility': (1) a visibility like that which comes into being when invisible white light crashes into a prism and is thereby splintered into visible colours. 'With this operation—precisely, reception—the given can begin to show *itself* starting from the outlines of visibility that it concedes to *l'adonné,* or rather that it receives from it.' Here I, myself, make a very specific contribution to the form of the other. Nevertheless, the form I contribute already belongs to the selfhood I receive in the other's arrival. Thus the second kind of visibility: (2) a visibility that provokes, in the same movement as the first, the visibility of *l'adonné*:

> In effect, *l'adonné* does not see itself before receiving the impact of the given . . . since, properly speaking, l'adonné is not without this reception, the impact gives rise for the first time to the screen against which it is crushed, as it sets up the prism across which it breaks up . . . The given is therefore revealed to *l'adonné* in revealing l'adonné to itself.[37]

This amounts to a phenomenal *reciprocity* 'where to see implies the modification of the seeing by the seen, as much as the modification of the seen

---

[33] Marion, *Prolegomena to Charity*, p. 82.
[34] Marion, *Prolegomena to Charity*, p. 84.
[35] Marion, *Prolegomena to Charity*, p. 87.
[36] Lévinas, *Totality and Infinity*, p. 266.
[37] Marion, *In Excess*, p. 50.

by the viewer.'[38] In this way, the resistance of the screen that I myself am, the very force of my act of receptivity, turns out to be the essential ingredient by which the invisible becomes visible. 'The greater the resistance to the impact of the given . . . the more the phenomenological light shows *itself.*'[39] In this view, my reception of the other implies passive receptivity, certainly, but it also demands an *active capacity*, a capacity (*capacitas*) that is able to increase to the measure of what is given and to make sure it happens. This work of reception, which the other asks from *l'adonné* 'every time and for as long as it gives itself,' explains why I do not receive myself once and for all (at birth) but, rather, receive myself anew in the event of each experience of the other giving *itself.*[40]

But what of language: how does the wordless, unseeing, gaze of the face-to-face find its way into a language and a conversation without destroying the ethical pre-eminence of one party or the other? Well, surprisingly enough, Marion finds a place for hermeneutics at this point. Hermeneutics, he says, is not only pragmatically necessary but actually *called for* in the face of the other. This because the other is always in at least as much doubt about the truth of its self-expression as I am. 'The other person cannot know more what his or her face expresses than he or she can see this face (because the mirror only ever sends back an image, and an inverse image).'[41] The other searches for his or her truth in me, as much as I search for my own truth in them. 'A face only says the truth about what it expresses—truth that in a sense it always ignores—if *I believe it and if it believes that I believe it.* Confidence, not to say *faith*, offers the sole phenomenologically correct access to the face of the other person.'[42] Thus, the face calls me to a faith/ful (and therefore risky) form of witness or substitution:

> To accede to this face demands . . . envisaging it face-to-face, despite or *thanks to* its absence from defined meaning—in other words, expecting that a substitute comes to give a meaning (to constitute, Husserl would say) and a significance to the expression which, of itself, is lacking from it. This substitute is named the event, in the double sense of what happens and, especially, of what fixes the result of an action or sanctions the unravelling of an intrigue.[43]

This means that the truth of the face is played not in what it says in the moment (whether in words or by expression) but in what it does through time, that is, across the whole 'story' of its life. To my mind, this insight represents a significant point of reconciliation between Lévinas and Ricoeur. The face

---

[38] Marion, *In Excess*, p. 50.
[39] Marion, *In Excess*, p. 51.
[40] Marion, *In Excess*, p. 48.
[41] Marion, *In Excess*, p. 120.
[42] Marion, *In Excess*, p. 122 [italics mine].
[43] Marion, *In Excess*, p. 122.

The Desire of God

resists interpretation, certainly. Yet, that exact fact *calls for* the telling of a story in which the other, as much as I myself, seeks to complete its own self-understanding. The story is retold over and over, never adequately, yet it is done so from a faith and a hope that the meaning of the story will one day be manifest.

In this situation, theology and phenomenology necessarily part company, according to Marion. Theology preserves the person as a meaning which is always arriving, as from an eschatological future in God. In faith it looks for a meaning beyond time, and a visible beyond invisibility (Heb 11.1). The revelation of the other person's meaning is therefore tied to the revelation of the meaning of God. The former only comes to its fulfilment in the latter. 'How could the finite face of the other person rise up in the glory of its truth, outside the glorification of the infinite Face? The hermeneutic of the saturated phenomenon of the other person becomes, in Christian theology, one of the figures of faith, thus of the eschatological wait for the manifestation of the Christ.' Phenomenology, on the other hand, cannot wait for the end of time. It can only wait *in* time.[44] Thus it is theology, specifically, that is able to help us understand that it is the impossibility of an absolute *fusion* in relationships that nevertheless calls for the interlocutionary *performance* of relationships. Relationships are 'impossible' to totalise, yet they are fecund also, giving rise to the intrigue of a story of becoming selves.

1.4 Body-language: A Speech before Interlocution

This is already borne out, I think, in what Lévinas writes about the 'correlation' of the 'saying' and the 'said'. We have seen how Lévinas places his emphasis on a 'language before language,' a language of the lover's mutual, unseeing, gaze. In *Otherwise Than Being or, Beyond Essence,* he names such a language the eventfulness of 'saying' over against the *détente* of the 'said.' The 'said,' he argues, is a word-game in which there is a constant attempt to outwit the other in one's own self-interest. The 'saying,' however, is a fore/word preceding language: 'it is the proximity of the one to the other, the commitment of an approach, the one for the other, the very signifyingness of signification.' Read in conjunction with *Totality and Infinity,* one is inclined to conclude that the 'saying' has to do with the pre-lingual expression of the body and with its 'gravity'. It is 'disinterested' in the sense of being unconcerned about compensation in an economy of exchange. Note, however, that Lévinas is *not* so naïve as to think that the saying is accessible in some kind of 'pure' form, apart from the said. In order to manifest itself, in order that its reality might be really *known*, the saying must 'correlate' itself with the said, and therefore with a linguistic system, with interlocution, and with being. Yet, it is in the miracle of language, according to Lévinas, that it allows itself to be betrayed; that is, the more 'original' reality of the saying becomes manifest by a kind of negative

---

[44] Marion, *In Excess*, p. 124.

capability, by our becoming aware of the said's non-coincidence with itself.[45]

This amounts, I suggest, to a plausible claim that the 'pure' language of love can remain itself even as it is disseminated throughout the otherness of ordinary, objectifying language. Or, to put things a little differently, the ordinary language of love—objective and manipulative as it is—may nevertheless become the means by which a more genuine love gains traction in the world without, at the same time, losing its identity as love.

1.5 The 'Saying' and Grace: Two Kinds of Substitution

The possibilities of this thinking for a fruitful intersection with the Christian language of grace are profound. Robert W. Jenson argues that the word of God must be understood as both law *and* gospel, and these should be neither separated nor confused. The law, he says, is a descriptor for our whole web of mutual address and obligation. It is culture, it is society, and it is language. In Lévinasian terms, it is the 'said.' Like Lévinas, Jenson does not wish to see the apparent necessity of law as some kind of 'fall' from grace or saying. For it is *God* who stands 'behind' the law, says Jenson. There is indeed a sense in which the law of obligation and command is rightly understood as the command and obligation of God. The 'gospel,' however, is a specifically Christian form of address, particularly as it promises itself in Christ. As *promise*, it signifies a fullness not (yet) arrived in presence. We might then compare the word of the gospel with Lévinas' 'saying'. While the law imposes obligation, the promise represents an address by which the one who stands behind the law, himself assumes obligation, and so opens a new kind of possibility for the one addressed. If the law commands freedom, the word of the gospel promises that God will guard and guarantee our freedom. While our own promises, promises made under law, are ordinarily *conditional* in that we are unable to control either the future or the past, the gospel promise is *unconditional* because it is offered by one who *is the power* to transcend such apparent necessities. According to Jenson's schema, law and gospel are not to be mixed up (any more than Christ's human and divine natures are to be mixed up), but neither are they to be separated from one another. For the law of God speaks for the legitimacy of our brother or sister's need; but it is the promise of the gospel that guarantees the transcending fruitfulness of our obedience. In this sense, the gospel's promise acquires our human action and language as its referent; and the promise of the gospel may be discerned as the transcendent quality towards which every act of law reaches.[46]

There is an affinity, I think, between this Pauline theology of promise and the proposals of Lévinas concerning the 'saying.' Both the promise and the saying are seen as essentially dynamic; they are, *like the body*, the un-made

---

[45] Lévinas, *Otherwise Than Being*, pp. 5-7.
[46] Robert W. Jenson, *Visible Words: The Interpretation and Practice of Christian Sacraments* (Philadelphia: Fortress Press, 1978), pp. 6, 7.

ground of all that is human language, culture and society. They are also, each of them, presented as the veritable way of salvation for egos trapped in the eternal return of their own sophistry. Like the body and its desires, promise and 'saying' contest such sophistry, interrupting culture and language in the figure of a primordial 'call'. Yet there is a crucial difference between the 'saying' and the 'promise,' a difference discernable in the way in which one person is said to be able to 'substitute' for another.

Recall, from chapter 1, Ricoeur's concern that, in *Totality and Infinity*, the Lévinasian self sometimes appears helpless to compensate for the asymmetry of the injunction toward justice and the good demanded by proximity with the other.[47] You will also remember that, in *Otherwise Than Being*, Lévinas makes no attempt to overcome that difficulty, choosing instead to push the asymmetry yet further by proposing the hyperbole of 'substitution.' Here the 'Other' is portrayed as the offender who needs pardon, a pardon which the 'I' seeks to affect by substituting itself for the other in a radical act of responsibility which is, in fact, never responsible enough.[48] Horner observes that such an *absolute* asymmetry is problematic because 'it leaves no prospect for my own alterity for the Other . . . And this is how Lévinas intends it to be, emphasising my own, always greater, share of the responsibility. There can be no reciprocity.'[49]

If this is what 'saying' finally comes to, in Lévinas, then the promise of the gospel must finally be distinguished from saying. Rather than laying upon us an ever-increasing responsibility which we will never be able to discharge, the gospel promises that in Christ God has done *for* human beings exactly that which we are unable to do for ourselves: the performance of the law's injunction to love one's neighbour as oneself:

> For what the law was powerless to do in that it was weakened by the flesh, God did by sending his own Son in the likeness of sinful man to be a sin offering. And so he condemned sin in sinful man, in order that the righteous requirements of the law might be fully met in us, who do not live according to the flesh but according to the Spirit (Rom 8.3, 4).

> We love because he first loved us. If anyone says, 'I love God,' yet hates his brother, he is a liar. For anyone who does not love his brother, whom he has seen, cannot love God, whom he has not seen (1 Jn 4.19, 20).

Here salvation comes as a free gift; it is not earned by us, and cannot be finally represented by us according to our own system of thinking. This far, the gospel and Lévinas agree. Where they disagree is in what 'salvation' actually means or makes possible *in the flesh*. In the end I would contend that Lévinas opts for an

---

[47] Ricoeur, *Oneself as Another*, p. 189.
[48] Ricoeur, *Oneself as Another*, p. 338; compare Lévinas, *Otherwise Than Being*, pp. 13, 25-6, 117, 135, 138.
[49] Horner, *Rethinking God as Gift*, p. 69.

ever-increasing burden of responsibility in which the 'I' is substituted for every other self. What the gospel envisions, on the other hand, is the coming of a Christ who substitutes for the 'I' in such a way that the real and proximate responsibility of the 'I' is performed by another, an other who is competent to do so because he has both suffered and conquered every human limitation, even death.

Crucially, the substitution of Christian atonement does not pretend to do away with the kind of ethical responsibility Lévinas wanted to preserve. For Paul, Christian people are, and remain, responsible before God and the neighbour. What we are given, in Christ, is not a dismissal of responsibility, but an example and power to perform those responsibilities as from a self which is already an *other* in the sense we have been enumerating: another self who is yet 'Christ in you, the hope of glory' (Col 1.27). I agree, therefore, with David Ford who says that it is possible to believe in the substitution of Christ without therefore negating the kind of radical ethical responsibility that Lévinas rightly champions.[50] In the schema I am proposing, the figure of Christ's *crucified body* can be read doubly: as God's salvific love for human beings, but also the fully unconditional love of human beings *for one another*, a love which we are empowered to perform by the atoning substitution of baptism, a passage at once Christ's and our own: our own death in Christ's death, our own resurrection in Christ's resurrection.

1.6 The Body as the Site of Covenant

It therefore suits my theological purposes to adhere more closely to Lévinas' earlier language, which appears to leave open (albeit obliquely, or marginally) the possibility of a genuine reciprocity or covenant. In *Totality and Infinity*, the body, and particularly that kind of embodied interaction known as 'facing,' acts as a crucial site or 'hinge' by which the negotiations of desire between a self and its other take place. With Charles Winquist we might say that the body is that place in which a person becomes available to our searching intention. It is therefore 'corrigible' in the sense that by its presentation in a body, a self becomes vulnerable to the constructive manipulations (either positive or negative) of both one's own self and other selves. At the same time, however, the body presents the world with a sense of the absence of its self from presentation. There are 'regions' of the body, as it were, which are 'incorrigible,' that is, capable of resisting the manipulations of society and culture absolutely. What the body limits is the tendency of imaginative subjectivity to know or construct the world as a wish-fulfilment, thus ignoring the bodily facts of pain, death, hunger, and the mysterious forces of material facticity.[51]

---

[50] David F. Ford, *Self and Salvation: Being Transformed* (Cambridge: Cambridge University Press, 1999), p. 70.

[51] Charles E. Winquist, *Desiring Theology* (Chicago: University of Chicago Press,

In a profound meditation upon the body in pain, Elaine Scarry argues that pain is the very opposite of the intentional imagination. It is that which both resists imagination and creation, and yet calls out for these responses as a way to endure.[52] In that sense one might draw an analogy between the encounter with one's own body and the encounter with another's. In both cases, the body is that reality which allows us to identify and converse with a person, a self; yet it is the body that also secrets away the very self we would want to engage with. The body is therefore a veritable presence of that absence which Kearney calls *persona* or *spirit,* a transcendent self that has either arrived already (and now is present only as the memory or trace of itself) or is yet to arrive (and is therefore promised).[53]

Jenson provides a useful summary of these findings when he defines body-interactions according to a fourfold taxonomy. First, the body is the *object-presence of a person for another person.* In order to become present for another I must grant that other the possibility of my becoming an object for them. Second, the body is the *object-presence of a person for themselves.* 'My body is myself insofar as I am available to myself, insofar as I am not merely identical with myself, but *possess* myself.' There is a sense in which I can cause my body to do and be things; but there is a sense in which my body dictates terms to me as well. I can therefore address myself in words only insofar as my body is a sense-object that participates in a society in which the body is addressed. Third, the body is the *to-be-transcended presence of a person.* 'I am beyond myself as a describable object in the world; and so am not merely a describable object.' This withholding or transcendence of self can be experienced as either the inalterability of the past or the promise/possibility of a future. (Lévinas would of course say that the unpresentable origin of such temporal absences is that which is not at all temporal—Infinity.) Finally, and crucially for our discussion of church and sacraments later on, the body is also the site in which *words become visible.* It is only visible words, argues Jenson, which become solid enough to resist the arbitrary replacement of words with other words.[54] In the visible speech of the face-to-face, we might say, words are governed not primarily by grammar, but by *gravity.* In the body, and therefore in the communal situation of interlocution, words take on traction and weight.

2. Biblical Poetry: Covenant Relations Embodied

What we have said about the body as a site of negotiation between the desire of self and other (even if that other is 'oneself as another') is borne out beautifully within the deeply covenantal canon of Hebrew Scripture, particularly in the

---

[52] 1995), pp. 7-12.
[53] Scarry, *The Body in Pain,* pp. 163-67.
[54] Kearney, *The God Who May Be,* p. 14.
Jenson, *Visible Words,* pp. 21-3.

Psalms and the *Song of Songs*. I should like to spend some time with these texts, because they also suggest a bridge to the next stage of my argument, i.e. that it is the sacred body of the church and its worship which provides the primary site for a specifically covenantal or *vowed* relationship between God and specifically Christian selves.

2.1 Psalms: Covenanting through Antiphonal Speech

The *Book of Psalms* has been described as Israel's most powerfully prayerful response to the speech of God in Torah. As such, it would be a mistake to classify the psalms as merely 'spontaneous musings or uncontrolled aspirations.' Rather, they are a paradigmatically *responsive* literature, which finds its origin and reference in a traumatic encounter between the psalmist and the word of God as it has been passed down in law and tradition.[55] Ricoeur notes that Psalmic prayer, as distinct from other modes of naming God in the Bible, actually addresses God from the first person 'I'. This implies, of course, that God is the other who, if not literally a person, is 'not less than a person.'[56] Such prayer proceeds on the basis that God has already spoken, and that this speech lingers on in the dependence of prayer on that address. As such, the Psalms perhaps inaugurate that tradition of bi-vocal performance that seems so essential to Scripture and liturgy: embodied words that present *antiphonally* as both prayer *to* God and the speech *of* God. We shall make much of this in the latter sections of this chapter.

Childs has written that the complex dynamism of this relationship can be usefully traced through the Psalmic understanding of 'righteousness' [$s^e daqah$]. Psalmic righteousness is quite unlike juridical conceptions of right, which pertain to some kind of absolute ethical benchmark or norm. Psalmic righteousness is rather about specific, and ultimately dynamic, negotiations of the good between covenanting partners. Thus, 'A righteous person was one who measured up to the responsibilities which the *relationship* had laid upon him.' [Italics mine]. Even when the term 'righteousness' is used of God alone, it refers not to a fixed norm, but to any action of God that bestows 'salvation' in the sense of a relationship that liberates. In the understanding of the Psalms, God's intervention in Israel's life 'established a bond between him and his people which was defined by the quality of his saving acts.' Human justice is then understood to be a free outcome, a *relationally* determined response to divine justice (cf. Pss 111, 112). Righteousness is therefore not earned or gained by human beings alone, but proceeds from God and is conferred on a person or community by virtue of God's free choice in making, and persevering

---

[55] Brevard S. Childs, *Old Testament Theology in a Canonical Context* (Philadelphia: Fortress Press, 1985), p. 207.

[56] Paul Ricoeur, 'Lamentation as Prayer,' trans. David Pellauer, *Thinking Biblically: Exegetical and Hermeneutical Studies*, eds. André LaCocque and Paul Ricoeur (Chicago: Chicago University Press, 1998), p. 213.

The Desire of God

with, a specific relationship through all of its ups and downs. Thus, 'The Psalmist can praise God, complain of his sufferings, plea for a sign of vindication, but through it all and undergirding his response, lies the confession that life is obtained as a gift from God.'[57]

2.1.1 LAMENT: OTHERING PAIN

The psalms of lament are particularly valuable as commentaries upon the complex relationship between the spirit or promise and a body in pain. Again we must repeat that none of the Psalms should be read as spontaneous expressions of religious emotions. They are feeling-states modified first by speech and then by the canons of Hebrew poetry, refined in both manifestations by memory, recitation and singing in the temple liturgy.[58] As such, the Psalms are inherently theological in character. So while it is rightly said that the Psalms do not, as prayers, speculate or theorize about the ultimate meaning of human suffering, they nevertheless assume and infer an implicit theology, which responds to the tradition that precedes their performance.[59] What is striking about the Psalms of lament, then, is that the process of formation should have chosen to *preserve* a sense of emotional spontaneity in such a way as to make it both communicable and exemplary in contexts beyond its specific existential origins.[60] Psalm 22 is a case in point. At one level, who can doubt that the prayer issues from a real and visceral experience of pain and persecution?

> Many bulls surround me:
> >strong bulls of Bashan encircle me.
>
> Roaring lions tearing their pray
> >open their mouths wide against me.
>
> I am poured out like water,
> >and all my bones are out of joint.
>
> My heart has turned to wax;
> >it has melted away within me.
>
> My strength is dried up like a potsherd,
> >and my tongue sticks to the roof of my mouth;
> >you lay me in the dust of death.
>
> Dogs have surrounded me;
> >a band of evil men has encircled me,
> >they have pinned my hands and feet.
>
> I can count all my bones;
> >people stare and gloat over me.
>
> They divide my garments among them
> >and cast lots for my clothing (12-18).

---

[57] Childs, *Old Testament Theology in a Canonical Context*, pp. 208-09.
[58] Ricoeur, 'Lamentation as Prayer,' p. 215.
[59] Ricoeur, 'Lamentation as Prayer,' p. 222.
[60] Ricoeur, 'Lamentation as Prayer,' p. 215.

Yet the language employed here is so slippery in its reference that the reader is left in some doubt as to the precise and specific origins of the pain being experienced. Who are these 'bulls of Bashan,' who are these 'lions'? How, precisely, is the protagonist's life being 'poured out'? Are his bones literally 'out of joint,' his hands and feet 'pinned,' or are these figures for the paralysis of fear? Such language succeeds in preserving 'enough concrete indications to keep the lament within the horizon of individual experience' and yet is calculatedly indeterminate enough 'to raise the expression of suffering to the rank of a paradigm.' The effect of that device, as Ricoeur notes, is to transform the 'I' of the protagonist into 'an empty place capable of being occupied in each new case by a different reader or auditor.'[61] That explains how the Psalms of lament have come to resonate so powerfully in contexts so different, so *other*, to their own (a context which is itself so very indeterminate, so *other* than *our* own).

2.1.2 PRAYER: THE SELF AS ANOTHER

The resonance of *otherness* in Psalm 22 may be discerned, I think, in three different modalities. First, it is my experience in reciting the Psalm privately that *another self* is praying the Psalm both with me and in me. It has often been pointed out that the Psalms of lament never present themselves as lament alone. Rather, their lament occurs within a paradoxical context of faith and praise. So, here in Psalm 22, a sudden reversal may be discerned in verse 22 and following, where the protagonist makes a 'vow of praise'. The change of direction continues the lament in the sense of heightening its power by a strategy of contrast, but it also strengthens the elements of faith and praise which have been 'waiting in the wings,' so to speak, throughout.[62] Walter Brueggemann would say that this 'imbrication of the one with the other'[63] is a consequence of the fact that we are many selves, and that 'we get through the day because we have arrived at some covenantal arrangements, within the self or among the selves, that are often tenuous and provisional, but enough to get through the day.'[64] On a day when I am feeling happy and grateful, in reciting this Psalm I become aware of a part of myself which is not like that, a self in memory or expectation which suffers the weight of the 'not yet' of faith and desire. Conversely, on a day when I feel that weight most acutely, in reciting this Psalm I become aware of another self who contests the ultimacy of my circumstances by *calling* me to faith and hope. Again, Brueggemann comments that we spend our lives gathering a strong self together. But sometimes, when that self is 'scattered' through trauma, displacement or disorientation, other

---

[61] Ricoeur, 'Lamentation as Prayer,' pp. 215-16.
[62] Ricoeur, 'Lamentation as Prayer,' p. 219.
[63] Ricoeur, 'Lamentation as Prayer,' p. 219.
[64] Walter Brueggemann, *The Covenanted Self* (Minneapolis: Fortress Press, 1999), p. 12.

The Desire of God

selves assert their right to be heard. We resist their power because we are afraid of losing ourselves. But in doing so, we fail to see that there can be another gathering, a re-gathering which is, perhaps, even more 'ourselves' than before. Without the scattering, there can *be* no regathering.[65]

Psalm 22 is perhaps the most radicalised instance of this phenomenon in the Psalter because the expressions of laments and praise are so extreme. On the one hand, the suffering of the protagonist is all the more acute because it is claimed as a suffering *before* God, and at the hands of God: 'My God, my God, why have you forsaken me?' (1). On the other, the supplicant's praise takes the form of a *commandment* to his brothers and sisters that they might praise God as well: 'You who fear Yahweh, praise him! All you descendents of Jacob, honour him!' How then are these two expressions, these two so *extremely* separated selves, regathered into some kind of unity? Perhaps through the flow of a narrative or drama, as we suggested in chapter 1. What mediates between them, what makes a renegotiation possible, is the threefold voice of a supplicant as he both remembers who God has been and invokes that God as from a not-yet-arrived future:

Yet you are enthroned as the Holy One;
    you are the praise of Israel.
In you our fathers put their trust;
    they trusted and you delivered them.
They cried to you and were saved;
    in you they trusted and were not disappointed (3-5).

Yet you brought me out of the womb;
    you made me trust in you even at my mother's breast.
From birth I was cast upon you;
    from my mother's womb you have been my God.
Do not be far from me, for trouble is near
    and there is no one to help (9-11).

But you, O Lord, be not far off;
    O my Strength, come quickly to help me.
Deliver my life from the sword,
    my precious life from the power of the dogs.
Rescue me from the mouth of the lions;
    save me from the horns of the wild oxen (17-21).

In narrative or dramatic terms, these interspersions remind the suffering 'I' of the reader that things have been different in the past and therefore may be different again. This pushes the reader along with the supplicant toward not only invocation, but, eventually, praise. It is as if what is looked for and desired

---

[65] Brueggemann, *The Covenanted Self*, p. 14.

is eventually found within the orbit of a peculiar kind of knowledge: faith.[66] Faith, it seems, is capable of gathering the different selves into a narrative whole. That is not to say that any particular whole is final! Narrative, as we discovered in chapter one, is never finished from the point of view of its main actors and characters. If there is a finishing, an ending, it is inscrutable . . . except, perhaps, for the author.

2.1.3 PRAYER: ANOTHER WITH THE SELF

Of course, as has been noted already, the Psalms are not simply internal dialogues between various selves. They are also the prayers of a gathered community at worship in temple, synagogue, home, or church. The history of their reception encompasses all these contexts. It is therefore the case that even if the Psalms are recited alone in one's lounge-room, they resonate with the voice of a gathered community. What I hear in recitation is not simply the voice of another self which is nothing other than my own, but a *synchrony* and *diachrony* of encounter with genuinely other, embodied selves. As a temple-worshipper, the author of Psalm 22 stood shoulder-to-shoulder with his or her fellow-worshippers. The Psalm was said or sung *antiphonally*, that is, according to a dialogical pattern of call and response. But the call or address would not only have been heard in the voice of the cantor; it would also have resonated in what was heard and felt alongside and in the body, as worshippers spoke or sung their responses in unison. In a similar manner, I share a synchrony with others of my congregation or tradition who pray the Psalms in the morning and the evening. Although the social patterns of life have changed over the centuries, so that it is rarely possible anymore to gather in the same architectural space with my *compadrés* on a daily basis, there remains a sense in which I hear them praying the Psalms along with me in a *common* of time, rite, language and spirit.

There is a sense, also, of what is called 'the communion of saints' in all this. Diachronically, I am aware that people of faith have been praying these Psalms for millennia. During recitation one certainly has a sense of the Psalmist as *other*. His voice is certainly not reduced or collapsed into my own. But one also has the sense of many other voices, many other selves, who perhaps prayed this Psalm in a time of great anguish. For example, I sometimes think of the early Christians who were fed to the lions as entertainment for the blood-thirsty Roman public. I imagine them praying this Psalm, with its extraordinary dialectic of despair and faith, as the gates open before them onto certain death. Diachronic connection of this kind has the effect of taking me beyond and even outside of the particular nature of my own difficulties and challenges such that they are relativised by another's.

For Christians, of course, the most potent of these latter encounters is with Jesus as he invokes the Psalm at the scene of his crucifixion (Mk 15.34).

---

[66] Ricoeur, 'Lamentation as Prayer,' pp. 218-19.

The Desire of God

Bonhoeffer, who was himself executed by an oppressive regime, made much of this. He wrote movingly that in praying the Psalms 'Someone else is praying, not we; that the one who is here protesting his innocence, who is invoking God's judgement, who has come to such infinite depths of suffering, is none other than Jesus Christ himself . . . The *Man* Jesus Christ, to whom no affliction, no ill, no suffering is alien and who yet was the wholly innocent and righteous one, is praying in the Psalter through the mouth of his Church.'[67] For Bonhoeffer, the Psalter was Christ's Prayer Book, which he continues to pray in and through the church as both the address of God to human beings, and the only paradigmatic human response to God's promises. Therefore, in attending to the Psalter, we learn to pray as Christ prays; we learn to pray even those things which do not spring from ourselves, but belong to Christ and the whole of his body, the church.[68]

2.1.4 PRAYER: ANOTHER AS THE SELF

We have already begun to explore a third mode in which *otherness* resonates in the Psalms: through the implied or explicit address of the one to whom the Psalm responds, 'Yahweh'. Yahweh appears, first of all, as one who has *already addressed* the psalmist in both tradition and personal experience. The rememoration of national liberation in verses 3-5 references the prior address of Yahweh in Torah and the events of the Exodus, while the rememoration of infancy in verses 9-10 is witness to the psalmist's belief in a more personal experience of address as a child.

Both these memories speak of a God whose word of address is one of care and liberation. And yet clearly, since the psalm as a whole is dominated by lament, there is another kind of God implied here, a God who has also abandoned the psalmist to the weight of his pain: 'My God, my God, why have you forsaken me? . . . you lay me in the dust of death.' It seems that the already established theology of Torah does not entirely account for this. Perhaps the more recent events of Exile, with the accompanying destruction of temple and state, have raised a question about God which as yet remains unanswered. Has God, perhaps, removed Godself from the history of Israel? How might these different Gods, or different God-selves, be reconciled? In the prophets, of course, the apparent abandonment of God is interpreted as a form of judgement. Here God abandons God's people in response to their prior abandonment of God (cf. Hos 4.6, 6.5, 13.6, 9; Isa 1.3ff, 5.13-17, 29.14b). The extreme form of that view is that of the Deuteronomists, who tried to exonerate God at the price of indicting the people. But clearly that reduction was not entirely acceptable in Israel. Psalm 22 and other psalms of lament bear witness to the perseverance of a question that remained unanswered. Here the fact of the people's sins is not

---

[67] Dietrich Bonhoeffer, *Life Together*, trans. John W. Doberstein (London: SCM Press, 1954), p. 31.

[68] Bonhoeffer, *Life Together*, pp. 32-4.

regarded as sufficient explanation.[69]

2.1.5 THE NON-SYNCHRONOUS SELFHOOD OF GOD

Scarry has noted just how often, in the Hebrew Bible, the relationship with God is mediated by the sign of a weapon. Such signs tend to emphasise the invulnerability of the creator and the vulnerability of the creature. Indeed, in some accounts, the already wounded or the disabled are sometimes understood to be at an even greater distance from God than the ordinary person (cf. Lev 21.16, 22.21; Deut 17.1).[70]

These very different experiences of asymmetry with God, at once a liberator and forsaker (or even a wielder of weapons), bear witness to a deep and abiding struggle in the Hebrew Bible which, according to Scarry, springs from the original scene of making or creation.[71] The act of God's making can be seen as either a positive, generative gesture, or as a negative wounding or destruction. Both involve an act of scarification upon material reality in which the creator 'objectifies his presence in the world through the alterability of his world.'[72] The *Book of Genesis*, it is noted, is dominated by the voice or word of God in the form of a generative command or promise 'Be fruitful and multiply.' It is a command or promise repeated over and over in the iterative sense we discovered in Derrida: the same repeated otherwise through a myriad of images.[73] The many genealogies of Genesis, along with the stories they suggest, are iterations of the first making. In the consistent pattern of this alternation of list and story Scarry discerns a repetition of the making or crossing from divine idea or promise into material substantiation. Here the human body becomes the substantiation of interior or non-material things.[74]

The Genesis language of generative promise sets up a particular kind of relationship between the word or voice of God, and the body-selves of human beings. 'The verbal enters the human phenomenon of generation by being placed before it and so coming to be perceived as its cause or agent . . . Hence the actual fact of the magnification of the human body, the literal event of procreation and multiplication, is never simply an event in and of itself but becomes in the first form an obedient acting out of the thing that had come before, and in the second form a divine fulfilment of the thing that had come before.' What Scarry wants us to note, here, is that no matter how much more powerful than human flesh is the word of God, that Word never substantiates itself apart from a change in human and material matter. In this generative schema, the body is understood to substantiate something other and beyond

---

[69] Ricoeur, 'Lamentation as Prayer,' p. 224.
[70] Scarry, *The Body in Pain*, pp. 182-83.
[71] Scarry, *The Body in Pain*, pp. 183-84.
[72] Scarry, *The Body in Pain*, p. 175.
[73] Scarry, *The Body in Pain*, p. 191.
[74] Scarry, *The Body in Pain*, p. 188.

itself: to make ample and evident the aliveness and realness of God.[75] Visible change represents the invisible. So the Scriptural stories, while not subverting the essential difference between God and human beings, nevertheless entwine the two together such that human beings can impersonate or represent God, and God can also impersonate or represent Godself in human beings.

According to Scarry, then, the difference between these scenes of generation and the scenes of wounding countenanced in lament is simply this: in scenes of generation/liberation both God and human beings are affirmed and magnified, but in scenes of wounding/forsakenness God is magnified at the expense of people:[76]

> As God in the scene of hurt is a bodiless voice, so men and women are voiceless bodies. God is their voice; they have none separate from him. Repeatedly, any capacity for self-transformation into a separate verbal or material form is shattered, as God shatters the building of the tower of Babel by shattering the language of the workers into multiple and mutually uncomprehending tongues (Gen 11.1-9).[77]

What are we to make of this difference? Or, to repeat our earlier question, how are God's two selves—liberator and forsaker—to be reconciled? Scarry's own solution is to re-read the scenes of destruction anthropologically: not as examples of disobedience and punishment before God, but as stories of doubt in which the conviction of God's *reality* is fading. In the absence of other evidence, the pain in one's own body or the bodies of one's fellows is produced as witness to God's presence and power, though now in a negative and destructive mode. To this way of thinking, which Scarry claims for the Hebrews, 'The failure of belief is, in its many forms, a failure to remake one's interior in the image of God, to allow God to enter and to alter one's self. Or to phrase it in a slightly different form, it is the refusal or inability to turn oneself inside-out, devoting one's physical interior to something outside itself, calling it by another name.'[78] I suspect, however, that this reduction is just a little *too* neat. God, for Scarry, is ultimately an artefact or product of human making, which then returns as an explanatory metaphor for the interior structure of making as such.[79] But clearly, in the belief of the Hebrew people, God is that reality which *precedes* both themselves and their need for explanations. So, if we are to accept that their stories are properly theological, that is, that they situate material and human history within a more expansive divinity, then the problem of a God divided against Godself still remains.

I am inclined, for reasons that will soon become clear, to read Psalm 22 as

---

[75] Scarry, *The Body in Pain*, p. 193.
[76] Scarry, *The Body in Pain*, pp. 198-99.
[77] Scarry, *The Body in Pain*, p. 200.
[78] Scarry, *The Body in Pain*, pp. 201-02.
[79] Scarry, *The Body in Pain*, p. 181.

part of a canonical shift in Jewish thinking toward the eschatological. In this view, the differing selves of Yahweh, as they are presented in Psalm 22, would not be seen as ultimate or definitive. They would be read, instead, as pieces of a puzzle that is not yet complete, or as signs of a persisting *inscrutability* with regard to the personhood of God. Recall Ricoeur's suggestion that the Psalm represents a persisting question. Questions, as Rilke wisely wrote, are ways of living toward a future that has not yet arrived.[80] In the late prophetic tradition of Israel there *are*, in fact, hints at a way in which the wounding-self and the liberating-self of God might be reconciled in covenant:

This is what the Lord says:

'Where is your mother's certificate of divorce
    with which I sent her away?
Or to which of my creditors did I sell you?
Because of your sins you were sold;
    because of your transgressions your mother was sent away.
When I came, why was there no one?
    When I called, why was there no one to answer?
Was my arm too short to ransom you?
    Do I lack the strength to rescue you? (Is 50.1-2a).

Why do you say, O Jacob,
    and complain, O Israel,
'My way is hidden from the Lord;
    my cause is disregarded by my God'?
Do you not know, have you not heard?
The Lord is the everlasting God,
    the Creator of the ends of the earth.
He will not grow tired or weary,
    and his understanding no one can fathom.
He gives strength to the weary
    and increases the power of the weak.
Even youths grow tired and weary,
    and young men stumble and fall;
but those who hope in the Lord
    will renew their strength.
They will soar on wings like eagles;
    they will run and not grow weary,
    they will walk and not be faint (Is 40.27-31).

Here one sees the beginnings of that kind of 'substitution' in which the perseverance of Yahweh in relationship is substituted for the weariness of the people. There is a hint, in these sermons, that Yahweh's abandonment is simply

---

[80] Rainer Maria Rilke, *Letters to a Young Poet*, trans. Joan M. Burnham (San Rafael, California: New World Library, 1992), p. 35.

The Desire of God

his suffering at being abandoned himself, and that it is precisely this that he offers as the genesis or source of a new possibility of salvation.[81] The second pericope looks for some kind of future marriage between the inscrutability of God's ways and God's action of liberation. I would claim that a future of that nature begins to arrive in Jesus of Nazareth. For here, as Jüngel has argued, God comes to God's *own* future through the pathways of the very *human* struggle against the threat of nothingness. In the career and cross of the crucified and risen One, who takes on his lips the cry of dereliction from Psalm 22 (cf. Mk 15.33), God makes himself known as one who *undergoes* the human experience of God's wounding and absence, but is not overcome by it. This effects a change in the character of nothingness, first of all. Nothingness, which God as creator has of course made possible, changes from being a nihilation, pure and simple, to being a '*concrete negation*' that gives the concrete affirmation of being a properly critical edge.[82]

But it also effects a change in the being of God. Now revealed as a God who '*exists for others*,' in the Crucified the different selves in God can be seen for what they are: not an irreconcilable hidden God, who wounds, and an historical God, who saves, but the relationship between a Father and a Son who are at once different and yet the same.[83] We caught a glimpse of that possibility in Lévinas' theory of paternity. In trinitarian perspective, the desire of the Father for the Son gives God a *human body*, a human *self* indeed, a self which can be identified historically and is weighted in presence; yet God's being does not terminate in a human self. For the Son's desire for the Father also gives human beings a *divine Spirit*, a transcendent kind of selfhood that arrives, as from the future, and is still arriving. Because this self is 'hidden with Christ' in a God who is still arriving at God's own selfhood, we too are still coming to ourselves through the pathways of God.

2.2 The Song of Songs: Finding Oneself in God

We have journeyed from the phenomenology of desire into the relationships of selves in the Psalms, and finally into the strange and mysterious theology of divine-human love. It is time, then, to delve into the character of that love as it is presented in the *Song of Songs*. There are those who would deny, of course, that the *Song* has anything at all to say about the divine. After all, God is never named in the poem.[84] But that would be to read the poem apart from both its thoroughly Jewish religious context, and the history of its reception in the canons of both Jews and Christians.

---

[81] Ricoeur, 'Lamentation as Prayer,' p. 226.
[82] Jüngel, *God as the Mystery of the World*, pp. 218-19.
[83] Jüngel, *God as the Mystery of the World*, pp. 220-21.
[84] Although a textual variant at 8.6 reads 'Love . . . is like the very flame of the Lord', most modern translations have chosen to leave this aside.

2.2.1 AN EROTIC ALLEGORY OF DIVINE-HUMAN LOVE

From the very beginning, the poem has been read as an allegory of divine-human love.[85] While the poem is certainly erotic in character, describing the mutual desire of a woman and her lover in radically fleshly ways, the canonical fathers and mothers clearly did not see the flesh, or erotic love, as somehow unworthy of God or God's people. That this is so might appear to be something of an oddity when one considers that Judaism and Christianity alone, amongst all the ancient Near Eastern religions, appeared to have no sacred rites of a sexually explicit nature. Kristeva explains this by reference to an analogy with the biblical canon as a whole. The *Song of Songs* imagines the desire of God as a desire without consummation. There is no love-making at the maternal hearth in this erotic poem. Therefore the *Song*, as with the canon as a whole, imagines God as one who loves, and is desired by human beings, but who remains absent, or not entirely present. Desire is not finally consummated, and so remains desire.[86] We shall return to this theme in a moment. Ricoeur, for his part, is happy to defend the traditional reading on the grounds of his now famous hermeneutics of reception. Allegorical reading, he says, is authorized by a long history of reading in which a text is cited in new contexts without the 'otherness' of that text necessarily being absorbed into such contexts. The only difference between the rabbinical and patristic readings and our own, he says, is a precise recognition of the difference, the gap, which necessarily remains between the cited and the citation.[87]

2.2.2 INDETERMINACY OF IDENTIFICATION

The Song of Songs indeed encourages such citation, for the precise identity of both its characters and its social milieu is notoriously difficult to pin down. Even the term 'Shulamite', primary subject of the poem, is not a proper name.[88] The plentiful signs of indetermination in the poem include: (1) The fact that pieces of dialogue often appear to include quotations from someone other than the one who is speaking, with the result that it is difficult to *identify* the speaker (1.4b, 1.8, 2.1, 6.10). (2) There are several dream-sequences that present a similar problem. Is the shepherd dreaming of being a king? (3.6-11). Is the Shulamite dreaming of being a peasant woman? (5.2-8), or is it the other way around? Or, are all these figures quite distinct from one another in the body? (3) There are evocations of memory that intertwine with the present in such a way that it is difficult to tell which is which. The mother figure returns again and

---

[85] Julia Kristeva, *Tales of Love*, trans. Leon S. Roudiez (New York: Columbia University Press, 1987), p. 86.
[86] Kristeva, *Tales of Love*, pp. 95-6.
[87] Paul Ricoeur, 'The Nuptial Metaphor,' trans. David Pellauer, *Thinking Biblically: Exegetical and Hermeneutical Studies*, eds. André LaCocque and Paul Ricoeur (Chicago: Chicago University Press, 1998), p. 277.
[88] Ricoeur, 'The Nuptial Metaphor,' p. 268.

again in 1.6, 3.4, 3.11, 6.9, 8.1, and 8.4, but whose mother is she? Or is she the beloved as a younger woman?[89] (4) The seven 'scenes' often referred to by commentators are said to begin with lover or beloved searching for each other, and to end with a consummation when they find each other. But these alleged 'consummations' are very difficult to find, in fact, because they are sung with a sense of longing rather than recounted with any sense of material gravity or traction. These features suggest that the *Song* is not a narrative in which characters can be readily identified, but a poem that explores the very formation of identity. The poem often asks the question 'who?' but the question is never entirely answered.[90]

2.2.3 THE NUPTIAL METAPHOR: LOVE INCARNATE

Following Origen, who said that it is the 'movements of love' in the *Song* which are more important than the identity of its characters, Ricoeur argues for an interpretation of the *Song* in which the 'nuptial' metaphor for the relations between the lovers is 'liberated' from a purely human reference. As we noted earlier, the Greek paradigm of erotic love tended to see the point of sexual entanglement as a means of ecstatic *escape* from the body into some kind of self-less and unconscious communion with the divine One. But that is not what is happening in the *Song of Songs*. There the profound play of desire in the possession and dispossession of selves suggests, instead, a view of love that is transcendent and yet powerfully incarnational at the same time. While the dominant metaphors in the *Song* are classically material in that human selves, animals, and landscapes tend to stand in for one another, the very intensity of these metaphors actually has the effect of dissociating the metaphorical network from its *support* in materiality. What happens here is not a doing away with the properly sexual reference but rather its putting on hold or suspension; this then effects a freeing of the whole metaphorical network of nuptuality for other embodied 'investments and divestments.'[91] That possibility is further enhanced by the radical mobility of identification between the partners of the amorous dialogue, a mobility that smacks of 'substitution' in the sense we have been using it.[92]

Kristeva agrees. The consistent play in the text between the lover as King and the lover as Shepherd is only explicable, she argues, if one accepts the Freudian doctrine of transference, i.e. that the absence of a beloved object (the King) is that which makes the *enjoyment* of a beloved subject (the Shepherd) possible. Transference love, she argues, is necessary for the very living of life because it avoids either (erotic) fusion with a beloved or (stoic) disengagement by rearranging life's accidents on the 'higher level' of symbolic organization.

---

[89] Ricoeur, 'The Nuptial Metaphor,' p. 269.
[90] Ricoeur, 'The Nuptial Metaphor,' p. 270.
[91] Ricoeur, 'The Nuptial Metaphor,' pp. 273-74.
[92] Ricoeur, 'The Nuptial Metaphor,' p. 278.

In the symbolic relation between an 'I' and an 'Other' the self can be destabilised and reorganised in the direction of innovation and rebirth.[93] On this basis, Kristeva argues that the lover in the *Song* can be legitimately interpreted as the cipher for an absent or incorporeal God who is nevertheless made available to the human beloved in ritual, as well as in the very ordinary movements of daily life:

> Supreme authority, whether it be royal or divine, can be loved as flesh while remaining essentially inaccessible; the intensity of love comes precisely from that combination of received *jouissance* and taboo, from a basic separation that nevertheless unites—that is what love issued from the Bible signifies for us, most particularly in its later form as celebrated in the Song of Songs.[94]

2.2.4 HUMAN LOVE AS THE PASSAGE FOR AN ESCHATOLOGICAL DIVINITY

Of course, that reading would only be possible if one were to read the *Song* in its canonical context as a book of the Jewish and Christian Scriptures. But that is what it is! In *that* context, one can see how it is that the appearance of God in the materiality of the burning bush of Exodus 3 might be amplified in the *Song* to include lover's bodies and whole landscapes. Furthermore, Kearney has made the important point that a canonical reading of the *Song* would also be an *eschatological* reading. In this view, the love between the Shulamite and her lover looks both back to Eden's innocence and forward to a time when God and human beings will gaze upon each other 'face to face'. Citing Rabbi Hayyim de Volozhyn (19th century), Kearney points out that the Song is filled with eschatological imagery. 5.1 speaks of love as entering a garden filled with milk and honey, an image of the Promised Land. Similarly, the kiss of 1.2 might be read as the promise that one day the revelations of God will be given mouth to mouth and face-to-face, rather than through the mediations of angel, fire, or ritual.[95] Such eschatology is subversive, according to Kearney, for it makes the powerful erotic charge of the poem into something more than (but still including) the erotic. If this is the case, then our received understandings of both God and desire are transformed. Law-based understandings of both God and the obedience of God are swept aside in order to say that 'burning, integrated, faithful, untiring desire—freed from social or inherited perversions—is the most adequate way for saying how humans love God and God loves humans. It suggests how human and divine love may transfigure one another.'[96]

In a similarly canonical move, Ricoeur compares the *Song* with two other biblical texts. The first is Genesis 2.23: 'This is bone of my bone, flesh of my flesh; this one shall be called *ishah*, for out of *ish* this one was taken.' He notes

---

[93] Kristeva, *Tales of Love*, p. 15.
[94] Kristeva, *Tales of Love*, p. 90.
[95] Kearney, *The God Who May Be*, pp. 54-6.
[96] Kearney, *The God Who May Be*, pp. 56-8.

that neither this nor the *Song* is literally about anything other than human love. The Genesis text witnesses to the birth of an interlocutionary speech, while the *Song* makes such speech into a discourse of love and desire. The Genesis text imagines a relation which comes between the birth of the good and the coming of evil, while the *Song* is perhaps witness to 'the innocence of love within the heart of everyday life.' Perhaps one could then surmise that the *Song* proposes a kind of realised eschatology in which the mythic birth of innocence is reiterated otherwise, this time as the promise of a rebirth of innocence in the midst of the profane love of the everyday. The two texts are also joined, perhaps, by a sense in which, while God is not named, it is nevertheless God who makes such love possible. God makes possible even a love that is unconscious of God in its performance.[97]

A second canonical point of comparison is that of the conjugal metaphor used in the prophets for the love between Yahweh and his people. Hosea 3.1 says: 'The Lord said to me, 'Go, show your love to your wife again, although she is loved by another and is an adulteress. Love her as the Lord loves the Israelites, though they turn to other gods . . .' There are clear differences between the prophetic image and that of the *Song,* but these nevertheless 'face' each other in a kind of 'mirror-relation'. In the prophets, the love of God is seen *as* conjugal love; so also, in the *Song*, conjugal love might be seen *as* the love of God. This kind of 'facing' of metaphorical fields invites the canonical reader to combine the two fields in such a way as to create a new kind of intertextual theology. If one were to intersect the divine love (invested in old and new covenants), and human love (invested in the erotic bond), then the nuptial metaphor common to both would be revealed as the very power of metaphorical inter-signification, the 'hidden root, the forgotten root of the great metaphorical interplay that makes all the figures of love refer to each other.'[98]

Conclusion

What have we discovered then? Perhaps that there is a fundamental uncertainty at play in theological discourse about whether the English phrase 'desire of God' indicates first a human desire for God, or else a Godly desire for human beings. You will recall our discussion of this particular conundrum in Derrida. Could it be that our desire for God is already occasioned by God's desire for us? Could it be that our sense of God's absence is the very sign of God's promised (but not yet arrived) presence? Kristeva says of the speech between lover and beloved in the *Song of Songs* that whenever a speech is uttered concerning the self, it is always already referenced in the reality of the other. There is a dialectic or dialogue here in which 'the protagonist constitutes himself as such, that is, as a lover, as he speaks to the other, or as he describes

---

[97] Ricoeur, 'The Nuptial Metaphor,' pp. 296-99.
[98] Ricoeur, 'The Nuptial Metaphor,' pp. 301-03.

himself for the other.' Such a dialogue, says Kristeva, is not dialogue as communication, but dialogue as 'incantation' or 'invocation'. *Prayer*, one might say. As such, it reveals 'at the very heart of monotheism,' a double dynamic of *ecstasy* (going out of oneself) and *incarnation* (welcoming the other into oneself).[99]

Jüngel has written, similarly, that in love 'the loving ego experiences both an extreme distancing of himself from himself and an entirely new kind of nearness to himself. For in love the I gives himself to the loving Thou in such a way that it no longer wants to be that I without this Thou.' 'Lovers' he says, 'are always aliens to themselves and yet, in coming close to each other, they come close to themselves in a new way.' He therefore repudiates, as the *Song of Songs* does, any theology of *agape* or unconditional love that does not include or encompass the *eros* of body and embodiment. For in love, a lover certainly *does* want to have or possess the other, but such possession actually transforms the structure of having in that it is only possible to do so by also possessing or having one's own self in a radically different way. What is both ontologically and theologically significant here is that the beloved other is desired by the loving I 'only as one to whom it may *surrender* itself.' In love, the 'I' only wants to possess the other in the form of *being possessed* by the other.[100] What the Psalmist says of the love of God is therefore true of every genuine love: 'Whom have I in heaven but you? And there is nothing on the earth that I desire beside you. My flesh and my heart may fail, but God is the strength of my heart and my portion forever.' (Ps 73.25, 26). Christian theology calls such desire and confidence 'covenant love'. It is to this history and theology that I should now like to turn.

It is time to consider the idea that the church's worship is perhaps the privileged place and time in which the Christian covenant is both constituted and performed. It will nevertheless be noted that it is precisely the worship of the church that points to the fact that neither God nor church are completed in worship. If, as Paul says, the Christian self is 'hidden with Christ in God' (Col 3.2), then the church cannot entirely be itself until such time as God is entirely Godself. And God is not, because the world is not yet what God intends for it to be. Of the coming of that eschatological 'day' we are able to surmise very little. What we can say, however, is that the church, precisely as the body of Christ, may know its identity and mission only insofar as it lives from the power of a reality which it cannot domesticate or tame because that reality comes, as it were, from a place of irreducible otherness.

---

[99] Kristeva, *Tales of Love*, pp. 91-5.
[100] Jüngel, *God as the Mystery of the World*, pp. 318-19.

CHAPTER 5

Written on the Heart:
Covenant in Israel and in Christian Worship

> *'The time is coming,'*
>   *declares the Lord,*
> *'when I will make a new covenant with the house of Israel*
> *and with the house of Judah.*
> *'This is the covenant I will make with the house of Israel after*
> *that time'*
>   *declares the Lord.*
> *'I will put my law in their minds and write it on their hearts.*
> *'I will be their God and they will be my people.'*
>
>   from Jeremiah 31

Introduction

The loving desire of which we have been speaking is made manifest in the interlocution of facing. As we learned in chapter 2, the theological meaning of that is that God addresses us in the face and form of the human Christ. In Pauline theology, Christ is understood to have inaugurated a 'new covenant' with God in which the relationship with God occurs through the mediation of his own body and face:

> We are not like Moses, who would put a veil over his face to keep the Israelites from gazing at it while the radiance was fading away. But their minds were made dull, for to this day the same veil remains when the old covenant is read. It has not been removed, because only in Christ is it taken away. Even to this day when Moses is read, a veil covers their hearts. But whenever anyone turns to the Lord, the veil is taken away. Now the Lord is the Spirit, and wherever the Spirit of the Lord is, there is freedom. And we, who with unveiled faces all reflect the Lord's glory, are being transformed into his likeness with ever-increasing glory, which comes from the Lord, who is the Spirit (2 Cor 3.12-17).

> The god of this age has blinded the minds of unbelievers, so that they cannot see the light of the gospel of the glory of Christ, who is the image of the invisible God. For we do not preach ourselves, but Jesus Christ as Lord, and ourselves as your servants for Jesus' sake. For God, who said, 'Let light shine out of darkness,'

made his light shine in our hearts to give us the light of the knowledge of the glory of God in the face of Christ (2 Cor 4.4-6).

The Christian claim is that God has and is a body, and that body is Christ. Therefore, in facing Christ, we face God, and find ourselves always already faced by God in an invitation to relationship. Not that this new, extra-Jewish, facing of God somehow manages to do away with God's mysteriousness. The face, as we have seen, is not an object for our projections. The face *is* the self, and yet because the self is still *becoming* itself, it can never be entirely *manifest* in a particular face.[1] This is perhaps even more so when we are speaking of the face of God in Christ. On the one hand, as Paul testifies, in turning to Christ the priestly 'veil' between God's glory and ourselves is taken away. Paul claims a particular 'knowledge' of God's glory as it shines forth from the face of Christ. John writes of having actually 'seen' the glory of God as it took flesh and dwelt in his midst (Jn 1.14; cf. 1 Jn 1.1-4). Mark, in turn, writes the death of Jesus as the beginning of a new era in which the temple veil that separates the holy from the profane is rent asunder (Mk 15.38). On the other hand, Paul can also talk of Christ as another self, a self inherent in what he calls the 'Spirit'. Spirit, as the etymology of the word suggests, is as elusive as wind [*pneuma*]. *Spirit* is that aspect of God in Christ that elides and eludes simple presentation. Derrida would perhaps compare her with the unpresentable 'X' in all discourse, the *différance* or supplement which has no name yet lends itself to many names.[2] John says that anyone born of the Spirit through baptism becomes like the Spirit themselves. 'The wind blows wherever it pleases. You hear its sound, but you cannot tell where it comes from or where it is going. So it is with everyone born of the Spirit.' (Jn 3.7).

The transformation of new birth apparently comes when one turns to Christ and finds that he has already fixed us in his gaze. The Spirit is the irresistible power of his transcendent personality, that aspect of God in Christ that is able to accomplish in us what we are unable to accomplish for ourselves. In that gaze we become mirror-selves who reflect, but also *become*, the self who is Christ. 'Transformation' is what the apostle calls it, literally the morphing of our body-selves into the image or likeness of Christ. Not that this happens overnight! Yet the apostles look for a day in which Christians will know who they are because they know who Christ is. 'When he is made known we shall be like him, for we shall see him as he is.' (1 Jn 3.2). 'When Christ, who is your life, appears, then you will appear with him in glory.' (Col 3.3b). The theology of the New Testament clearly posits Christian selves that only become who and what they are by conjoining themselves, in covenant love, with an *other* who is, at once, God, a human person, and an elusive *persona* or spirit. In this chapter, I should like to explore the ways in which that covenant is both created and

---

[1] Ford, *Self and Salvation*, p. 21.
[2] Derrida, 'How to Avoid Speaking,' p. 4.

maintained by the experience of communal, embodied, worship. But first some essential background on the origins and development of the covenant in Hebrew and Jewish theology.

1. The Covenant in Israel

1.1 The Covenant as a Mutual Choosing

It is impossible to understand the Christian covenant without first acknowledging its indebtedness, in both theology and practice, to the Jewish covenant which preceded it. In his thorough study of the Hebrew tradition, Ernest Nicholson writes that 'covenant-language served as the focal point for that desacralisation of religious society of which the prophets were the chief agents. The concept of a covenant between Yahweh and Israel is . . . the concept that religion is based, not on a natural or ontological equivalence between the divine realm and the human, but on *choice*: God's choice of his people and their 'choice' of him, that is, their free decision to be obedient and faithful to him.'[3] Nicholson rejects the influential idea that the Hebrew covenant was based on ancient Near-East treaty traditions. Earlier research had suggested that the covenant between God and Israel was modelled on that contract in which a conquering king would grant rights to his vassals only insofar as they served his own interests.[4] Nicholson responds by claiming that the texts themselves support a more nuanced understanding. The theology of covenant emerged, he contends, during the late monarchical period when Hosea was preaching, and subsequently received its most extended treatment at the hands of the Deuteronomic writers between the late pre-exilic period and the 6th century BCE.[5]

What was distinctive about the preaching of Hosea and his contemporaries was their contestation of any kind of 'naturally' conceived alliance between God and human society that guaranteed Israel 'safe passage' through history so long as it appeased the wrath of Yahweh. Yahweh, at this time, was most often considered to be some kind of chief amongst a more extensive pantheon of fertility deities which symbolised the apparently necessary cycles of nature. The idea of covenant, of freely chosen moral responsibility and commitment, sought to challenge and demythologise these notions.[6] If, from ancient times, Israel had believed that El-Yahweh guaranteed its well-being, then Hosea was to preach that 'You are not my people and I am not your God' (1.9). While the

---

[3] Ernest W. Nicholson, *God and His People* (Oxford: Clarendon Press, 1986), pp. vii-viii.

[4] A discussion of this research may be found in Norman K. Gottwald, *The Hebrew Bible: A Socio-Literary Introduction* (Philadelphia: Fortress Press, 1985), pp. 204-07, 226-27.

[5] Nicholson, *God and His People*, p. 191.

[6] Nicholson, *God and His People*, pp. 192-205.

Zion tradition said that God would lay waste any enemy that attacked Jerusalem, Isaiah announced that Yahweh was about to summon exactly those enemies as his own warriors (7.18). All four prophets, Nicholson notes, consistently preached a condemnation of Israel according to a newly conceived ethical sphere of interpersonal relationships. In their hands, religion became an agent for the delegitimisation of state ideology. The 'naturally' conceived divine-human continuum is rent asunder and monotheism comes to be. The world is no longer something which God sustains, but rather something God transforms by virtue of God's free and 'other' transcendence. 'Hence Israel is more and more viewed as having been called by God as a manifestation of his will for righteousness in the world, and is eventually conceived of as the divine means of bringing blessing, salvation, Yahweh's righteousness, to the world.' In this way, a nascent soteriology is developed.[7]

1.2 The Conditional Covenant

According to Nicholson, the main feature of this new religious situation in Israel was a sense of bi-laterality in which Israel no longer followed a pre-destined path, laid out by the mythological cycles of nature-gods, but was free and responsible to choose its own future in a genuinely *historical* sense. While Yahweh asymmetrically sought and commanded an absolute and exclusive commitment and obedience, that vocation had to be chosen and re-chosen in each new generation. A covenant like that carries within it the possibility of separation and divorce, as the language of Jeremiah's 'new covenant' makes explicit (Jer 31). Possibly the earliest description of covenant-making, Exodus 24.3-8, already makes that point. The Lord commands, but the people must freely choose to bind themselves to the commandment. The covenant is then ratified in a liturgical ceremony. Exodus 34.10-28 repeats the formula. God binds Godself to a covenant with Israel but also expects Israel to bind itself to God through obedience. The same goes for Deuteronomy 26.17-19, where Israel declares that Yahweh is Israel's God, while Yahweh declares that Israel is his own possession. Israel is to fulfil its covenantal vocation by becoming 'a people holy to Yahweh' its God.[8]

Brueggemann calls this Sinai tradition of covenant the 'conditional' tradition, which is distinguished from a more 'unconditional' tradition associated with the patriarchs and with David.[9] It is conditional because, while Israel remains free to accept or reject the covenant, it is nevertheless *Yahweh* who asymmetrically determines the terms of the covenant through command and law giving. The conditional covenant is bilateral to the core, yet the options for Israel were circumscribed from the beginning. What Yahweh promises the Hebrew people is another kind of bondage in exchange for their freedom from

---

[7] Nicholson, *God and His People*, pp. 206-08.
[8] Nicholson, *God and His People*, p. 211.
[9] Brueggemann, *The Covenanted Self*, p. 36.

the bondage of Egypt. From the first, Yahweh says 'Let them go that they may *serve* me' (Ex 5.1). 'Thus,' says Brueggemann, 'the 'freed slaves' have a freedom that is a new servitude, under new commands and new demands. The new commands are given at Sinai. But before they are given, there is a particular interchange where God declared that if the people will 'obey my voice' [infinitive absolute] and 'keep my covenant' [infinitive absolute] then they will be the chosen possession of Yahweh (Ex 19.5-6).'[10] Here the people are free, certainly, but only within a circumscribed field which God makes possible. Bilateral and yet conditional: that is the covenant of Sinai.

1.3 The Unconditional Covenant

According to Childs, however, the conditional covenant should be read as in some sense subordinate to the unconditional covenant. The latter reveals God as one who is *faithful*, keeping the promises that have been made to patriarchs, kings and prophets, regardless of the behaviour of the people.[11] Psalm 89.30-37 is typical in this regard:

> If his sons forsake my law and do not follow my statutes,
>   if they violate my decrees and fail to keep my commands,
> I will punish their sin with the rod, their iniquity with flogging;
>   but I will not take my love from him, nor will I ever betray my faithfulness.
> I will not violate my covenant or alter what my lips have uttered.
> Once for all, I have sworn by my holiness—and I will not lie to David—
>   that his line will continue forever and his throne endure before me like the sun;
> it will be established forever like the moon, the faithful witness in the sky.

This Davidic tradition of covenant expresses a perseverance in God's faithfulness, even where that of Israel fails. It is therefore 'unconditional' in Brueggemann's sense, a covenant more like a promise than a command or law. It promises that God will be faithful to the terms of the covenant, even when Israel is not. Hosea 11 takes the tradition a step further. There we find Yahweh raging against Israel like a father who despairs at the waywardness of his son. 'The more I called to Israel, the more they fled from me' says Yahweh. Despite his love and care—here the commandments are called 'cords of human kindness' and 'ties of love'—Israel was faithless, turning instead to Baal and other gods of fertility. So Yahweh contemplates Israel's destruction by the hand of Assyria, refusing to relent even if they call out for help. Yet, at precisely this moment in the text, there is a sudden turning, even a repenting in the heart of God:

> How can I give you up, Ephraim?
>   How can I hand you over, Israel?

---

[10] Brueggemann, *The Covenanted Self*, p. 24.
[11] Childs, *Old Testament Theology in a Canonical Context*, p. 43.

> How can I treat you like Admah?
> > How can I make you like Zeboiim?
> My heart is changed within me;
> > all my compassion is aroused.
> I will not carry out my fierce anger,
> > nor will I turn and devastate Ephraim.
> For I am God and not man—
> > the Holy One among you.
> I will not come in wrath (11.8-9).

There is evidence here for the kinds of claims I made in chapter 2. God is not forever the same, enshrined in the heavens as some kind of 'unmoved mover'. God is rather one who is deeply affected, to the very core of the divine being, by what human beings do and say. Further, it seems that no matter what human beings do, no matter how far they stray from God's purposes, this God is not one who will simply cut the umbilical cord in a cold and calculating manner. This God is really, and quite literally, a *father* in the sense that Lévinas understands paternity, one whose own being and selfhood is implicated in, and affected by, what his children do or fail to do. There is both bilaterality and asymmetry here, although these differ from that of the 'conditional' covenant. In the conditional covenant, Israel can release both itself and God from the terms of the covenant, thus annulling the relationship altogether. The covenant is asymmetrical in the sense that it is God who commands, therefore outlining a circumscribed field of possibility within which Israel may then exercise its freedom. The unconditional covenant, by contrast, presents another kind of asymmetry. Here God chooses to stick by Israel whether the specific terms of the covenant are honoured or not. There is a sense in which God undertakes to both *undergo* and *suffer* whatever future Israel chooses for them both.

1.4 An Unfolding Covenant: Both Conditional and Unconditional

What are we to make, then, of these two covenantal trajectories—the one conditional and the other unconditional? Should we read the former under the aegis of the latter, as Childs appears to suggest, or do we need to somehow choose between them? Intriguingly, all of our commentators point to the proclamation of Jeremiah as some kind of breakthrough that is able to leave the tension between conditionality and unconditionality (law and grace, if you like) in its wake:

> 'The time is coming,' declares the Lord,
> > 'when I will make a new covenant
> with the house of Israel
> > and with the house of Judah.
> It will not be like the covenant
> > I made with their forefathers
> when I took them by the hand

>   to lead them out of Egypt,
> because they broke my covenant,
>   though I was a husband to them,' declared the Lord.
>
> 'This is the covenant I will make with
>   the house of Israel after that time,' declares the Lord.
> 'I will put my law in their minds
>   and write it on their hearts.
> I will be their God,
>   and they will be my people.
> No longer will a man teach his neighbour,
>   or a man his brother, saying, 'Know the Lord,'
> because they will all know me,
>   from the least of them to the greatest,' declares the Lord.
> 'For I will forgive their wickedness
>   and will remember their sins no more.' (Jer 31.31-34).

As we noted earlier, Nicholson regards the use of *heperu* (annulled, broken) in this passage as the sign of a radical transition from one kind of relationship—what we have called the Sinai or conditional covenant—to *another*, which nevertheless retains the same structure and goal as the old one. What is different in the new situation, he says, is that Yahweh now undertakes to so change the hearts of the people that they will *spontaneously choose* to keep God's commandments. The same thought is expressed in Jeremiah 32.36-41 and Ezekiel 37.15-28.[12] One might add Ezekiel 36.24-32, where the prophet promises a kind of divinely performed heart transplant whereby 'hearts of stone' are replaced by 'hearts of flesh'. In reading these passages it becomes clear that the 'new' covenant cannot be mistaken for the unconditional covenant of Davidic tradition. For these preachers imagine a time in which Israel actually *obeys* God and *does God's will*. It is not that God simply chooses to keep the divine promises in perpetuity, regardless of what Israel may decide. Rather, as Childs puts it, God now undertakes to do for Israel what it proved unable to do for itself, that is, *trust and obey.*[13]

One is left to ask, then, how that might actually happen on the ground. *How* might God do for human beings what they seem unable to do for themselves, and how could such a thing be done without violating the human *freedom* so valued by both conditional and unconditional versions of the covenant? Brueggemann suggests a solution that resonates strongly with my reflections on the *Psalms* and the *Song of Songs*. Our relationships with God and one another are, in fact, both 'profoundly unconditional and massively conditional'. Even in formally unconditional relationships like that between marriage partners and between parents and children, there remain high levels of expectation. When

---

[12] Nicholson, *God and His People*, p. 212.
[13] Childs, *Old Testament Theology in a Canonical Context*, p. 96.

these expectations are not met, there can be much pain, and even a high degree of rejection, even though the wounded party is highly committed. 'The truth,' says Brueggemann 'is that there is something inscrutable about such relationships that are both conditional or unconditional; or perhaps we should say neither unconditional nor conditional. If one seeks to make one term or the other final in characterizing such a relationship, we destroy the inscrutability that belongs to and defines the relationship.'[14] In Brueggemann's view, the categories of conditional or unconditional vows need to be seen as subsets of that more embracing reality he simply names 'covenant'. In the covenant human beings have with God, it is the holy other who initiates, responds to, and watches over the relationship.[15] But, equally, human beings are granted the freedom, precisely by God's will and initiative, to legitimately assert their needs and wants over and against what God seems to be doing at any particular time. 'It is through urgent insistence that God can be bonded to my issues, so that I may be bonded to God's expectations.'[16]

What Brueggemann appears to have in mind here is something like a developmental view of covenant which begins, asymmetrically, with the experience of God's sovereign command, but necessarily passes through periods of transition or disillusionment as the human subject comes to terms with the apparent injustice or incomprehensibility of God's purposes. It is legitimate and necessary, during such periods, to complain and cry out to God, precisely on the basis of the covenantal promises. But ultimately, in the Hebrew canon, the commands of God are not seen as impositions but rather as belonging to, and even definitional of, 'the very fabric of our existence.' From self-assertion, Hebrew spirituality moves toward a point where it can see that the possibility of joy in life is intimately tied up with the joy of both God and neighbour. Here the juridical approach to obedience is transformed into a trusting acceptance that joy for God and our neighbour is the very means by which one's own desires are fulfilled.[17] In this perspective, the best 'good' that one might achieve for oneself comes through a prior recognition of, and working for, the good of another. This is amply illustrated in Deut 6.5-6 and Psalm 119, where the language of 'loving' and 'keeping the commandments' is paralleled in order to create a sense of equivalence between desire and obedience.[18] One might say, with Kearney, that the desire or love of God exists in the accusative before it exists in the nominative. Our desire for God is

---

[14] Brueggemann, *The Covenanted Self*, pp. 36-7.
[15] Brueggemann, *The Covenanted Self*, p. 38.
[16] Brueggemann, *The Covenanted Self*, p. 7.
[17] Brueggemann, *The Covenanted Self*, pp. 38, 40-1. Although this work is never cited by Brueggemann, I detect in the background something of the 'faith development' model advanced in James W. Fowler, *Stages of Faith: The Psychology of Human Development and the Quest for Meaning* (Melbourne: Collins Dove, 1981), pp. 117-211.
[18] Brueggemann, *The Covenanted Self*, p. 45.

already God's desire for us. It is given us in excess, gift, grace; so much so that our desire should be seen not as a lack or gap to be somehow fulfilled by God, but rather as an affirmative 'yes' to the summons of a superabundant, impassioned God in whom we find our deepest desires—which are already God's desires—fulfilled.[19]

1.5 The Covenant Formulated in Worship

What remains to be said about Israel's covenant is essential to my thesis in this chapter: that the worship of Israel played a decisive role in the formation of the sacred texts by which the covenant is known and received. Chauvet notes that both the historical and hermeneutical activity of Israel is likely to have begun around the early shrines of Hebrew worship at Shechem, Gilgal and Shiloh (amongst others).[20] These beginnings set the pattern for much that was to follow. We have already noted the decisive *theological* role of the temple liturgy as it was expressed in the Psalms. But we should observe, also, that the great story-cycles of the Yahwist, Priestly, and Deuteronomistic histories were both formed by, and formative for, the worship of Israel. The preaching of the prophets, of course, happened in and around key liturgical events, and became Scripture through liturgical recitation. Chauvet summarises the results of much recent scholarship when he says that the canonical texts have survived precisely because of their use in the liturgy. The Bible as we have it was designed for public reading and became authoritative by that public reading.[21]

This well-attested fact has two important consequences for our study of vowed selves. First, the covenantal thinkers of the Jewish people did not simply *use* the liturgy to express their pre-formed ideas. The liturgy was in fact the *workshop* in which their ideas were formed. The experience of worship shaped their theology at least as much as their theology shaped the liturgy. Second, and even more importantly, if (1) the Hebrew Bible is a thoroughly liturgical book (in both origin and transmission), and (2) that text is largely about the negotiation of a covenant with God, then one simply must conclude that the worship of Israel is *itself* the very work of *per/forming the covenant over and over again* in each new generation. The liturgy is the covenant itself; or, to put things a little differently, the liturgical body of the community is the material hinge by which the relationship between God and human selves is negotiated.

2. The Covenant in the Worship of the Church

2.1 The Church as a New Covenant

The Greek word *ekklesia,* or church, originally referred to a secular gathering

---

[19] Kearney, *The God Who May Be*, p. 54.
[20] Chauvet, *Symbol and Sacrament*, p. 191.
[21] Chauvet, *Symbol and Sacrament*, pp. 191-92.

brought into being by the summons of a herald. It was first used in a religious context when it translated the Hebrew phrase 'people of God' in the Septuagint. The writers of the New Testament took over the term to describe their own communities, which they regarded as a legitimate continuation of the people of God, the true Israel, in the form of a *new covenant* mediated though Jesus the Christ.[22] The new or 'Christian' covenant of course retains a crucial relation with the old or 'Jewish' covenant. No-one is more explicit on this point than Paul in Romans 11.17ff, where he argues that Christian converts are like recently grafted branches who therefore have no grounds whatsoever for exalting themselves over the root of the tree from which their very life is drawn. And yet the new covenant is genuinely new. It is a covenant that seeks to transcend the tensive categories of law and grace through the absolutely singular and messianic action of a God who reveals Godself to be irrevocably human. One might therefore say, with Derrida, that the old covenant repeats itself otherwise, that the new covenant reveals that the old is 'iterable,' subject to 'drift' or eschatological indeterminacy.[23]

Invoking Paul's language of the face, we might summarise the New Testament's ecclesiology in a fourfold manner. First, and in parallel with Hebrew usage, the church is a *gathering*, a congregation of people, which forms according to the asymmetrically original call and promise of God. Here God faces the community God calls into being. Second, the church is that community that claims to have 'heard' and 'seen' God's address in *Jesus*, who lived God's life, was crucified, and is risen in the power of the Spirit. Here God faces the community in and *as* the man, Jesus Christ. Third, the church is a fellowship or *koinonia* of those who are responding to God's summons by vowing themselves, in faith, to the way and worship of Jesus. Here God, in Christ, substitutes Godself for the church so that the church might become a bodily substitute for Christ, capable now of mirroring the face of God in and for itself. Fourth and finally, the church is that community which resolves, in the power of the untameable Spirit, to work with and for God in God's eschatological *mission* for peace and justice in the whole creation. Here God faces the world in the face of the church. This language of the face emphasises that the Christian covenant with God is interlocutionary and embodied; it also reminds us of the pivotal role of Jesus in the whole communicative drama. The fourfold taxonomy emphasises that the church both *is*, and *learns to be,* itself only as it worships. For worship, as I will argue now, is a fourfold performance of covenantal relation: summons/gathering, address/listening, embodiment/ transfiguration, and sending/mission. Let us spend a little time with each of these claims.

---

[22] Gerhard Ebeling, *The Nature of Faith*, trans. Ronald Gregor Smith (London: Collins, 1961), pp. 140-46.

[23] Derrida, 'Signature Event Context,' p. 8.

2.2 The Covenant as Summons and Gathering

The New Testament affirms and repeats the Jewish experience of God as essentially asymmetrical. God creates, God calls, God promises, and human beings have no other choice than to navigate within a circumscribed set of determinations made possible by God in the form of a gift. John's gospel begins with an affirmation of the priority of God as the *creator per verbum*: by the Word of divine address, every form of being receives its possibility from God (Jn 1.3). The *Letter to the Hebrews* affirms the Christian belief that 'the worlds were prepared by the word of God, so that visible things were formed from invisible things' (Heb 11.2). In Romans 4.17, Paul describes God as the one who 'gives life to the dead and who calls into being the things which do not exist [*kalountos ta me onta hos onta.*]' This is a coming-to-be which befalls us from the outside, as it were, establishing us in being not as a consequence of some kind of immanent unfolding, but rather because God *calls* us into being by a specific word of address, in a manner quite indifferent to the apparently 'natural' processes of being so beloved by philosophers.[24]

What such divine indifference might mean for the formation of personal identity is made clear by another Pauline text, this time in 1 Corinthians 1.26-29: 'Consider your own call, brethren: not many of you were wise by human standards, not many were powerful, not many were of noble birth. But God chose what is foolish in the world to shame the wise; God chose what is weak in the world to shame the strong; God chose what is low and despised in the world, and also the things that are not, in order to annul the things that are [*kai ta me onta, hina ta onta katargese*], so that no-one may boast in the presence of God.' What we learn here is that God is essentially indifferent to either our 'natural' or our 'socially-constructed' selves.[25] God reserves the right to interrupt us, even in the midst of what seems most 'natural' or 'inevitable', with a word of command or promise which relativizes it all. From the perspective of the apostle, what seems 'natural' or 'necessary' is far from it; indeed, what seems natural or necessary is a form of slavery which God comes to contest and transform (cf. Gal 4.21-5.1; Jn 8.31-38). Not that God *forces* people to leave their slavery behind. The apostle says that God leads people to *metanoia* not by means of a whip or gun, but by the virtues of kindness and forbearance (Rom 2.4, 5).

For the New Testament, God's gathering call is heard and seen most clearly in the life and death of the risen Jesus. In him the community learns that the call is intended to save us from slavery and oppression—'I have come,' he said 'to seek and save the lost' (Lk 19.10). From Jesus the writers of Scripture also learned that by far the most important modes of God's call are *invitation*, *promise* and *question*. In John's account, Jesus is always *inviting* people to receive him as food or drink or light or life, so addressing a desire, which he

---

[24] Marion, *God without Being*, pp 86-9.
[25] Marion, *God without Being*, pp 89-95.

evokes in them, for a deeper satiation or salvation. In doing so, he *promises* that any who receive him in trust and faith will be given a miraculous new name and identity: children of God.[26] The form of this invitation-promise is of course conditional: 'If . . . then . . .' The possibility of freedom has been offered by God, but liberation remains conditional upon the existential assent of the people. The synoptic gospels combine these elements with a parabolic pattern of *questions* in which people are invited by Jesus to reconfigure who they are in relation to the claims of the coming kingdom upon their lives.[27] Questions invite hearers to consider their experience anew, to enter into what Jüngel has aptly called 'a new experience with experience':

> In this new experience, all that has been experienced until now under the aspect of its nothingness is experienced once more. The new quality of this experience makes it impossible to align it with other experiences. Rather, it is related to those experiences from which it differs in that 'old becomes new' . . . In view of the possibility of non-being, man has a qualitatively new experience with his being. I call it a new experience with experience, because it is not only every experience already had, but experience itself is experienced anew.[28]

Questioning forms a crucial dimension of parabolic speech, for it introduces *within* the discourse of an enclosed ego or culture a perspective from *beyond* it, from God. Parables are not forceful in character, but playful. They play with the counters of a familiar game, but introduce elements that make the familiar seem suddenly unfamiliar.[29] Frank Rees has pointed out that the question, as a key mode of God's address, is an essential component of the Jewish tradition as well: from the question 'where are you?' (Gen 3.9) to the sustained questioning of the book of Job (chapters 38-42), human beings are invited to ask their own questions, and so begin upon a journey of transformation in God.[30]

What the call of God promises, first of all, is a gathering of selves into the new space and time of God's own becoming. The letter to the *Ephesians* says:

> With all wisdom and insight God has made known to us the mystery of his will, according to his good pleasure which he set forth in Christ, as a plan for the

---

[26] Cf. Jn 1.12, 13, 43-51; 3.16-21; 4.10-15; 5.2-9; 6.35-51; 7.37-39; 8.12, 31-38, 51; 10.7-18; 11.25-27; 12.26; 14.1-7, 11-14; 15.7, 10-11; 16.20-33.

[27] Cf. Mk 2.8; 3.4, 24, 33; 4.21, 40; 5.9, 30-31, 39; 6.38; 8.17-18; 8.27, 36-37; 9.33; 10.38; 11.30; 12.10; 12.16; 12.35; 14.37, 41; 15.34; Lk 2.49; 5.32; 6.39, 46; 10.36; 11.9-13; 12.13, 14, 22, 51, 57; 13.2, 15-16, 18, 20; 14.3, 28, 31; 15.4; 16.12; 17.7, 9, 18; 18.8, 19; 22.35; 24.17, 19, 26, 38, 41; Mt 5.17; 6.25, 28, 31; 9.28; 13.27, 51; 17.25; 20.13, 15; 21.31.

[28] Jüngel, *God as the Mystery of the World*, p. 32.

[29] Jüngel, *God as the Mystery of the World*, pp. 289-91.

[30] Frank D. Rees, *Wrestling with Doubt: Theological Reflections on the Journey of Faith* (Collegeville, Minnesota: Liturgical Press, 2001), pp. 151-57.

fullness of time: to gather up all things in him, things on heaven and things on earth (1.8b-10).

God, who is rich in mercy, out of the great love with which he loved us even though we were dead through our trespasses, made us alive together with Christ— by grace you have been saved—and raised us up with him and seated us with him in the heavenly places in Christ Jesus (2.4-6).

God, we are told, wants to gather up absolutely everything, without remainder, 'in him,' that is, in *Christ*. For Christ is understood here, as elsewhere, as that personal reality in which the very great difference between God and the universe is overcome or traversed by a still greater similarity.[31] In Christ our very great distance from God becomes the possibility for a genuine relation or proximity with God. Because God chose to face God's human other by gazing into the face of Christ, human beings may now face their divine other by gazing into that same face. In this manner God traverses the distance; God does not, as the Chalcedonian doctrine of Christ makes clear, annihilate the distance altogether. The human Christ is 'one substance' with the Father, and yet he is 'personally' distinct. In Christ, God embraces the human without ceasing to be God, and human beings embrace divinity without ceasing to be human. What this means for those whom God addresses is this: that Christ becomes the place of crossing or congregation for everything. 'In Christ,' God is gathering God's other, human beings and the whole creation, into the divine becoming. When God is arrived at Godself, then we shall all arrive at *ourselves* as well. Note that the wholeness or peace of arrival is not imagined in pagan terms, as a monadic stillness in which the divine and the human are fused. Rather, the New Testament imagines a gathered unity in which 'oneness' remains both dynamic and relational. Christ prays in John that his disciples may be one as he is one with the Father: neither the same, nor distinct, but 'filiated,' as Marion says (Jn 17.11, 21).[32]

The Trinity is Christianity's best imagining of this, for here the Father, the Son and the Spirit become themselves by constantly ceding themselves in and for the other *as* other. We noted in chapter 3 that the circle-dance of the Trinity has been widened in Christ to include the life of human beings and the world. Insofar as we are able to cede ourselves to God, to project ourselves into the *othering* space that is 'in Christ,' God is able to include us in the othering of God's own divine *circumincessio*. So it is the mission of God in Christ to gather all of us who are 'far off,' strangers to God, into the covenant promise, so that we might no longer be aliens, but citizens of God's commonwealth—the very dwelling-place of God (Eph 2.17-22).

In Sunday worship this theology of gathering is performed in a number of inter-related rites. First there is the 'call to worship' in which a portion of

---

[31] Jüngel, *God as the Mystery of the World*, p. 288.
[32] Marion, *The Idol and Distance*, p. 110.

Scripture is read, usually from the genres of command, promise, or invitation that we have referred to. Here God is understood to be the initiating agent, the one who gathers (as the etymology of *ek-klesia*, from *kaleo*, 'to call,' makes plain),[33] and the worshippers respond by *actually* gathering—coming together in body, mind and spirit from places and experiences of radical difference. Usually this is followed by a hymn of praise to, and/or an invocation of, the Trinity. The purpose here is to remind worshippers that they are crossing a threshold in which profane space and time becomes sacred space and time. As well as gathering in a building or a garden or whatever, the community congregates, with Christ, in the eschatological space and time of the trinitarian communion.

To do so is to enter that order of signification which Chauvet calls the 'symbolic'. Symbol is of course a 'contract, pact, or covenant' that, unlike juridical contracts, exists from time immemorial: it is the language-world by which distinct entities or persons are gathered together into interlocutory relationship (from the Greek *sym-ballein*, 'to put together'). The symbolic is to be distinguished from the 'imaginary,' which, in Lacanian theory, is that force by which the mediated distance between the real and the subject is erased in order to create the illusion of immediacy. Such immediacy, in the symbolic order, is problematised by reference to a 'third' in any covenant or relation, who both transcends and possibilises the relationship precisely as a relationship of *others*.[34] In worship, I suggest, this 'third' can be any member of the Trinity who is not, at that moment, being specifically addressed. For each of God's *personae* function as the author(iser) and origin of life for their others, whether divine or human. The transition into the symbolic purview of the Trinity therefore has a profoundly transformative effect on the identity of worshippers. In worship one both seeks for, and is offered, another self, a *me* in the accusative rather than an *I* in the nominative—perhaps even the 'we' of filiation in a new family under God. Not the adding of an 'I' to a 'you,' but the creation of a new, complex, person.[35] David Ford expresses this well. In worship,

> God posits the self in community without that necessarily being a dominating heteronomy. Likewise, there is no 'shattered cogito' in fragmentation, but there can be a complex gathering of self in diverse relationships (including forms of self-dispossession that require a letting go of control and mastery, often an existential equivalent of shattering) before a God who is trusted as the gatherer of selves in blessing.[36]

---

[33] Chauvet, *The Sacraments*, p. 34.
[34] Chauvet, *The Sacraments*, pp. 14-16. cf. the discussion of the imaginary and the real in Žižek, *On Belief*, pp. 79-88.
[35] Chauvet, *The Sacraments*, p. 32.
[36] Ford, *Self and Salvation*, p. 99.

What is theologically important here are not just the words that are spoken, but the architecture of facing as well. Kristeva is right to note that the Christian Scriptures rarely tell us to love God except through the mediating otherness of other human beings.[37] Paul actually downplays the love of human beings for God in favour of the more original love of God for human beings. Instead of urging people to love God, he assures them of God's love and challenges them to imitate that love in their dealings with other people (Rom 5.6-8; cf. Rom 13.8-15-13; 2 Cor 8.8-15). For the writers of the New Testament, the best path to a love-allegiance with God is through the love of that body-self which is the neighbour (Eph 5.1ff; 1 Jn 3.11-24; Mt 25.31-46). What the church learns in worship, then, is that God faces and calls the worshipper *in* and *as* the material voices and bodies that belong to our fellow worshippers; and also that worshippers address *God* in praise and love by a facing of *one another*. If the church is the 'body of Christ,' as Paul insists, then Christ is addressed and loved by the addressing and loving of human selves. In some traditions, the gathering rites include some kind of 'litany of the saints' in which the voice and address of God is closely associated with the lived charity of particular human lives. Saints are not, of course, worshipped as God, but rather venerated as icons or vessels of God's glory and voice. Saints are exemplars of that vow or covenant by which the enclosed self is ceded or given away in favour of a new self which is Christ. In the gathering rites, their presence reminds worshippers that Christ loves, and is loved, in a diachronic community of saints through time, not only through the synchrony of encounter within the present moment.

The final movement in the gathering rites is often confession and absolution.[38] Having heard the command and call of God, the worshippers inevitably become aware of the inadequacy of their attempts to perform God's law. Far from bypassing the seriousness of this situation, the New Testament declares that we are indeed responsible for ourselves as well as others. Paul declares that 'there is no-one righteous, not even one . . . all have sinned and fall short of the glory of God.' (Rom 3.10, 23). Matthew has Jesus say that there is no getting around the requirements of the law, or the indictment of the prophets on all who fail to keep the law:

> I tell you the truth, until heaven and earth disappear, not the smallest letter, not the least stroke of the pen, will by any means disappear from the Law until everything is accomplished. Anyone who breaks one of the least of these commandments and teaches others to do the same will be called least in the kingdom of heaven, but whoever practices and teaches these commands will be called great in the kingdom of heaven. For I tell you that unless your righteousness surpasses that of the Pharisees and the teachers of the law, you will certainly not enter the kingdom of heaven (5.18-20).

---

[37] Kristeva, *Tales of Love*, p. 140.
[38] Confession and absolution may also take place as a response to the liturgy of the Word and a preparation for communion in the body and blood of Christ.

Recall our earlier reflections upon the dialectic of law and grace in the gospel story. God asymmetrically commands, not for our oppression, but for our liberation. Yet it is clear that if there is to *be* such liberation, it will not come by a self-funded success in performing what is commanded. The whole of the Hebrew Scriptures might be understood as a hard-won testimony to this fact. The 'new covenant' proclaimed by Jeremiah is at once a confession of the same, and a promise that God will somehow make possible the performance which seems so very *impossible* from the human side. In the Christian witness, the possibilising power of that promise is seen in the cross of Christ. There both defeat and victory in the performance of the law coincide in 'proximity'. In the cross of Christ, defeat becomes the condition for victory, and victory is forever inscribed with the scars of defeat. In the cross of Christ, God takes responsibility for the performance of the law, but in such a way that human beings are accorded a new kind of responsibility. David Ford writes that the dead face of Jesus on the cross

> resists any notion of substitution which is about replacement of the one substituted for and which sponsors irresponsibility. Instead, it represents the full person of Jesus Christ, but in an absence which demands a comparable responsibility. It signifies simultaneously the ultimate carrying out of responsibility and the complete handing over of it. Before this dead face one can recognise both someone who gave himself utterly for God and for us, and the fact that being dead is not a matter of doing anything for us: it is a being dead for us, being absent for us, being one who creates by his death a limitless sphere of responsibility for us. As in Jesus's parables of masters who go away and leave stewards in charge, the dead face is the embodiment of a call to responsibility in absence.[39]

In Jesus we discover that the way to fulfil God's righteous demands is not, first of all, about pretending that we can do so from the enclosure of our own selves. Rather, as Paul famously argued in Romans, it is about throwing ourselves, in faith and trust, upon the mercy of God 'in Christ' (3.21-26). By dying to ourselves with Jesus on the cross, by giving up on the possibility of self-funded righteousness, we pass beyond the borders of the enclosed ego, and find ourselves in the proximate space of Christ's passion. There we are no longer ourselves but 'ourselves as another,' we are Christ (Gal 2.20). 'In Christ' we remain responsible before God, as Christ was responsible, but we live from the power of *Christ's* faithfulness, not our own. Christ alone has offered the true worship and sacrifice God requires: a life lived entirely for God, in utter faith toward God, without remainder (Heb 4.15; 5.8-10). Matthew, at the beginning of the passage cited above, has Jesus say that he had come to 'fulfil,' that is, to perform, the law's righteous demands in a way that no-one else had managed to do (Matt 5.17). Therefore it is only as we vow ourselves to Christ, giving ourselves entirely over to him, that we gain the forgiveness and

---

[39] Ford, *Self and Salvation*, p. 206.

acceptance of God. When the Father looks upon Christ, he looks also upon those for whom Christ died. For the sake of Christ, God raises them from the dead with Christ, forgiving their sins and remembering them no more (Rom 6.1-14). *This* is liberation. As Ford notes, the resurrection can be interpreted as a vindication of the life of responsibility in forgiveness. The responsible life could then be understood as a mirroring of two practices: an ongoing faith in God's forgiveness, and the practice of forgiving others.[40] The confession and absolution practised in the liturgy seeks both to promise, and to form, responsibility like this.

2.3 The Covenant as Address and Listening

So much for the gathering rites. Let us talk now about the 'service of the Word'. It has often been said that in the formation of Christian theology, Jesus the parable-speaker eventually *became* the parable. Thus John's designation of Jesus as the very Word of God, who says nothing except what he hears from the Father (Jn 1.1, 14; 7.16; 8.28. cf. 5.19). Stanislas Breton notes that while some contemporary scholars reject the Johannine prologue as too onto-theological because it speaks the language of the Greek *logos*, in fact it does obeisance to neither the Greek nor Jewish conceptions of God. It is naïve, he says, to imagine that one may simply do away with the language of either the Greeks or the Jews. From the beginning, Christians have been speaking their *unique* message in languages that people already knew. 'The new wine demands the ancient bottle that contained it. And if it had to break it, as it had to do, it did so after having used it.' The new wine of the Christian message could only flourish by modifying an old discourse's resonances.[41] John's use of pre-Christian ideas should not be taken, therefore, as a slavish repetition of pre-established patterns, but rather as a *rupturing* of those patterns from within. According to Breton's careful analysis, it is ordinary human language which gives to God a being in the world which God would not otherwise have; and this not because of our own decision, but because God chose, from time immemorial, to come to us as the Word who is also a body, a person, named Jesus.[42] 'For the God who is beyond the forms of being, of wisdom, and of power, far from dispensing us from this body of the world and of humanity to render homage in spirit, requires these attributes in order to come amongst us *in truth*. It is precisely because he is nothing of that which is that he must *become*.' Breton notes, finally, that in God's *becoming* God seems to take the form of the least: the vulnerable, the naked, the nothings (Matt 25.31-45; cf. 1 Cor 1.28). In these God acquires a human self that is also God's *other*.[43] This

---

[40] Ford, *Self and Salvation*, p. 207.
[41] Stanislas Breton, *The Word and the Cross*, trans. Jacquelyn Porter (New York: Fordham University Press, 2002), p. 110.
[42] Breton, *The Word and the Cross*, pp. 112-14.
[43] Breton, *The Word and the Cross*, pp. 121-22.

analysis dovetails rather well with Jüngel's comment that the word is the right 'place' for a thinking about God because language unites in itself both perishability and the power of becoming.[44] As language deconstructs and destroys itself in order to construct and communicate new meanings, so God joins Godself to human perishability on the cross, in order that human beings may experience the power that transcends even death.

The Word that once became flesh becomes Word again in the worship and proclamation of the church. This by virtue of the resurrection: Christ is raised into the *kerygma* and into the *liturgy*, thus making them the indispensable pathways by which God fulfils God's becoming. Now this is a mystery most profound. How is it that human words and ideas could become, at the same time, the very speech of God, God's own self-communication? I think Marion would answer 'by the gift'. The gift of God's speech, Marion would say, is not so much an interruption of human speech as a power that makes human speech possible and puts it into play.[45] God, as the giver of this speech, would give Godself to be 'seen' or heard in human speech, yet not in such a way as to be simply *identified* with that speech. There remains a sense of appropriate 'distance' and 'disproportion' between the giver and the gift. In christological terms, one might say that God only appears in the disappearances of cross and resurrection.[46] So, while Christ is able to abolish this distance in himself, because he is himself both the giver and the gift, the speaker and the spoken, Marion says that we ourselves are unable to do so because we remain human, without at the same time being God.[47]

The word of God in Christ, as it appears in human speech, must therefore transgress the common order of human speech or meaning. In practice, this means that even as we attempt, in all integrity, to speak the word of Christ, we shall only do so by recognising that Christ himself must take these words to himself and make them mean something other than what we intend. Only by our abandoning the need to control the meaning of our language will Christ be heard to speak his own self *in* our language.[48] For this is what happens in Luke's Emmaus story (chapter 24). Like ourselves, these disciples live in a time after the event of Christ's passion. Like ourselves, their only access to this event is in memory and interpretation; the event itself is unavailable. What happens then, however, is a *new* event: 'the referent in person redoubles, completes and disqualifies the hermeneutic that we can carry out from this side of the text, through another hermeneutic that, so to speak, bypasses its text from beyond and passes on this side.' Here Christ, the referent, 'transgresses the text to interpret it to us . . . less explaining the text than explaining himself through

---

[44] Jüngel, *God as the Mystery of the World*, p. 190.
[45] Marion, *God without Being*, p. 101.
[46] Marion, *God without Being*, pp. 104-06.
[47] Marion, *God without Being*, pp. 140-41.
[48] Marion, *God without Being*, pp. 143-44.

it.' Hence the language of the church in liturgy, theology, or preaching stands upon solid ground only insofar as it regards its own utterance as transgressable by Christ's own speech.[49]

Jüngel appears to agree with Marion to a large degree. Right speech about God, he says, is only that kind of speech that allows God to speak for Godself. Speech about God is therefore dependent upon God's self-revelation, which has already happened in the crucified and risen Jesus. *Our* speech must therefore recognise and orient itself around *that* event or Word. In practice, this means that our speech about God will only become God's speech insofar as we are able to be self-critical, recognising that God is something *other* than what we assume or know much of the time. Faithful thinking will only be that if it constantly refers back to its source in God's self-expression.[50]

The criterion of Christian speech (*logos*) about God is therefore the word of the cross (*logos tou staurou*). Paul says that 'the word of the cross is folly to those who are perishing, but to us who are being saved it is the power (*dunamis*) of God' (1 Cor 1.18). Here, as Jüngel correctly notes, the event-character of the crucifixion, its *dunamis*, is shared with the speech that speaks of it. The word of the cross is not, therefore, simply a statement which shares information *about* the crucifixion; it actually participates in the event of which it speaks. In Pauline thought, the cross, the word of the cross, and hearing the word of the cross are all part of the same event. Why? Because it is God who speaks in both the event and the apostolic word that speaks it. The human word of the apostle is Word of God because it 'lives from' the word and event of the cross. Certainly it is a translation, but such translation is made possible by the christological fact that God has become human 'in the execution of his divinity'. Thus human speech is able to become divine speech because of God's choice and decision alone. It is not that we have somehow attained to the very speech of heaven.[51]

Breton, for his part, regards the act of preaching as a paradigmatic example of that piece of theatre which Paul names becoming a 'fool for Christ' (1 Cor 4.10). The eccentricity of the fool for Christ is a decentring of the self in favour of the preacher's model, who is Christ. In preaching the word of the cross, the preacher goes 'out of himself' so as to participate in the very events of which she or he is a witness. Ecstatic, outside the self in Christ, the preacher's 'I' begins to see things as God sees them; and also becomes a beneficiary of the salvation she or he proclaims. This is a performative self, a self who cannot help being implicated and transformed by the story being told. In the witness to faith before others, the preacher makes a vow that is, in one and the same movement, the vow of faith, but also the vow of Christ as to his servant. Preachers acts out their beliefs even before such beliefs can become an object

---

[49] Marion, *God without Being*, pp. 147-48.
[50] Jüngel, *God as the Mystery of the World*, pp. 227-29.
[51] Jüngel, *God as the Mystery of the World*, pp. 287-88.

for them, in the form of a creed, for example. From this 'outside' of *ekstasis*, the world can be judged, remembering that the 'outside' is inside the world. In preaching, the current world is relativised so that it becomes only one possibility amongst others. In preaching, the world also becomes the subject of Christ's compassion and grace. This is a love that participates in Christ's love for those who, as far as the world is concerned, do not exist. This is to imitate the God who creates goodness where there was none, *ex nihilo*, rather than to find a spark of goodness in everyone (cf. 1 Cor 1.28).[52]

Thus, in the liturgy of the Word, the preaching is preceded by at least *one* recitation from the Bible, and preferably three or four, each from different parts of the canon. This signifies the willingness of both preacher and congregation to place themselves under the authority of the Christ-Word as he speaks himself in the word of Scripture. There is a distinctively sacramental tone to this practice and belief. Chauvet recalls that in the first two centuries of the church, the words '*mysterion*,' '*mysterium*,' and '*sacramentum*,' were used exclusively in relation to the Scriptures. They were extended to describe the pastoral rites of the church only during the third and fourth centuries.[53] A sacrament, I submit, is a material, audible or visible reality in which the eschatological promise, will or Spirit of God may be discerned in such a way that human beings are enabled to respond with faith and devotion.[54] A sacrament can therefore function like an icon in the sense that Christ is the visible image (*ikon*) of an invisible God (Col 1.15; Heb 1.3). But it can also function as the hearing of God's inaudible word in the human Christ's audible words. The Scriptures are read as Scripture precisely because they are said to participate in this divine-human speech of Jesus. As such, they are apostolic testimony, which hears and repeats the word of Jesus even as Jesus hears and repeats the word of the Father in the Spirit (Jn 8.28; 16.12-15). In that they are venerated. Like the bread and the wine, the Scriptures are a holy place in which Jesus Christ, precisely as Word of God, may be encountered. But the Scriptures are not identical with Jesus, any more than an icon of Jesus may be mistaken for Jesus himself.

In the Christian assembly, the Scriptures are read for their christological content. The earliest Christian communities, when they gathered for worship, would read the Hebrew Scriptures as apocalyptic and proleptic testimony to the necessity of a new covenant, which the messiah would inaugurate. The New

---

[52] Breton, *The Word and the Cross*, pp. 42-4.
[53] Chauvet, *The Sacraments*, p. 43.
[54] Cf. Chauvet, *The Sacraments*, p. 44. Augustine said 'The Word comes to the element; and so there is a sacrament, that is, a sort of visible word.' This theology assumes that the divine Word is invisible in itself, but comes to us in the incarnate Jesus, who gave us rites which convey the Word, himself, visibly. In Reformation usage, the visible or material is contrasted not so much with the invisible or immaterial, but with the 'audible' (cited in Jenson, *Visible Words*, p. 4).

Testament is itself the concrete performance of that kind of reading. It arose from the early church's worship, and more specifically from the proclamation of Christ's life, death and resurrection as these were discerned and received *in the pages of the Hebrew Bible*. There are two lessons to be taken from this fact. First, against any simple or reductionist understanding of the Lutheran doctrine of *scriptura sola*, the Christian Scriptures clearly live in and from the church's worshipping faith. As Chauvet says, the Bible lives in the church as a fish lives in water.[55] 'In other words, the Bible never reaches its truth as Word of God as fully as in the liturgical act of its proclamation where the ancient text is, as it were, raised from its death by the living voice of the reader, then by that of the homilist who unfolds its timeliness.'[56] But that affirmation implies and requires precisely the kind of lesson that the *sola scriptura* was intended to teach: that the faithful reading of Scripture in the church is predicated upon the prior speech of God in *Christ*, to which the Scriptures are authoritative and apostolic witness. According to Ebeling, Luther taught that the word of God comes as our adversary. It does not confirm us in what we think we are, but negates the illusions we have about ourselves. Yet this is how the Word draws us into our truer selves, thus affecting the possibility of relationship with God.[57] One might conclude, then, that the service of the Word repeats and performs a covenant between God and worshippers in which (1) the Word takes human language and material discourse as its vehicle and vessel, thus risking the possibility of misunderstanding and manipulation even as such understanding is made possible; yet (2) in doing so, the Word still manages both to contest the 'profane' self and renew it according to the baptismal promise of a new self 'in Christ'.

2.4 The Covenant as Embodiment and Transfiguration

The dialogical nature of the covenant is perhaps even more explicit in the third movement of worship, in what is usually called, in shorthand, 'the liturgy of the Sacrament.' Of course (as we have just seen with the liturgy of the Word), worship as a whole is deeply sacramental, and in this worship simply repeats and performs the sacramental structure of Christian *existence* in its whole breadth and depth. Still, the liturgy of the sacrament, as it is enacted in Sunday worship, proclaims and embodies this fact as perhaps no other Christian sign or symbol is able to. For what is encountered in that ceremony variously called 'The Lord's Supper,' 'the Eucharist,' or 'Holy Communion,' is Jesus Christ in his most deeply Chalcedonian form: at once encompassing our material and human selves, but also 'at one' with the Father in a rich covenant of love made

---

[55] Chauvet, *The Sacraments*, p. 46.
[56] Chauvet, *The Sacraments*, p. 47.
[57] Ebeling, *Introduction to a Theological Theory of Language*, p. 17. See also Martin Luther, 'The Babylonian Captivity of the Church,' trans. A.T.W Steinhäuser, *Three Treatises* (Philadelphia: Fortress Press, 1970), p. 169.

possible by the eschatological movement of the Spirit. This encounter has a deeply *converting* effect on the selves who participate, principally through its association with baptism: both Christ's and ours. In the injunction to remember and face Christ's baptism—a figure for his life, passion, and resurrection (Mk 10.38, 39; Lk 12.50)—Christian worshippers are also taken back to the rites of their own baptism. In baptism the candidate consents to 'die with Christ,' there putting to death their enclosed selves that they might rise as different selves 'in Christ'. There is a profound sense in which the rite of communion simply repeats, in a non-identical way, the rite of baptism, so that believers are reminded that they no longer belong to themselves, but to Christ (1 Cor 6.19, 20), and so are maintained in a present-continuous conversion of life.[58]

The primary mode by which the Supper converts or transfigures is through its concentration upon ordinary and material things: bread, wine, and human bodies. In each case, the supper aims to *make a change*. In summary, the bread is changed into the broken and bloody body of Christ (Mk 14.22; 1 Cor 11.23, 24); the tragic blood/wine of the old covenant is changed into the celebratory wine of the new (Mk 14.24, 25; 1 Cor 11.25, 26); and the individual bodies of the worshippers are changed into a single corporeal vessel by which Christ continues to carry out his mission in the power or *persona* of the Spirit (1 Cor 10.17; cf. 11.29; 12.12, 13). It is not surprising that the Supper should focus itself on bodies in this way, for the body is the arch-symbol of the whole symbolic order. Anthropologically, it is widely recognised that every relation or conversation crosses through the mediating inter/face of the body. We saw this clearly in our investigation of the *Song of Songs*. As Chauvet says, 'no word escapes the necessity of a laborious inscription in a body, a history, a language, a system of signs, a discursive network. Such is the law. The law of mediation. The law of the body.' Neither can Jewish or Christian theology escape this determination. For God, it seems, has determined to come to us in body, in voice, and in writing. Thus, '*The anthropological is the place of every possible theological.*' Or, in terms of worship, there can be no insight into divine communication apart from the arch-sacramentality of embodiment. In sacramental rituals the faith is 'put to work' in people's bodies, where symbols converge in gestures, postures, spoken and sung words, and silences.[59] Jenson comments that sacramentality is something unique to Christianity. In non-Christian religion, he says, the embodiments of God are temporary, only to be overcome in the movement towards a higher 'spiritual' fusion between the self and God. Here material vessels are seen as mere signs or instruments of non-material forces. This God, says Jenson, ends up being an entirely silent and entirely still God, a Nothing. By contrast, the God of Jesus actually speaks and acts in material being. So while other religions regard sacraments as precarious

---

[58] I will explore the full implications of this point in the final chapter, which concentrates on the foundational nature of the baptismal covenant.
[59] Chauvet, *Symbol and Sacrament*, pp. 151-52.

or penultimate, Christianity sees them as its distinguishing mark.[60]

The change that is wrought in the Eucharist can be seen as an inscription or copying of Christ the Word onto the materials brought to God in that part of the liturgy known as the 'offertory.' In this moment, which immediately precedes the Eucharistic prayer, the worshipping community offers itself to God, along with the bread and the wine, for whatever purpose God would choose. It is a moment of unconditional surrender that comes, in the logic of worship, as an immediate response to *the preaching of the Word* (with all the positive ambiguity of that phrase). Here the Word himself comes to effect a veritable transfiguration of the materials placed before him after the face and form of his own self. One cannot help but recall Paul's words in Romans 12.1-2:

> Therefore I urge you, brothers and sisters, in view of God's mercy, to offer your bodies as living sacrifices, holy and pleasing to God—this is your spiritual act of worship. Do not conform any longer to the pattern of this world, but be transformed by the renewing of your mind. Then you will be able to test and approve what God's will is—his good, pleasing, and perfect will.

The offertory comes after God has called the people to worship and spoken to them, in the figure and example of Christ, of how life is supposed to be lived. Having heard the gospel of God's grace and mercy, there is an invitation for everyone to submit themselves to God's way and will, to put off the economy of accumulation which dominates 'the world', and put on the new way of faith and love (1 Thes 5.8). By participating in the liturgy of the sacrament, beginning with the offertory, the worshippers determine to *accept* this invitation. They offer their bodies, along with their most sustaining artefacts, for the new designation and inscription, 'the body and blood of Christ'.

This kind of visibility nevertheless implies a great degree of vulnerability on Christ's part. Chauvet says that the Word becomes visible in three ways: christologically, he becomes visible as bread, wine or water (and, I would add, community); liturgically, he comes already 'clothed,' to some extent, in the churchly themes, lections and colours of the day; sacramentally, he comes as the priest and host who himself says the prayers of sacrifice and thanksgiving at the table.[61] But Marianne Sawicki has written that 'seeing' the risen Lord in this way strongly implies that there is a sense in which *we*, as human beings, 'make' Jesus for our own consumption. 'Seeing the Lord was rendered possible through *making* the Lord, in all the senses that 'making' carries in colloquial American English usage: to construct, to recognise, to confect, to coerce, and even to sexually abuse.' The construction of Jesus in the liturgy follows on inevitably from the construction of Jesus in the gospels, she argues. There Jesus was *made* for the purpose of his becoming visible, discoverable, identifiable, in

---

[60] Jenson, *Visible Words*, pp. 30-1.
[61] Chauvet, *The Sacraments*, p. 48.

circumstances subsequent to Calvary where otherwise his involvement might have gone unnoticed.[62] The Eucharistic Christ, in continuity with the Christ of the gospels, therefore gives himself into the hands of others, others who now possess the power to do with him as they wish—even to the point of political torture and crucifixion. 'After Calvary, the church has Jesus on her hands. The body of Jesus that came down from the cross fell into the lap of the teaching church. Michelangelo's carving of the *Pietà* represents mother church as well as mother Mary.'[63] In a pertinent comment on exactly this illustration, Elaine Scarry points out that in the history of Christian art, Jesus is portrayed mostly at the time of either his infancy or his death, the two times in any person's life when they are most vulnerable and dependent. The *Pietà* conflates these two in Jesus' life, thus underlining a thematic connection between embodiment and passion: in taking a human body, Christ allowed himself to be described, inscribed, and even manipulated by others.[64] He allowed human beings to *make* him as a predicate, thus enabling him 'to enter and be held in a human mind, just as the larger fact of his having a body enables him to enter and be held within the narrow perceptual field of human vision, the slender realm of touch'.[65] This is the case as much with the Eucharist as with the historical Jesus of Nazareth. In the Eucharist, Christ takes on the body the worshippers fabricate for him in the offertory.[66]

This is not to say, of course, that the vulnerability of Christ in the Eucharist means that we can simply *use* him for our own theologico-political purposes. Whenever Christ has been enrolled in specific *causes* in the history of the church, he has managed to evade capture—slipping away, not into a bodiless realm of spirit, but into another form of body. One can see this happening in a number of New Testament accounts of the resurrection. In Luke's Emmaus Road story (24.13-49), for example, Christ joins the disciples on the road in a form they do not recognise. He is definitely *there*, as an available body, but clearly in a manner somehow discontinuous with the kind of Jesus the disciples have appropriated into their discourse, a Jesus who is dead and buried, whose cause is no more. That Jesus is able to deconstruct their version of himself, and then appear to them as someone recognisable but materially *different*, I take to be a theological presentation of his resurrection-self: a self which, having overcome death, is also able to overcome the death we human beings would render his irreducible *otherness* with our most reductive liturgy and theology.

---

[62] Marianne Sawicki, *Seeing the Lord: Resurrection and Early Christian Practices* (Minneapolis: Fortress Press, 1994), p. 8.
[63] Sawicki, *Seeing the Lord*, p. 9.
[64] Scarry, *The Body in Pain*, p. 216.
[65] Scarry, *The Body in Pain*, p. 217.
[66] For a fuller discussion, see Garry J. Deverell, 'The Making of the Body of Christ: Worship as a Technological Apocalypse,' *Australian Journal of Liturgy* 9.1 (2003): 19-35.

I have been arguing throughout this chapter that while God makes Godself available to us in and as a voice, a text, and ultimately a body, God may not be simply or exhaustively identified with the capture of a particular body—not even the particular body of the crucified Jesus. Recalling Lévinas' discussion of nakedness, I suggest that the resurrection accounts of an appearing-disappearing Christ testify to the *transcendent* nature of Christ's body-self. No body-self, least of all Christ's, can be simply objectified or captured, *even in the exposure and vulnerability of nakedness*. This is something that every torturer knows only too well. The *persona*-self evades such capture, even when every region of the body has been exploited and violated.[67] So, too, the Eucharistic body of Jesus escapes even our manipulations, returning again and again to contest our objectifications and re-write his own, more authentically *eschatological* self, on the bodies of bread, wine and worshipper.[68]

2.5 The Covenant as Sending and Mission

What we are describing here is clearly covenantal in its dynamism. God takes the initiative in calling worshippers to Godself. That we cannot perform the Trinitarian dance as enclosed selves is forgiven us. God comes to us in the Word who is Christ, accomplishing as a human self that which we cannot accomplish for ourselves, empowering us to dance in the face and form of *another* self, that is, Christ. Of course, to the point we have reached in the liturgy, Christ is still not entirely body; he is a material voice and text, but not yet a body in its fleshly fullness. Neither, yet, are the worshippers entirely *God's* body, full participants in the corporeal dance which God is. Christ finally *becomes* a body because we offer him one in bread, wine, and human selves. As a result, and in that same moment, the worshipping selves *become* God's body, since God is forever 'in Christ,' reconciling the world to Godself (2 Cor 4.19). What God therefore contributes to the covenant is a promise, a command, and a body. What human selves contribute to the covenant are faith, obedience, and a body. The body therefore becomes the common site of negotiation or crossing between God's promise and command, on the one hand, and human faith and obedience, on the other. Even now, though, as the worshippers imbibe the very personhood of Christ, the promised incarnation is not yet fulfilled. Worship is certainly *not* the culmination or fullness of what God is doing with the world.

In the perspective of the New Testament, while the Messiah has indeed arrived, he has not yet arrived in his fullness. Indeed, God's purposes for the world, despite having taking a decisive turn with the coming of Jesus, are far from finished. Both Paul and John illustrate the tension between this 'now' and 'not yet' in the imagery of labour in childbirth:

---

[67] Kearney, *The God Who May Be*, p. 13.
[68] Sawicki, *Seeing the Lord*, p. 327.

> We know that the whole creation has been groaning as in the pains of childbirth right up to the present time. Not only so, but we ourselves, who have the firstfruits of the Spirit, groan inwardly as we wait eagerly for our adoption as children, the redemption of our bodies. For in this hope we were saved. But hope that is seen is no hope at all. Who hopes for what he already has? But if we hope for what we do not yet have, we wait for it patiently (Rom 8.22-25)

> I tell you the truth, you will weep and mourn while the world rejoices. You will grieve, but your grief will turn to joy. A woman giving birth to a child has pain because her time has come; but when her baby is born she forgets the anguish because of her joy that a child is born into the world. So now with you: now is your time of grief, but I will see you again and you will rejoice, and no one will take away your joy (Jn 16.20-22).

As Mary gave birth to Jesus, the church now labours to give birth to Christ's *parousia* (Gal 4.19; cf. Eph 3.17-19; Col 1.27), a veritable presence of God, we are told, that will fill 'all in all' (1 Cor 15.28). The child has been conceived in the watery womb of baptism (Jn 3.5), by a covenant marriage between God in Christ and the church (Eph 5.27), but the child promised there has not yet been born. We wait in hope for that which is not entirely here, except, as Derrida says, in the eschatological rupture of the promise itself.[69] The precise reason for this waiting is difficult to discern. Sometimes the texts speak of the mercy of God in waiting for more people to come to a decision of faith in the promise. In these texts, it seems that the coming of the reign of God is in some sense dependent upon whether or not human beings ultimately allow God's Torah to become the dominant historical fact. It is what we bind and loose on earth that God will bind or loose in heaven (Mt 18.18-19 cf. 2 Pet 1.10, 11; 3.8, 9). These texts parallel what we called the 'conditional' covenant of the Hebrew Bible. Sometimes, however, the New Testament speaks of a 'growing' of the reign in such a way that human decision has little or nothing to do with it. God has mercy on some and not on others, and this mercy is in no way predicated upon what human beings have chosen (Mk 4.26-29; Jn 15.16; Rom 9.14-18). There is a sense here of the inevitability of God's arrival which parallels the 'unconditional' covenant of the Jewish experience. Such texts, of course, need to be read within the canon as a whole. The authors emphasise one aspect of the covenant or another, usually as a response to the particular nature of the theological controversies within their own homiletic contexts.

With Brueggemann, I tend toward the 'both/and . . .' rather than the 'either/or' on this question. There will come a 'day' when the reign of God has arrived in its fullness; that this day will come is a matter of God's sovereign choice and decision, not our own. Yet we learn from Christ that God moves towards God's own chosen destiny through a process that is irreducibly human

---

[69] Derrida, 'Faith and Knowledge,' pp. 66-7. See also my discussion of this passage in chapter 1.

and historical, which implies that God's day will arrive in and through the historical struggles and negotiations of the interlocutionary face-to-face. To this way of thinking, God is 'in amongst it' as the eschatological Spirit who relentlessly invites, cajoles, and seduces us into the space and time of the ecstatic self, who is Christ. In Christ is salvation, and nowhere else (Acts 4.12; Jn 14.6). There is choice in this, of course there is. But the Spirit, who is closer to us than we are to our own selves, is able to so convert the aim of our desire that we choose for God's own choices, without in any sense being forced or programmed to do so. That is a big claim, I know. But I really can't see any way around it if I am to remain a Christian who hopes. Hope, of course, has its object in something, or someone, who is not present (Rom 8.24). Anyone who hopes actually looks to another to complete the performance of what is hoped for; and such looking, or facing, takes the form of confession or testimony. Marion asks what publicly acquired qualification, in Austin's sense, could make the confession 'Jesus is Lord' perform the truth of its claim to everyone's satisfaction. Certainly not any qualification already attached to the one who so confesses. For Jesus is not available, in any publicly verifiable way, as the referent of confessing speech. Marion argues that the only one who could possibly verify such a confession would be the one who said 'Me, I am' (Ex 3.14=Jn 8.24, 58). If Christ, as the one who traverses the distance between the language of God and the language of human beings, took the confession to himself and made it his own speech, then perhaps the confession could be verified. But to claim that Christ is the hidden speaker in every testimony, as Christians do with regard to Scripture and the liturgy, is simply to repeat the problematic over again at another remove.[70] It appears, then, that any way one moves, a confession of faith remains exactly that: a confession in and from faith. Faith, in Marion's schema, is precisely the confession that one can never perform that which one confesses. One must wait upon the arrival of another.[71] Jesus had to do the same of course. He died a liar, as far as most of his interlocutors were concerned. And yet God vindicated his claims, as well as his cause, by the resurrection (Rom 1.4; 1 Tim 3.16; Phil 2.9-11).

The faith and hope of waiting upon Christ are transformed, in the Christian mission, into the charity that Christ exercised in his own mission. For it is in charity that the eschatological Christ of faith and hope begins to arrive in the *facing* of relationships, first in church, but then spilling out into the world at large. Paul writes to the Philippians saying that if they take any encouragement from being united to Christ in his sufferings, or any comfort from his love in

---

[70] Marion, *God without Being*, p. 188. It would be an interesting study to compare Marion's argument with that of the Johannine Jesus as he wrangles with the 'Jews' over the source of his authority. There Jesus claims that his speech is not his own, but the Father's, that he speaks only what he has already heard from the Father (8.28). The 'Jews' are, of course, not so easily convinced!

[71] Marion, *God without Being*, pp. 191, 194-95.

the fellowship of the Spirit, then they ought to take to themselves—to their own bodies and communities—the very same mind, love, spirit and purpose that motivated Christ himself (Phil 2.1-5). The dialectic of presence in eschatological absence is unmistakable here. The disciples are suffering as Christ suffered, that is, they are experiencing that vulnerability in persecution that leads to the questions 'Where is God? Has God abandoned us?' Paul's response is to remind them that God's self-emptying love for *humankind* was most evident at precisely that point when *Christ* felt most abandoned: in the nothingness and slavery of the cross (2.6-8). He therefore asks the Philippians to take comfort from such selfless love, which, while no longer present in the dying face of the crucified, is nevertheless present in the Spirit which inhabits their fellowship; and then he asks them to repeat for each other what Christ repeated for them: the delivery of God's love through an emptying of the self *in favour of the other* (2.3-5). In that gesture, God is given a new body, a new vehicle by which to love the world (2.13).

We noted earlier Kristeva's remark that, in Christianity, the Deuteronomic injunction to love God (Deut 6.5) is largely displaced into *faith* towards God, and *love* towards one's neighbour.[72] Following Luke's Emmaus story once more, Chauvet says that faith is basically an assent to the loss of some kind of 'Gnostic' immediacy with Christ in favour of the displaced communion made possible by Scripture, sacrament, and mission.[73] These three go together, and may not be separated, for the Scriptures inscribe the Paschal presence onto the sacraments, and the sacraments train the believer to recognise the face of Christ in friend and neighbour. In the Johannine corpus, faith in God is demonstrated and performed in the love of one's brother or sister in need:

> This is how we know what love is: Jesus laid down his life for us. And we ought to lay down our lives for our sisters and brothers. If anyone has material possessions and sees his brother or sister in need but has no pity on them, how can the love of God be in him? (1 Jn 3.16, 17).

> This is love: not that we loved God, but that he loved us and sent his Son as an atoning sacrifice for our sins. Dear friends, since God so loved us, we ought also to love one another. No one has ever seen God; but if we love one another, God lives in us and his love is made complete in us (1 Jn 4.10-12).

The movement here, in every instance, is from God to disciple to neighbour. The Father is 'unseen' apart from the performance of his love in and as the sacrificial death of Jesus 'for our sins.' It is *this* love (and not one of our own imagining) that the apostle recommends as the model and structure of our own love. Indeed, if we repeat this love by a mimetic abandoning of self in favour of our neighbour, the apostle promises that our own love will be taken into God's

---

[72] Kristeva, *Tales of Love*, p. 140.
[73] Chauvet, *Symbol and Sacrament*, pp. 39-41.

love, even to the point of *becoming* God's love. Our own love will be taken into the mission of God. Furthermore, despite the fact that the Father remains 'unseen,' and is therefore no object for any idolatrous gaze, the apostle tells us that the love of God, so repeated, *is* God. 'God is love. Whoever lives in love, lives in God, and God in him' (4.16b). Here the love of God is paralleled with the Word of God in John's gospel: 'In the beginning was the Word, and the Word was with God, and the Word was God' (1.1). For John, then, the *love* of God in Christ is also *God*. The *mission* of God in Christ is also *God*. The Son receives from the Father what the Father already is, in himself, so that what the Son enacts in his sacrificial death is also the self-giving love of the Father. For Christian disciples, this means that as we repeat this act in the love of neighbour, we also receive God to ourselves, in Christ, through the Spirit. '[The Spirit] will bring glory to me by taking from what is mine and making it known to you. All that belongs to the Father is mine.' (Jn 16.14, 15a). There can be no greater paradox! By loving his or her neighbour, the disciple enacts the mission of God and shares, thereby, in trinitarian communion *with* God.

The final rite of the Sunday liturgy is about sending the disciples out on mission. Having gathered to hear the Word, and having imbibed that Word in the sacrament, the community is newly constituted as the community in which the Spirit continues to execute the mission of Jesus—but in a more expansive form than any individual body could manage! The Johannine corpus challenges us to so locate ourselves in this love of God for God's others, for human beings, that we absorb God's own compassionate drive, and own it for ourselves. There is an intriguing interplay in both gospel and epistle between the language of abiding in God's circle and the language of being sent, somehow, beyond the circle to 'bear much fruit' (Jn 15.5). The love of God is described as a love which is not self-interested or self-directed. Rather, it is the kind of love that looks upon the other, the world of people and their sins, with compassion. The Father sends the Son into the world to be its saviour. Yet even there, in the midst of the smeared, bleared world of darkness, betrayal and death, even in this place so very far beyond the circle of God's presence and power, the Son yet continues to abide with the Father, and teaches his people to abide with the Father as well. Here John teaches that abiding in God's love is not about locking yourself in a safe place and feeling the warmth, but actually taking that safe place with you beyond the circle, into the land of the *other*, which is far from safe. The image of the vine and the branches is instructive (Jn 15.1-8). The branches of a vine can grow to a place a very long way from their source. They are 'sent out' from the root in order to be fruitful, and they cannot be fruitful unless they are sent. Yet even in their great distance from the vine, in the act of bearing fruit, they are nevertheless connected with the vine in a vital way. Without this connection they will die, nor will they bear any fruit. So it is with us. God sends us out beyond the circle to bear the fruit of love and justice in a world that has ceased to believe that these are possible. It is not safe outside the circle. Yet it *is* safe, safe because we carry the love of God with us, in our acts of self-giving love. Such love is powerful in its apparent weakness, powerful enough to cast the fear from our hearts and disarm our enemies. It is the power of the resurrection, which is stronger even than death.

Conclusion

In the second part of this chapter I concerned myself with that quintessentially Pauline image of the church as the 'body of Christ'. I argued that since the church is the body of Christ, but Christ's body is also the body of God, then the church should also be regarded as the body of God. I went on to explain, at length, how it is that the mission and activity of God come to *be* embodied in this way. In keeping with my focus on vows, I argued that the church is essentially a *covenant* community, that is, a community called into being by the command and promise of God as they come to us in the 'visible word' who is Christ. Of course, the call is only half of the equation. The church cannot exist without the response of obedience and faith, which itself takes the form of a series of covenant vows. These vows—both God's and ours—come together in an embodied form through the bi-vocality of Christian worship. Here the church gathers at the summons of God to hear God's commands and promises anew each week; and to renew its own vows in response to what it sees and hears of God in preaching, sacraments, and community.

I will therefore conclude by foreshadowing a discussion I mentioned only in passing in this chapter, a discussion nevertheless at the very heart of my whole thesis: that Christian worship is not genuinely Christian unless it constantly repeats and recapitulates the *baptismal* covenant by which human beings leave themselves behind and become wedded to Christ. Baptism is the rite by which human beings become Christian. It embodies, at once, the asymmetrical command and promise of God toward transformation and the vocative response of human beings in obedience and faith. In the rites of baptism, as I will argue in the remaining chapters, the worshipping body actually becomes a non-identical 'copy' of the body of Jesus, a body which lived and died in a certain way, and shall also rise again by the power and intervention of the Spirit who comes from the future. The primary means by which that covenant is remembered and performed, I will argue, is through the weekly gathering of the community around the Eucharist, which may be understood as a meal which recollects the covenant sealed by Christ, and re/presents its claims upon those gathered in such a way that participants are invited to re-commit themselves to God's ways anew. Eucharistic worship is therefore to be regarded as indispensable for the formation and maintenance of that Christian identity that is formed in baptism.

CHAPTER 6

The Baptised Self:
Formation 'in Christ' as Parable

In a flash, at a trumpet crash,
I am all at once what Christ is, ' since he was what I am, and
This Jack, joke, poor potsherd, ' patch, matchwood, immortal diamond,
  Is immortal diamond.

Gerard Manley Hopkins[1]

Introduction

This chapter, and the next one, will explore the notion that the formation of Christian identity is intimately related to that immersion of the Christian in Christ I have called the baptismal covenant. In baptism the promise of God toward forgiveness and salvation is received by a sacrifice or displacement of the human self in favour of its other, here identified as the crucified and risen Christ who is present in the Spirit. Such displacement, being a repetition in the self of Christ's own self-sacrifice in the Trinity and on the cross, establishes the Christian in the liminal identity of covenant responsibility. Responsibility, paradoxically, is both a faithful acceptance of the superabundance of God's blessing over and above anything that we might pretend to perform or work out for ourselves, but also the equally faithful acceptance of a mandate and a mission to become Christ-like vessels of blessing for others. For baptism reconfigures the human self for a Christ-like identity and mission whereby the love of God is written upon the human and material body of Christians. The Eucharist, as the regular celebration and performance of this blessed and blessing self, may therefore be understood as a fundamental repetition and recapitulation of baptismal identity, and this for the purpose of *maintaining* Christians in conversion of life.

Beginning with an investigation of the New Testament's language concerning baptism, I will in the present chapter demonstrate that such language is parabolic, that is, strategically designed to deconstruct the meaning of the human self through a transformative encounter with Christ as the

---

[1] From the poem 'That Nature is a Heraclitean Fire and of the comfort of the Resurrection' (1888).

'parabler become parable' (Crossan).[2] The implications for an understanding of the Christian self will be shown to be several. First, that the Christian self is reconstructed from the ruins of a merely human self after the pattern of Jesus Christ; thus the Pauline rhetoric about a salvation that unfolds 'in Christ'. Second, that Christian experience can be defined as a 'new experience with experience' (Jüngel) in which despair becomes hope, death becomes life, separation becomes love, and failure becomes victory. Third, that each Christian recapitulates the Christ-self in a unique and unrepeatable *haeccietas* or 'isness' (Osborne). This means that baptism can never be finally understood in mythic terms, that is, as a deep structure that manifests itself over and over in an eternal return of the same. Baptism is, rather, a privileged mode of Christ's ongoing incarnation as God's *other*, constantly disrupting the human project by an eschatological in-breaking of Holy Spirit. Baptism will therefore be defined, in this chapter, as *the othering of the self in the parable of Christ's Pasch*.

1. A Biblical Theology of Baptism: Covenanting with God through Immersion in the Pasch of Christ

It is widely agreed that amongst the most important sources for a theology of Christian baptism is the baptism of Jesus by John in the Jordan River.[3] This event, as it is presented by the evangelists in narrative form, forces a number of otherwise disparate theological traditions and themes to interact with one another intertextually, themes drawn from both Jewish and nascently Christian communities. The result is a radically new understanding of the covenant God forged with Israel, now forged anew for the church 'in' Jesus Christ.

The evangelists present the baptism as follows:

> And so John came, baptising in the desert region and preaching a baptism of repentance for the forgiveness of sins. The whole Judean countryside and all the people of Jerusalem went out to him. Confessing their sins, they were baptised by him in the Jordan river . . . At that time Jesus came from Nazareth in Galilee and was baptised by John in the Jordan. As Jesus was coming up out of the water, he saw heaven being torn open and the Spirit descending on him like a dove. And a voice came from heaven: 'You are my Son, the Beloved; with you am I well pleased (Mk 1.4-5, 9-11).

> John said: 'I baptise you with water for repentance. But after me will come one who is more powerful than I, whose sandals I am not fit to carry. He will baptise you with the Holy Spirit and with fire . . . Then Jesus came from Galilee to the Jordan to be baptised by John. But John tried to deter him, saying, 'I need to be

---

[2] See below, section 2.6.
[3] Osborne, *The Christian Sacraments of Initiation*, p. 25. cf. Aidan Kavanagh, *The Shape of Baptism: The Rite of Christian Initiation* (Collegeville, Minnesota: Liturgical Press, 1978), p. 10.

baptised by you, and do you come to me?' Jesus replied, 'Let it be done so now; it is proper for us to do this to fulfil all righteousness.' Then John consented. As soon as Jesus was baptised, he went up out of the water. At that moment heaven was opened, and he saw the Spirit of God descending like a dove and lighting on him. And a voice from heaven said, 'This is my Son, the Beloved; with him I am well pleased.' (Mt 3.11, 13-17).

The people were waiting expectantly and were all wondering in their hearts if John might possibly be the Christ. John answered them all, 'I baptised you with water. But one more powerful than I will come, the thongs of whose sandals I am not worthy to untie. He will baptise you with the Holy Spirit and with fire . . . But when John rebuked Herod the tetrarch because of Herodias, his brother's wife, and all the other evil things he had done, Herod added this to them all: He locked up John in prison.

When all the people were being baptised, Jesus was baptised too. And as he was praying, heaven was opened and the Holy Spirit descended on him in bodily form like a dove. And a voice came from heaven: 'You are my Son, the Beloved; with you I am well pleased.' (Lk 3.15-16, 21-22).

The next day John saw Jesus coming toward him and said, 'Look, the Lamb of God, who takes away the sin of the world! This is the one I meant when I said, 'A man who comes after me has surpassed me because he was before me.' I myself did not know him, but the reason I came baptising with water was that he might be revealed to Israel.' Then John gave this testimony: 'I saw the Spirit come down from heaven as a dove and remain on him. I would not have known him, except that the one who sent me to baptise with water told me, 'The man on whom you see the Spirit come down and remain is he who will baptise with the Holy Spirit.' I have seen and I testify that this is the Son of God.' (Jn 1.29-34)

1.1 Baptism for Repentance and Forgiveness of Sins

Jesus' baptism by John the Baptist indicates that Christian baptism retains an important continuity with John's baptism which, we are told, represented a washing of 'repentance for the forgiveness of sins' (Mk 1.4).[4] The call to repent is a prophetic theme, stretching back into Israel's long history as a bearer of the covenant law of Moses. The Torah, God's law for the just ordering and conduct of Israel's complex covenant with Yahweh, land and neighbour, was rarely realized in practice. In times of national crisis, so the story goes, the prophets would be raised up by God to proclaim judgement on the people for their lack of covenant stewardship. Importantly, the word of judgement was usually accompanied by a promise: if the people would repent of their madness, then God would forgive their sins and restore their fortunes. The baptism of John stands firmly in this tradition. The washing with water, as with many first century Jewish ablutions, signified a washing away or forgiveness of sin as a

---

[4] Jenson, *Visible Words*, pp. 126-27.

person turned (*metanoia*) both *away* from evil and *toward* God in a more thoroughgoing trust and obedience (cf. 1 Pet 3.10-12, 20-21).[5] The importance of the repentance/forgiveness theme for Christian baptism is underlined in *Acts*, where Peter declares baptism to be the appropriate sign of both human repentance and God's forgiveness of sins (2.38).

Furthermore, it is the imagery of baptism—with its plunge into a watery death—that best exegetes the meaning of repentance. The Pauline (or deutero-Pauline) epistles often describe its turning as the putting aside or death of an 'old' self, and the putting on or raising of a 'new' self by the power of God alone:

> You were taught, with regard to your former way of life, to put off your old self, which is being corrupted by its deceitful desires; to be made new in the attitude of your minds; and to put on the new self, created to be like God in true righteousness and holiness (Eph 4.22-24).

> Put to death, therefore, whatever belongs to your earthly nature: sexual immorality, impurity, lust, evil desires and greed, which is idolatry. Because of these, the wrath of God is coming. You used to walk in these ways, in the life you once lived. But now you must rid yourself of all such things as these: anger, rage, malice, slander, and filthy language from your lips. Do not lie to each other, since you have taken off your old self with its practices and have put on the new self, which is being renewed in knowledge in the image of its Creator (Col 3.5-10).

That Christian baptism preserved an insistence on personal turning or repentance is further evidenced by the fact of a certain embarrassment that *Jesus* should be baptised. There was a widespread belief, in early Christianity, that Jesus lived an entirely sinless life (cf. Heb 4.15; 1 Pet 2.22). Matthew clearly shared this belief, for when Jesus requests baptism from John, we are told that John tried to deter him, saying 'I need to be baptised by you, and you come to me?' (Mt 3.14). Clearly Matthew's community *practised* a baptism of repentance, else it would not require an explanation for why Jesus himself, being sinless, should be baptised.

1.2 Baptism as the Arrival of An/other Self or Vocation

The explanation in fact given by Matthew takes us further into what it might mean to turn to God in baptism. Jesus was baptised by John, we are told, 'in order to fulfil all righteousness.' (Mt 3.15). Embedded in this rather cryptic remark is something about the resolute surrendering of one's life into the hands of God. For here Jesus declares his intention to live according to a script authored by neither John nor himself, but by God. Something of the content of that script is revealed in the voice that comes from heaven—'This is my Son, the Beloved; with him I am well pleased.'—a midrash on Psalm 2.7 and Isaiah

---

[5] Kavanagh, *The Shape of Baptism*, pp. 7-9.

42.1.[6] The Psalm refers to the anointing of a king as God's chosen 'son,' and Isaiah to the messianic figure of Yahweh's servant who is destined to 'bring forth justice' through his suffering in the cause of God (Is 42.3; cf. 53.4, 5). Gathered into the baptism story, the midrash effects a divine commissioning which charges Jesus' life with a unique meaning and purpose. The self that he *might* have become is asymmetrically put aside in favour of the messianic self God has *ordained* him to be. The new self arrives as if from the Father in the Spirit, who descends upon Jesus as he rises from the waters (Mk 1.10; Mt 3.16; Lk 3.22; Jn 1.32). The covenant references in this gesture are plentiful. In the story of creation, the Spirit hovers, like a bird, over the waters of chaos in order to perform, to make real, the words of making that God will speak (Gen 1.2). The Spirit is also like the dove who arrives for Noah as a sign that God's wrath is past, that a new age is beginning because the Spirit has driven back the waters of destruction (Gen 8.1, 11). The waters of the Jordan are significant, too, for they signify the place of crossing for the people of Israel from the wilderness of Sin to the land of Promise (Josh 3).

The message from the evangelists is clear. From this point onward a new, messianic, age has arrived. The kingdom of God is at hand (Mk 1.15) and it has begun to arrive in Jesus, who now lives from the power and purpose of God's Spirit. This is particularly clear in Luke's account, where, from the moment the Spirit descends at his baptism, Jesus is said to be 'full of the Holy Spirit' (4.1). After being tempted by Satan, he returns to Nazareth 'in the power of the Spirit' and declares himself the anointed of God in the synagogue: 'The Spirit of the Lord is upon me, because he had anointed me to preach good news to the poor, freedom for the captives, recovery of sight for the blind, release for the oppressed, and the arrival of God's year of favour' (4.14-21). At his baptism, then, Jesus is marked with a uniquely baptismal identity and vocation: beloved messiah of God, and suffering servant of Yahweh. The consequences of these namings for a New Testament theology of baptism are fivefold.

1.3 Baptism as an Immersion in the Pasch of Jesus

First, by naming Jesus 'messiah' and 'suffering servant', the evangelists accomplish a decisive theological connection between Christian baptism and the specifically *paschal* events of Jesus' passion, death, and resurrection. That this is so can be seen from two important gospel trajectories. In Mark, Jesus explicitly describes his passion and death as both a 'baptism' and a 'cup' (10.38, 39; cf. 14.23, 24). In John, it is following the baptism that Jesus is identified as the sacrificial lamb who takes away the sin of the world (1.29-34). In both passages, the baptism is presented to the reader as both an anticipation of the paschal events and a radical and total immersion in the messianic meaning of those events. The paschal sacrifice of Jesus therefore takes baptism

---

[6] Jenson, *Visible Words*, p. 127.

to itself as a primary sacramental symbol.[7]

Now, that means that *every Christian baptism* is to be read as a repeat inscription of Jesus' own paschal identity onto the bodies and souls of candidates. Every baptism now orients itself toward the life, death, and resurrection of Christ as its hermeneutical centre. In the passage already cited, Mark has Jesus tell his disciples that they, too, will share in the baptism of suffering he must undergo (10.39). But it is Paul who develops this theology most extensively. In Romans 6.1-14 he interprets Christian baptism as a saving participation in the Pasch of Christ. In baptism, he says, we die with Christ to the sin of the world. As a consequence of that death, sin no longer has any power over us. Having been buried with Christ, we are also raised, 'with' him and 'in' him, to live the life of freedom which God wills and intends for us, the very life which Christ himself lives. This is a life oriented not toward sin, but toward God. In baptism, the selfhood of the Christian is displaced or refigured in favour of another self, a self 'hidden with Christ in God' (Col 3.3). It is this 'new' self which is able to live the divine vocation fully and totally, in a way that the 'old' self could never have done on its own. 'It is no longer I who live,' says Paul, 'but Christ who lives in me. The life I live in the body I live by faith in the Son of God, who loved me, and gave himself for me.' (Gal 2.20). Kristeva writes that baptism is therefore the experience of both 'total loss' and 'total gain'. The former self is lost, but then recovered in its entirety as it is invested, totally, in God.[8]

1.4 Baptism as Transfiguration

Another way of thinking about the transformation wrought in baptism is through the lens of that peculiarly synoptic term 'transfiguration' (Lk 9.28-36). According to Luke, Jesus took Peter, James and John up a mountain with him to pray. In the middle of their prayer an amazing thing happened. The appearance of Jesus' face changed and his clothes became all dazzling white. In the Greek text, Luke actually says that while Jesus was praying, 'the aspect of his face (*prosopon*) was changed (*heteron*) and his clothing became sparkling white.' This means, literally, that Jesus' face was *othered*, that his eschatological and divine self, the self that was soon to break out in resurrected excess, suddenly became manifest in his ordinary human face, without at the same time negating that face or humanity in such a way that it became somehow false or unreal.[9]

Now, in Luke's version of the story, this event—rightly called the 'Transfiguration'—has a doubly parabolic purpose. First, as a narrative strategy internal to the story, it shows Peter, James and John—disciples about to join Jesus in his pilgrimage to the cross—that their journey shall not be in vain. Yes,

---

[7] Jenson, *Visible Words*, p. 14. See also Chauvet, *Symbol and Sacrament*, p. 476.
[8] Kristeva, *Tales of Love*, p. 142.
[9] Kearney, *The God Who May Be*, p. 40.

there are difficult times ahead. There will be misunderstanding and suffering, there will be the fracturing of the community of disciples, and there will even be torture and death. But the Transfiguration assures the disciples that for all this, God will not abandon them. God will be as present and active in this *future* as in the messianic figure of Christ who stands before them in this moment. The Transfiguration shows them that while Christ's glorious self may usually be hidden, it is nevertheless real. *More real*, in fact, than their usual experience of reality—excessively real. Out of death will come life, out of crucifixion will come resurrection, out of darkest night will spring the glory of morning, the morning of an 'eighth day'. Jesus had already promised as much in the intentionally Paschal pericope immediately prior to this one in Luke's chronology (9.18-27). The Transfiguration, I suggest, may therefore be read as a baptism-like sacrament, a visible event that serves to confirm and translate the word of God's promise into more concrete and material terms. Reinforcing the point is the fact that the voice from heaven repeats the nomination of Jesus as 'Son' and 'anointed', thus reinscribing the specifically Paschal vocation of Jesus, given first at his baptism (9.35; cf. 3.22).

But these lessons are directed at Luke's readers, first of all, the congregation for whom he is a theologian and spiritual guide. It is likely that they, like most modern readers, identified themselves with Peter, James and John. Like the disciples in the story, Luke's congregation understands itself to be witness to an event it can barely understand. And yet that event holds within it a precious testimony for all who would prepare themselves to die with Christ in baptism: that whoever would lose their lives for the sake of Christ will also gain it anew, and this through the arrival of a *divine* self whom God has raised from death (9.24. cf. 9.35). Similarly, in 2 Cor 3.7-18 Paul assures his listeners that all who turn to face Jesus can expect to be transformed in the very depths of their beings. For the glory of Christ's divine image is not only to be witnessed from the outside, in such a way as to receive an impression on the face, like sunburn, that fades with time. By the Spirit, says Paul, the image witnessed takes up residence in our very souls and spirits, burning as if from the inside, changing us (as Paul says) from 'glory into glory' so that our human selves are *refigured* or *transfigured* into the very selfhood of Christ. That it is the Spirit who effects such change should alert us to the fact that transfiguration is not an instantaneous event. The Spirit comes from God's *eschaton*, drawing the human self into God's own becoming.[10] Therefore, the New Testament imagines that the transformation begun at baptism will only become complete on that 'day' of reckoning when history and eschatology are reconciled (Rom 8.23, 29-30).[11] The agency of the Spirit also reminds us that we do not become who we are apart from others. For the Spirit baptises us into a *communal* body (1 Cor 12.13). Christ is a body with many members. Only together may

---

[10] Jüngel, *God as the Mystery of the World*, pp. 344-47.
[11] Rowan Williams, *On Christian Theology* (Oxford: Blackwell, 2000), pp. 286-87.

Christians aspire to become his embodiment in the world.

1.5 Baptism as the Formation of a New Covenant in God as Trinity

A third consequence of the interweaving of Jesus' baptism with his messianic identity is that Christian baptism can then be seen as the sacramental means by which God forms a new, filial, covenant with human beings. Jesus is called God's 'beloved Son,' not simply God's 'prophet,' 'messiah,' or 'servant'. It was Lévinas who famously argued that filial relationships are both more intimate and more mysterious than other kinds of relationships. 'By a total transcendence, the transcendence of trans-substantiation, the I is, in the child, an other. Paternity remains a self-identification, but also a distinction within identification—a structure unforseen in formal logic.'[12] My child is at once me, but also a stranger: at once issuing from myself, but yet not of my own making. So the relationship performed in the baptism of Jesus is strikingly trinitarian. The Son receives his Son-self from the Father in the Spirit and, in the same movement, the Father receives his Father-self from the Son in the Spirit. In both cases, a familial self comes into being only as it is received from the other, dynamically, through the mediating power of the Spirit. Interestingly, the Spirit, as the trinitarian partner who somehow escapes a familial name, remains somewhat mysterious. One may conclude, therefore, that the relationship between the Father and the Son is intimate, and yet mediated by an undomesticable alterity that keeps them from fusing together as some kind of pagan monad.[13] Any truly loving relationship, as Marion often notes, is predicated upon the persisting distance of strangers.[14]

By their free choice for baptism into the Pasch of Christ, human beings are drawn into this differential *circumincessio* of the Trinity. In Galatians, Paul says: 'You are all children of God through faith in Jesus Christ, for all of you who were baptised into Christ have clothed yourself with Christ . . . Because you are children, God sent the Spirit of his Son into our hearts, the Spirit who calls out 'Abba, Father.'' (3.26, 27; 4.6). In baptism, according to Paul, we receive the Spirit of filiation. This makes us heirs, with and in Christ, of all God has promised God's children. As children of God, we receive our truest selves, our Christ-selves if you like, from God as Father. Equally, by facing the Father in the place of Christ (*in persona Christi*), there is a sense in which the Father receives his own selfhood from us. Just as, in Jesus, the Father receives a certain humanity or anthropological naming from the Son so, in the body of Christ, which is the church, the Father becomes vulnerable to the particularity of our own nominations. By the participation of the baptised in the Son's face-to-face with the Father, the Father of Jesus becomes 'our Father,' the one who

---

[12] Lévinas, *Totality and Infinity*, p. 267.
[13] Cf. a similar reflection in Chauvet, *Symbol and Sacrament*, pp. 510-17.
[14] Marion, *Prolegomena to Charity*, p. 81.

hears our prayers and is *changed* by them.[15] In this way, a genuinely familial bond or covenant is established between God and human beings. In Christ, the baptised experience *God* as another self; in Christ, God experiences the *baptised* as another self. By participating in the gift of Christ's baptismal Pasch by faith, we therefore attain to a bonded participation in the trinitarian communion.

1.6 Baptism as the Formation of a New Bond with Others

A further consequence of the baptismal bond with Christ is the establishment of a new kind of relationship with our fellow human beings. Bonhoeffer, in his little book *Life Together,* speaks about the church as 'community through Jesus Christ and in Jesus Christ . . . we belong together only through and in Jesus Christ.' What he means to say is that communal life apart from Christ is frustrated by the ego-demands of individuals. Each jostles to improve his or her own position at the expense of others. In baptism, however, the ego is ceded in favour of Christ's will and purpose.[16] Jüngel says that the ego is taken out of itself, into a space and time that contests the ultimacy of the ego's attempts at self-possession. The address of God in baptism problematises the human self as a self-grounding presence in the 'I think'. The address distances the ego from itself, taking it into what Jüngel calls an *'eschatological spiritual presence,'* which amounts to a new way to be present in the world. This has the effect of 'destroying or negating' every dimension of the here and now which is focused on itself, and for itself, alone.[17]

In that movement, every claim to status or power at the expense of another is relativised. As Paul says, in the wake of baptism 'There is no longer Jew nor Greek, slave nor free, male nor female, for you are all one in Jesus Christ.' (Gal 3.28). In baptism we are initiated into a new communal reality, in which we each approach the other 'in' and 'through' the mediating love of Christ. Again, Bonhoeffer says: 'Jesus Christ stands between the lover and the others he loves. I do not know in advance what love of others means on the basis of the general idea of love that grows out of my human desires—all this may rather be hatred and an insidious kind of selfishness in the eyes of Christ. What love is, only Christ tells in his Word. Contrary to all my own opinions and convictions, Jesus Christ will tell me what love toward the brethren really is.'[18] For the letter to the Ephesians, the baptised self is the person who no longer lives in their own space alone, but in that space disposed over by God's grace in Christ Jesus. Christians are those who 'imitate' Christ's loving sacrifice, submitting to one

---

[15] See the discussion of this point in chapter 3 above; cf. Kearney, *The God Who May Be,* pp. 29-31.
[16] Bonhoeffer, *Life Together*, pp. 10-12.
[17] Jüngel, *God as the Mystery of the World*, p. 175.
[18] Bonhoeffer, *Life Together*, p. 25.

another out of reverence for Christ (5.1, 21).[19]

1.7 Baptism as In/corporation into the Church as the Body of Christ
Finally, no discussion of baptism would be complete without exploring its relationship with the church as the body of Christ. In 1 Corinthians Paul writes: 'The body is a unit, though it is made up of many parts; and though all its parts are many, they form one body. So it is with Christ. For we were all baptised by one Spirit into one body—whether Jews or Greeks, slave or free—and we were all given the one Spirit to drink.' (12.12, 13). We noted above that baptism repositions us in relation to other human beings. This is particularly the case in that fellowship known as the church, for there each person immersed by the Spirit into the Pasch of Christ emerges from the waters of death to inhabit a body which is no longer simply personal or private: it is a body that belongs, simultaneously, to Christ and his brethren. The church is rightly called the *koinonia* of the baptised, for baptism is the primary rite of initiation into that corp/oration which both receives its life from Christ, and lives that life anew in a communal 'we'.

Chauvet has written persuasively about the priority of the church in the formation of baptismal identity. Baptism implies the taking to oneself of a name and identity that is already 'there,' written on the church's body in its Paschal identification with Jesus. This is made clear, he argues, in three Lukan stories about the structure of Christian initiation—Acts 8.26-40 (Baptism of the Ethiopian official), Acts 9.1-20 (Saul's Conversion), and Luke 24.13-35 (Encounter on the Emmaus Road). It is noted that each of these stories is placed in the *time of the church* following the resurrection, and in the *missionary spatiality* of a departure from Jerusalem. In each case, the initiative and promise toward transformation comes from God, *extra nos*, but this is mediated to the people concerned by the *embodied action of the church*. That mediation is attested at three different levels: (1) God addresses each person in a language of faith that is already at work in the church's kerygma; (2) the movement of faith born in each person through their asking of a question is then informed by a sacramental gesture: a baptism, the laying on of hands, the breaking of bread; (3) the eyes of faith are then opened, yet they open onto a space—an absence—henceforth filled with presence of the church. What is decisive in each of the stories, according to Chauvet, is that faith begins with a necessary *renunciation* of any valid seeing or knowing of Christ apart from the mediating witness of the church in word and sacrament. This by virtue of a realization that Christ is absent by his precisely *eschatological* presentation in the church, a community which might then be legitimately described as Christ's 'basic' sacrament or icon.[20] The competence to be Christian, to assume a genuinely Christian identity, therefore comes from a willingness to *disenthrall oneself* of the need

---

[19] Ford, *Self and Salvation*, pp. 118-19.
[20] Osborne, *The Christian Sacraments of Initiation*, p. 89.

for proofs in the form of one's own preconceived ideologies in favour of a symbolic mediation of Christ from the church.[21] It is therefore the church that forms Christians, not individual Christians that unite together to form the church. The new baptismal self spoken about by Paul in Colossians 3.9-10 is not simply Christ, but the body of Christ, which is the church.

2. Baptism, Parables and the 'Other'

2.1 Parables as Destabilising Agents

According to John Dominic Crossan, a parable is a narrative that is able to subvert the stabilising logic of myth, by which the world is rendered both liveable and predictable. While myth wants to reassure us that the world is stable, parable wants to both change human beings and destabilise the world.[22] Parable therefore stands at the opposite end of the narrative spectrum to myth. 'Myth establishes world. Apologue defends world. Action investigates world. Satire attacks world. Parable subverts world.'[23] According to Crossan, parable is 'story grown self-conscious and self-critical'. Indeed, 'To be human and to remain open to transcendental experience demands a willingness to be 'parabled'.'[24]

This last affirmation implies a kind of analogy between stories and people. *People* are perhaps like *myths*. We tend towards stasis, seeking always to effect a reconciliation between what has been received as common wisdom and the apparently 'new' thoughts, feelings and experiences encountered in the still-arriving present. The experience of parable, however, is not so easily reconciled. It is like the 'other' we found in the philosophy of Lévinas, Ricoeur and Derrida. It faces or *regards* us from the vantage point of an interlocutor whose world, whatever our efforts to know or understand it, nevertheless perseveres in mystery. Parable therefore possesses a power to confront and contradict our mythic expectations about both self and world. If myth is like the 'ownmost' self (Heidegger), parable is like the surprising claim of another person (Lévinas). 'It takes two to parable' says Crossan. 'One can tell oneself stories but not parables. One cannot really do so just as one cannot really beat oneself at chess or fool oneself completely with a riddle one has just invented. It takes two to parable.'[25]

2.2 Parable Transforms Myth

In that light, I suggest that parable is able to get 'under one's skin,' so to speak,

---

[21] Chauvet, *The Sacraments*, pp. 19-28.
[22] John Dominic Crossan, *The Dark Interval: Towards a Theology of Story* (Sanoma, California: Polebridge Press, 1998), p. 39.
[23] Crossan, *The Dark Interval*, p. 42.
[24] Crossan, *The Dark Interval*, pp. 39-40.
[25] Crossan, *The Dark Interval*, p. 69.

in a way similar to that of the phenomenological 'other'. But that raises questions about the structural and temporal dualism that characterizes Crossan's account. What if the parable is able to possess one's ownmost mythology in such a way that one experiences aspects of that mythology as somehow unfamiliar or alien, even from the beginning? We discussed in chapter 1 Ricoeur's account of a threefold experience of otherness at the heart of human subjectivity: in the passivity we have (1) toward our bodies, (2) toward the other person who is somehow able to 'gestate' or reproduce themselves within our ownmost subjectivity, and (3) toward the apparently internal voice of *Gewissen* or conscience.[26] What is worth noting at this juncture is that Ricoeur draws each of these experiences into a precisely narrative theory of the self in which the story one tells to *make oneself as a self* is forever being disrupted by a polysemy of address from elsewhere, which is nevertheless experienced *within and as the self*. Tellingly, for our purpose in this chapter, Ricoeur names this self an *attested* self. Unable to posit itself as the ultimate foundation of reality (in some quasi-scientific or epistemological sense), the attesting self is nevertheless an act of *credence or trust* in 'the power to say, in the power to do, in the power to recognise oneself as a character in a narrative, in the power, finally, to respond to accusation in the form of the accusative: 'It's me here' [*me voici!*], to borrow an expression dear to Lévinas.'[27] Ricoeur therefore defines attestation as 'the *assurance of being oneself acting and suffering*' even as that assurance, in some sense, comes from another.[28]

On that basis, it is necessary to tweak Crossan's understanding of parable a little. Rather than seeing parable as myth's 'binary opposite',[29] a phenomenon that arrives late on the scene to challenge myth's hegemony, I would prefer to see it as an apprehension or address that helps to constitute and transform mythology from the beginning. Myth, as myth, is open to transformation, just as the self, as self, is open to transcendence. Myth changes, and has changed from the beginning, because of the actively illocutionary power and effect of the parabolic other in the very heart of myth's competence to be itself.

2.3 Sacraments are Parables

In a parallel observation, David Power suggests that Christian sacraments may be understood as a parabolisation of the mythic and cosmic structures of ordinary ritual. Christian sacraments are distinctive, he says, in putting their emphasis on domestic rites rather than festive or cosmic ones, even as these latter forms are respected in the performance. 'The ritual transfer from sacrifice, rites of passage, cosmic rites, indeed from the whole language of

---

[26] Cf. Ricoeur, *Oneself as Another*, pp. 318-51.
[27] Ricoeur, *Oneself as Another*, p. 21.
[28] Ricoeur, *Oneself as Another*, p. 22.
[29] Crossan, *The Dark Interval*, p. 38.

cosmic identity, to the loaf and the cup, to the tub of water, to the jar of oil, shared in daily living, parallels the transition of the Christ-story into a people's parabolic language.'[30] In Christianity, all those mythic longings for communion with the world and with the universe are transformed into the ordinary face-to-face across a meal-table or a bathing-pool. In this the connections with the cosmos are not lost (water, bread, wine, and bodies are, of course, elemental), but rather *gathered* into the ordinary and historical memory of a particular event: Christ's Pasch. What the sacrament teaches is that communion with one another is only really possible through communion with the other who is Christ crucified, the Christ who is God's choice for the particularity of the lowly and weak over the religious, mythic and philosophical systems of the world (1 Cor 1.27-29). This amounts to a practical and parabolic renunciation of the final authority of such systems. Thus, 'The domesticity of Christian ritual and the teaching of parable go together in constituting the setting within which the proclamation of the Cross and the transformation of the [cosmic] elements into divine gift takes place.'[31]

2.4 Parable is God's Excessive Address

In chapter 5 I showed, at length, how the church's self-expression in liturgy might become, also, the address of God which constitutes the church as church. In Jüngel's terms, God is the 'other' who traverses the distance between Godself and the world in such a way that God's own reality becomes even more 'obvious' over and against that which was already 'obvious' about the world.[32] This is what Barth called the 'analogy of faith,' in which human words become capable of correspondence to their divine other only because that other has first come close, in the figure of Christ's incarnation, to refigure such words as divine speech. Not that this coming close becomes an absolute identification between the human and the divine. The difference between human beings and God is preserved within the precisely relational terms of an 'even greater similarity within a great distance.'[33] That, I submit, is how parable works as well.

Theologically, parable is the address of God to human beings according to a language which is anthropologically familiar (myth); yet it performs this address according to a logic of excess, so that the hearer's world is drawn into a realm which literally *others* it's meaning. The effect is a form of dissonance: the hearing and seeing of one's own intentions and understandings according to a new register, the *strange* register of an/other's voice and vision. Jesus'

---

[30] Power, *Sacraments*, p. 144.
[31] Power, *Sacraments*, pp. 145-46 [my addition].
[32] Jüngel, *God as the Mystery of the World*, p. 258.
[33] Jüngel, *God as the Mystery of the World*, p. 288; cf. Karl Barth, *Evangelical Theology: An Introduction*, trans. Grover Foley (Grand Rapids, Michigan: Eerdmans, 1963), pp. 16-18, 20-3; cf. Barth, *The Humanity of God*, pp.46-7.

parables were apparently like this. They shattered the 'deep structures' of his hearer's beliefs about what God was like, and how God worked in the world.[34] But they did so in a playful way, presenting the possibility that things may indeed be other than what they seem, yet without force or coercion in any ordinary sense of those words. The *force* of the parable, according to Jüngel, comes not from a sense of urgent necessity, but rather from the surprising quality of non-necessity. 'It is not necessary to call Achilles a lion. It was also not necessary to call Jesus God's Son'. Yet, 'in such talk, a certain reality is expressed through *possibilities* in such a way that this possibility leads forcefully to the discovery of a new dimension of reality and to greater precision in talk about what is real. Metaphors and parables thus express more in language than was real until now.'[35]

2.5 Baptism Reveals the Self as More than Itself

It is this superabundant 'more', I contend, that baptism into Christ makes 'visible,' though in a strictly metaphorical mode.[36] For baptismal language is parabolic through and through. Performed and experienced by real selves, using ordinary words, and materials such as water and oil, the rite of baptism nevertheless bears witness to the yet *more real* reality of another self—Christ—in and by whom the Spirit incorporates ordinary people and things into the relational field of the Trinity. Here they become capable of bearing a more expansive or excessive meaning than was hitherto possible. Baptism in the Spirit seals the *covenant* between God and the one who is baptised (2 Cor 1.18-22; Eph 1.13). It is therefore a carrier of all the complex dynamisms of that relationship as we explored it at length in chapter 3. In baptism, Christ comes closer to the candidates and their sponsors than they are to themselves.[37] In him, God becomes the yet more foundational call and promise to which the candidate's attestive selves are only the answer. At the same time, it is only in and *as* this substituted Christ-self that the candidates become capable of answering the call, promising with assurance to desire as God desires, and do as God does.

In narrative terms, the baptised person becomes another Christ in the unfolding of the theo-drama of God—perhaps not *another* Christ so much as a member of the one Christ who alone is capable of pleasing God. What Christ does, the baptised person does. Where Christ goes, the baptised person follows. By participating 'in Christ', the baptised person demonstrates that he or she has both died with Christ to the elemental powers of this world, and risen to life with God in the new world of promise. As a ritual, baptism therefore performs

---

[34] Crossan, *The Dark Interval*, p. 100.
[35] Jüngel, *God as the Mystery of the World*, p. 291.
[36] In using this language of 'superabundance' or 'excess', I am drawing upon the discussion of Marion's theology in chapter 3 above.
[37] Jüngel, *God as the Mystery of the World*, p. 295.

the Paschal life of both Christ *and the Christian* in miniature. Baptism is like a theatre production that is simultaneously able to mirror life as most of us live it, with all of its comic ambiguities and tragic contradictions, and yet reconfigure the possibilities of that life according to the way Christ lived it. It is a passion-play in which the one who dies finds his or her salvation only because they die *in persona Christi*, within the larger personal *gravitas* of one who has overcome sin and death already (cf. Eph 4.8).

2.6 The Pasch of Jesus as the Parable of God

In that same narrative sense, Jesus is for the church not simply a teller of parables, but the very speech or parable of God. Crossan, a first-rate historian as well as a Bible critic, says that in the wake of the crucifixion Jesus' followers had to decide whether, in this event, God was punishing Jesus or not. After all, the Hebrew Scriptures taught that anyone hung on a tree was cursed (Lev 18.5; cf. Gal 3.13). Jesus had taught them, by his parables, that God would be encountered 'where and when their world was overturned and challenged at its very depths', and now they were confronted with a decision about whether they really believed that or not. According to Crossan, they decided that the event of the cross now replaced the parables told by Jesus. It became the supreme Parable.[38]

Paul unfolds the parabolic nature of the cross in the celebrated 1 Corinthians 1.18-28 which, as we noted in chapter 2, critiques the dominant *mythoi* of his time. According to Breton, Paul saw Greeks as 'seekers' who sought after the reason of things, typified in the Platonic motto *logon didonai*, 'to realize, to give reasons.' Jews, on the other hand, were not seekers so much as people who *claimed.* They claimed signs and wonders which erupted into everyday life as evidence of an 'Excellence who can generously dispense exception.' The principle at work in the Jewish *mythos* was not a supreme Reason or Idea, but an untameable and unpredictable Sovereign who is constantly undercutting the ground from which an enquiry could be made about God.[39] What the apostle did, in his proclamation, is to critique both Jewish and Greek mythologies according to the rupture he called the *logos tou staurou*, the word of the cross. The word of the cross, he contends, is the power and wisdom of God to save. It saves by a parabolic critique of both Greek reason and Jewish sovereignty, reconfiguring both according to the 'weakness' and 'foolishness' displayed in the crucified one. Here, in this extraordinary sign of contradiction, the apostle discerns God's call to a fundamental revaluation of all values. From now on it is the weak and foolish ones, the 'nothings' of the world, who are both wise and strong! For in the cross, God makes a free and sovereign choice for all the weak and despised who would cling to the weak and despised Christ in baptism.

---

[38] Crossan, *The Dark Interval*, pp. 102-03.
[39] Breton, *The Word and the Cross*, p. 5.

2.7 'Fools for Christ': Living Parables

The 'fools for Christ,' the company of the baptised, come to walk the way of the cross out of their desire to respond to or answer for the cross of Jesus. Paul wrote: 'May I never boast except in the cross of our Lord Jesus Christ, through which the world has been crucified to me, and I to the world.' (Gal 6.14). Here, as Breton notes, faith takes up the parabolic excess of the cross and performs it theatrically. The excessive 'word' of the cross, which can never be finally contained in any particular *mythos*, is converted into a bodily form of speech that says far more than a discursive form of speech could ever say. Here the disciple carries his or her own body, his or her own self, in a staurological manner. Breton again: 'This supplementary body that Christ 'takes on from the faithful' is indeed a crucified body, of which that on the first Cross remains the exemplar. In giving up the spirit, Jesus diffused his breath into the world . . . Our fools take hold of it again, reincarnate it in somewhat animal 'spirits,' supplementing it with body rather than soul.'[40]

In baptism, and in the life of discipleship it configures, one might say that the marks of Christ's crucifixion are forever inscribed upon the bodies of the neophytes such that they no longer belong to themselves alone, but first and foremost to Christ. 'Let no one cause me trouble,' says the apostle in the same passage, 'for I bear on my body the marks of Jesus.' (Gal 6.17). In another place he says: 'The one who was a slave when he was called by the Lord is the Lord's freedman; similarly, the one who was a freedman when he was called is Christ's slave. You were bought at a price; do not become slaves of men.' (1 Cor 7.22, 23). In baptism the disciple dies to his or her own will and way, rising instead to the birth of a new sense of self saturated by Christ. In this the disciple is freed from the values of the *mythos* in which he or she has lived until now, but only by becoming the free and willing slave of God. The eccentricity of the fool for Christ is exactly this: a decentring, perhaps even a maddening, of the self in favour of Christ.[41]

2.8 Christ the Lacunae of God

It is perhaps worth repeating, at this juncture, that while parable is certainly able to release human beings from the static, totalising, properties of myth, it cannot be performed or exist *apart* from myths. As we noted earlier, Lévinas said something similar about the 'said' and the 'saying.' In order to manifest itself, in order that its reality might be known, the saying must 'correlate' itself with the said, and therefore with a linguistic system and an ontology.[42] A

---

[40] Breton, *The Word and the Cross*, p. 37.

[41] A pertinent passage from the desert fathers: 'Abba Anthony said, 'A time is coming when people will go mad, and when they see someone who is not mad, they will attack him saying, 'You are mad, you are not like us.'' Benedicta Ward, ed., *The Sayings of the Desert Fathers* (Kalamazoo: Cistercian Publications, 1975), p. 6.

[42] Lévinas, *Otherwise Than Being*, pp. 5-7.

parallel notion in Derrida is the relationship between narrative and its parabolic '*lacunae*', a relationship he traces in Freud:

> Freud's use of Aristophanes' *Symposium* is not total. He relates only that which is essential to his purposes. And that is the case for everyone who draws on what has gone before. 'Each one makes himself into the *facteur*, the postman, of a narrative that he transmits by maintaining what is 'essential' in it: underlined, cut out, translated, commented, edited, taught, reset in a chosen perspective. And occasionally, within the narrative, lacunae are again pointed out, which makes a piece of supplementary history. And this supplement can embed itself in *abysme* within another lacuna that is bigger or smaller. Bigger or smaller because here we are within a logic that makes possible the inscription of the bigger in the smaller, which confuses the order of all limits, and forbids the *arrangement of bodies*'.[43]

Parable operates as a 'secret', in the mode of an uncontainable supplement or *lacunae* in every myth. It is that property of *indeterminacy* in myth that enables myth to change. In Derrida's thought, the origins of the secret are archaic and eschatological, as from a place without place and a time without time.[44] In Christian perspective, the secret or 'mystery' is 'Christ crucified' (1 Cor 2.1, 2)—an event that resists simple definition and yet, precisely because of that, is able to call into being that most unstable of narrative genres known as a 'gospel'. It has often been noted that the gospel of Mark, as the paradigm performance of this genre, has no definitive *telos* or ending. The reader is left to speculate on exactly where or how the missing Christ might show himself anew. It is a gospel of secrets in which, even when the secret is revealed, the reader can never be entirely sure that the secret *has* been revealed (Mk 4.11, 22). Yet the very mode of the gospel's performance, the creation of a story about Christ's passion, suggests that the secret is nevertheless a revelation that has a history-like substance and meaning.

A story there must be, it seems, even a myth. Yet each new performance of the story, each new preaching, responds to the call of a secret that has not yet presented itself *in toto*. The Pasch of Christ may indeed be a 'foreclosed event,' as Marion says, yet it is inscribed on the bodies of the baptised over and over, with each new celebration of the sacrament. For, as Marion also says, in each celebration of the sacrament a 'new event' occurs. The 'secret' comes to inscribe *himself* anew, transgressing even the paschal texts that warrant the rite in order to interpret their meaning to us as if the story has never been told before, 'less explaining the text than explaining himself through it'.[45] Ford rightly refers to this phenomenon as 'non-identical repetition'.[46] Here it is Christ himself who does the baptising: writing his paschal identity over and

---

[43] Derrida, *The Post Card*, p. 373.
[44] See my discussion of Derrida in chapters 2 and 3 above.
[45] Marion, *God without Being*, pp. 146-47.
[46] Ford, *Self and Salvation*, pp. 123, 152.

over, crossing the gap between practice and referent in a way that the church, as ritual and cultural host, is never able to accomplish by itself.

2.9 Baptism as a Singular Event

That is why Kenan Osborne insists that each new celebration of baptism is an entirely new event, even though it is patently obvious that baptism can only be recognised *as baptism* because of its ritual and social character:

> ... baptism is not a replication, a verbal phrase emphasising an action, nor is baptism a replicated clone, a substantive phrase emphasising a thing. Each baptism is not a duplication of a rote activity, nor is each baptism the enfleshing of a duplicative reality. Rather, each baptism is an existential event, an existential action, an existential *Ereignis*. Each baptism is an individualized, historically discrete, temporally unrepeatable moment in the life of an individual, of a particular community of Christians, and of the temporal-historical presence of an active God. *There is no such thing as generic baptism*, just as there is no such thing as generic eucharist. Each baptism is a unique event; each eucharist is equally a unique event. To use a Scotistic term, there is an *Haecceitas*—a 'thisness'—about each sacramental celebration [italics mine].[47]

What makes each new baptism really 'new' is precisely the presence of Christ in the Spirit. It is not that Christ is being ritually memorialised by the church, but rather that the crucified and risen one *arrives* in the Spirit to fill the words, the rituals, and indeed the candidates with himself. Of course, if Christ were not alive and active, if the meaning of Christ could be circumscribed by historical or anthropological investigation, then repeat-performances of the passion would be most unlikely. For what drives the church to perform the story over and over, if not a sense that the story remains a mystery? The ritual of repetition is certainly not motivated by a desire for sameness, and certainly not the 'eternal return' of the same! It is motivated by a sense that the Christ is 'bigger' (Derrida) than any particular re-staging of his story, any particular arrangement of acting bodies on a ritual stage. While traditions and meanings are indeed handed on, there is innovation of meaning with each particular celebration. Even when church authorities try to control the meanings of baptism, the meanings engendered escape control. 'There is something very wise to the saying that any priest who thinks that the people think what he thinks when he baptizes a child had better think again. What happens, what exchange of grace occurs, is specific to each sacramental event, granted that it happens within a certain universe of meanings, rituals, and encounters.'[48]

---

[47] Osborne, *Christian Sacraments in a Postmodern World*, p. 58.
[48] Power, *Sacraments*, p. 59.

Conclusion

In this chapter I have argued that the covenant between God and Christians is formed in and by the paschal event of Christ's death, burial and resurrection. There God faces human beings with a call and promise to life in all its fullness; there, also, a human being faces God with a uniquely free response of faith and obedience. The covenant that Christians enjoy with God is therefore mediated in and through Christ, and especially the figure or parable of his paschal passage. There God becomes a human person in order that human beings, *as human beings*, may be enabled for participation in the divine *communio* of the Trinity. Baptism is both the symbol and the performance of this passage. It repeats the essentially mysterious and eschatological event of the Pasch in such a way that its accomplishments are made available for a non-identical *reaccomplishment* within the lives of ordinary human beings in any time or place. Here the baptism of Jesus is inscribed upon the body of Christians in such a way that the unique event of the Pasch is nevertheless 'copied' into the world in a supreme event of paradox: revealing itself over again in a unique ritual, and yet preserving itself as a unique and unrepeatable secret at the same time. Baptism is therefore the inauguration and commencement of that covenant with God in Christ known as 'discipleship'.

CHAPTER 7

The Baptised Self:
Formation 'in Christ' as the Church

Introduction

We are ready now to investigate, in detail, how the parabolic excess of the New Testament language concerning baptism may be 'converted' into the bodily *practice* of baptism by contemporary rites. In what sense do the contemporary rites of the Western, English-speaking, churches perform the parable well, and in what sense would reforms seem desirable? By attempting to answer these questions in a discursive mode I will of course be indulging in a form of *practical* or *liturgical* theology, that is, a theology that emerges out of a critical reflection upon the actual performance of baptism in contemporary ecclesial communities.

After a brief discussion about the significance of worship to theology as such, I will engage in a critical commentary concerning the rite of baptism as it is practised by contemporary English-speaking churches. It shall be noted that baptism, as a ritual, makes little sense apart from an integral strategy for the formation of *Christian selves* within local ecclesial communities. Traditionally, that strategy was called the 'catechumenate', a comprehensive programme of action and reflection in which candidates for baptism learned how to *be* Christians by participating in Christian practices and learning the substance of the faith from specially appointed educators. The chapter will conclude with a plea for a more thoroughgoing engagement of catechumenal strategies by the church as it seeks to prepare people for baptism. For without such intentionality, I will argue, it is unlikely (but certainly not impossible) that a genuinely *Christian* self will emerge from the waters.

1. The Idea of a Liturgical Theology: Interpreting Christian Existence in and through Worship[1]

The recently arrived discipline of *liturgical theology* has been particularly concerned to take Christian *worship practices* as the key source for its

---

[1] An earlier version of this section appeared as part of Garry J. Deverell, 'Uniting in Worship? Proposals Towards a Liturgical Ecumenics,' *Uniting Church Studies* 11.1 (2005): 21-36.

reflections.[2] The movement has taken a saying of Prosper of Aquitaine at the Council of Carthage (418 CE) as its motto: *legem credendi lex statuat supplicandi,* 'the law of worship constitutes the law of belief'. (The maxim is often presented in its shorter form: *lex orandi, lex credendi,* 'worship shapes belief'). In some parts of the movement, the saying is invoked to elevate the worship practices of the church to a place of pre-eminent importance for theological reflection in general. Aidan Kavanagh, for example, argues that worship is not just one source of theology amongst others, but the 'ontological condition' of theology, the context in which the originating Word is best heard and performed in the faith of the church. 'The liturgy' says Kavanagh, 'does not merely reflect but actualises concretely and in a sustained manner that basic repertoire of faith which is irreducible; it does this to a degree of regular comprehensiveness no other mode or level of faith-activity can equal.'[3]

At first glance, Protestants may wonder at Kavanagh's apparent lack of regard for the normativity of Scripture. Is not the Bible the norm of norms in that it presents unique and apostolic testimony to the Word of God who is Christ? Should not worship therefore conform to the patterns and practices hallowed in Scripture? Others, Orthodox and many Catholics, may argue that while worship is indeed normative, it is itself normed by the traditional teaching of the Episcopal orders of the church or, occasionally, by the experience of the Spirit in a saintly life of mission, performed in imitation of Christ. For is it not the bishops or other Episcopal authorities who approve any changes to the liturgy; and isn't it the ever-new call of the Spirit of love in missionary situations of poverty and need that (eventually) forces the church to adapt its rites, thereby acknowledging a certain normativity from mission?

In view of these questions, some have argued for a three-fold interplay of *lex orandi, lex credendi,* and *lex vivendi* ('the law of living') in the norming of the Christian life, where none of these dimensions is allowed to 'norm' apart from the co-inherent authority of the others.[4] Don Saliers, for example, argues that

> The mutually critical correlation of liturgy and ethics is part of the critical reciprocity between *lex orandi* (pattern of prayer) and the *lex credendi* (pattern of belief). But these issue in the *lex agendi* (pattern of intention-action) of the church. Hence we may say that true doxology issues in fitting orthodoxy as

---

[2] Some trace the beginning of the liturgical theology movement to the publication of Alexander Schmemann, *Introduction to Liturgical Theology* (New York: St. Vladimir's Seminary Press, 1966). See, for example, Don E. Saliers, *Worship as Theology: Foretaste of Glory Divine* (Nashville: Abingdon Press, 1994), p. 13.
[3] Kavanagh, *The Shape of Baptism,* p. xii.
[4] E. Byron Anderson, *Worship and Christian Identity: Practicing Ourselves* (Collegeville, Minnesota: Liturgical Press, 2003), p. 27.

reflective faith, and both in orthopraxy of the church's servanthood in the social order in which it is placed.[5]

Chauvet, who poses the problem in terms of a hermeneutics of ecclesial identity, offers a more nuanced account. *The church is most itself*, he says, *in worship*. That affirmation should not be taken to imply that Christians do not belong to or do the work of Christ in their scattering during the week, but only that the church 'manifests its identity best as a concrete liturgical assembly'.[6] Why? Because the sacramental character of worship provides the primary site for a 'symbolic' or hermeneutical 'exchange' between the address of God in Christ and the existential world of ethical and missional decision. By this he means nothing other than what we have been talking about under the rubric of 'covenant' in this book: that Christian worship effects a unique and real exchange of identity and vocation between God and human beings, albeit in a way which acknowledges God's priority in the process.[7]

The model of symbolic exchange is useful to theology because it posits a relationship between God and human beings that is not a market but a divine economy in which gifts remain gifts even as they are received. You will recall our discussion of the controversy between Derrida and Marion on this point. Derrida is sceptical about whether a gift that is recognised as a gift can remain a gift: for the recognition of a gift is already a gift returned. But Marion replied that there are ways of receiving the gift that do not circumscribe its gratuitousness. Chauvet suggests that *faith* is such a way. For faith is not the 'return-gift' demanded by a market-economy, but rather the shaping or formation of a life in which the gift of God may remain, precisely, a gift. Chauvet calls such a life 'living gratefully.' Ford, as we have seen, calls it 'the responsibility to forgive'.[8] In such a life, grace can never be made into an object for human manipulation. If one tries to use or store it for the coercion of others, it will rot away like the manna given Israel in the desert.[9] The call of God in the experience of grace is to repeat and embody such grace in one's living toward God and others. In this way, grace remains grace; the gift lives on not as an exchange-gift, but as the ever-widening mission of the self-giving Trinity into the creation and beyond. Thanksgiving or gratefulness is the pattern, if you like, of a life in which grace is received as the *performance* of grace.

Now, if worship is anything, it is the performance of grace in the shape of Eucharistic thanksgiving or blessing. Worship communicates the radically *new*

---

[5] Saliers, *Worship as Theology*, p. 187. cf. Gordon W. Lathrop, *Holy Things: A Liturgical Theology* (Minneapolis: Fortress Press, 1993), pp. 4-11 and Kevin Irwin, *Liturgical Theology: A Primer* (Collegeville, Minnesota: Liturgical Press, 1990), pp. 68-72.
[6] Chauvet, *The Sacraments*, p. 34.
[7] Chauvet, *The Sacraments*, p. 123.
[8] Ford, *Self and Salvation*, p. 207.
[9] Chauvet, *The Sacraments*, p. 124.

blessing of God in and as the human act of repeating God's former blessings, performatively, in a non-identical *anamnesis*.[10] Marion says that it is a 'fundamental rule of revelation' that 'There is no presence of God among men, if men do not bless him and the one he has sent'. It is not that God is unable to present Godself anyway, whether we recognise it or not. Rather, because this God gives Godself as grace or blessing, only the person who also blesses is able to *recognise* the gift without disfiguring its meaning.[11] Since worship (precisely as *Eucharist*), is exactly the blessing which Marion describes, it is worship that is able to *reveal* the grace which would otherwise remain hidden or implicit within the Christian life as a whole. It is therefore unique, in Christian existence, as the place of graced experience which also enables participants to both *recognise* and *perform* that experience in all the business of life. All of which is to say that Kavanagh may be right. Perhaps worship *is* unique in what is makes possible ontologically. I have argued throughout this book that worship is a transformative encounter by which God takes on a body- or existential-self and human beings take on a spirit- or eschatological-self. In worship, identities are ex/changed—changed as from a different 'here' and a different 'now'—in such a way that both the realm of God and the world of human beings are ontologically, that is *really*, altered.

Liturgical theology, then, represents an explicit attempt to interpret the whole of Christian existence in and through the language and symbols of worship. Worship is neither the expression of an overwhelmingly *human* life, understood as that realm somehow beyond the reach of God, nor the expression of an overwhelmingly *divine* life, understood as somehow beyond the reach of the human. Worship is, rather, the privileged site of negotiation or exchange whereby each of these realities comes to accomplish themselves as truly divine or truly human in and through the interlocutionary agency of the other. In this worship simply repeats, ritually but not identically, that *paradigm* of worship we have been calling the Pasch or passage of Jesus of Nazareth. For the Christ, in his life, death, and resurrection, is precisely that confluence-in-difference of the divine offering of love and the human offering of faith that we have been examining under the rubric of worship.

So it should be noted, from the outset, that the theology of the New Testament concerning baptism is *already* a practical and liturgical theology. It is more than likely that most of the key metaphors and symbols used by Scripture to imagine and describe baptism are partly derived from actual baptismal practice in the communities from which the texts emerged.[12] So, when Paul talks about 'putting on' the new self, or 'clothing' oneself in Jesus Christ, he is calling to mind the existing practice of being clothed in a white garment as a neophyte emerges from the baptismal pool (Col 3.10; Rom 13.14;

---

[10] Ford, *Self and Salvation*, pp. 154-55.
[11] Marion, *Prolegomena to Charity*, p. 129.
[12] Kavanagh, *The Shape of Baptism*, p. 6.

cf. Rev 6.11; Mk 16.5). Similarly, the texts which interpret the coming of the Spirit at Jesus baptism as an 'anointing' by God for his messianic mission are drawing not only upon the ancient Jewish practice of anointing kings (1 Sam 9.16), but also upon the practice of anointing the baptised with oil (Acts 10.38; Lk 4.18; 2 Cor 1.21, 22; 1 Jn 2.20). Such anointing may have happened either before the washing, symbolising the preparation of the candidate for burial with Christ (Mk 14.8), or after the washing, thereby symbolising the healing, salvation, and joy that the Spirit brings to that event (Mk 6.13; Heb 1.9). It may even be that the imagery of 'burial' with Christ, so prominent in Pauline theology, reflects a particular baptismal practice amongst his churches: the complete immersion of the candidate under the water, before rising to greet the community of the redeemed (Rom 6.4; Col 2.12; 1 Cor 15.4). These examples indicate that Christian *theology*, from the very beginning, has benefited from a symbiotic relationship with the ritual *practices* of the faith. From the beginning, practice has formed reflection, and reflection has formed practice.

2. The Ecumenical Liturgy of Baptism: A Commentary

Having examined the most recent rites of a great many English-speaking churches, I do not think that it is too far-fetched to claim that there is a common ecumenical vision amongst them concerning baptism, especially at the level of liturgical performance.[13] The rites are strikingly similar with regard to:

their placement in time and space,
the *ordo* followed,
the ritual status of the principal participants,
their use of textual and material symbols,
and their relationship with the liturgy of the Word and of Eucharist.

Because theological meaning is both made and performed in such things, the rites actually agree in theology to a very large extent. Even where there are notable differences, these tend to represent variations upon a common theme

---

[13] The rites consulted for the writing of this section were those of the Anglican Church in Australia, the Baptist Union of Great Britain, the Church of England, the Church of Scotland, the Episcopal Church in the USA, the Methodist Church of Great Britain and Ireland, the Presbyterian Church in the USA, the Lutheran Churches of North America, the Roman Catholic Church in Australia and New Zealand, the United Church of Christ in the USA, the Uniting Church in Australia, and the United Methodist Church in the USA. These churches represent the latest incarnations of Anglican, Congregational, Lutheran, Reformed and Roman traditions. The churches of the Anabaptist and Pentecostal traditions tend not to publish collective worship books or even instructions for the ordering of worship. Thus it is difficult to offer any comment about worship in these traditions that could realistically be said to represent anything more than the practise of individual congregations.

rather than serious divergences about the substance of baptismal faith.[14] It would be prudent to offer a broad exposition of that agreement before I move into a more critical mode of analysis. Obviously, in doing so, I will be describing a rite which does not really exist, anywhere, in its totality. Clearly that would present a serious problem for my account if I then went on to claim that this virtual, non-existent, rite somehow *manifested* itself in the practices of each of the different churches. But that is *not* what I am claiming, not a bit. I am simply exercising what David Tracy calls an 'analogical' imagination. I am spotting similarities made possible by difference, and I am doing so out of a post-structuralist sensibility that relationships are structured by genuine alterity rather than by some kind of underlying ontological oneness.[15] What is offered here should be understood as a taxonomy of baptism that is curious about the *conversations* that have clearly been going on between contemporary English-speaking liturgists.

2.1 The Placement of Baptism in the Ordo and the Sacred Calendar

The first thing I notice is that every single rite, without exception, agrees that the normal place and time for the celebration of baptism is following the homily and before the Eucharist during the regular Sunday service of Christian worship. This reveals a common sensibility regarding the relationship of baptism to the rest of the liturgy. The precise placement of the rite in the *ordo* makes it clear that in baptism the Word of God's love, having been read and proclaimed, now takes human flesh as its own body-self; and, at precisely the same moment, a human being takes to his or herself, in faith, the spirit-self of the crucified and risen Christ. Baptism therefore signifies a repetition-in-difference of the covenant established in the unique selfhood of Christ: divinely begotten and human in being, yet without either confusion or division.[16] As such, baptism is a *sacrament*, and this in the two-fold sense we have been unfolding in this book: first, that baptism is a visible and sensible sign-event in

---

[14] The convergence of contemporary rites is due, in no small part, to that extraordinary flowering of historical and theological scholarship known as the 'Liturgical Movement'. Beginning in France in the late nineteenth century, these historians and theologians turned to the practice of the Early and Patristic churches as inspiration for the renewal of contemporary rites. Good historical surveys are available in James D. Crichton, *Lights in Darkness: Forerunners of the Liturgical Movement* (Collegeville, Minnesota: Liturgical Press, 1996), Osborne, *Christian Sacraments in a Postmodern World*, chapter 1, and Frank C. Senn, *Christian Liturgy: Catholic and Evangelical* (Minneapolis: Fortress Press, 1997), chapter 17.

[15] David Tracy, *The Analogical Imagination: Christian Theology and the Culture of Pluralism* (New York: Crossroad, 1981), pp. 408-29. Note, here, that Tracy's *positive* and *constructive* concept of analogy has, at its heart, a radically dialectical and deconstructive sense of the *mystery* of God's ways with the world.

[16] Kearney, *The God Who May Be*, p. 41.

which the crucified and risen Jesus arrives as God's Word of *promise*;[17] and second, that baptism is a visible and sensible sign-event in which a candidate, with the support of the church, accepts God's promises in *faith*.[18]

That all of this takes place on a Sunday, called by some in the early church the 'eighth day of creation', means that baptism is intimately connected with the resurrection of Jesus, which is the first event of the new creation. That many of the rites we are examining recommend, in addition, that baptism be celebrated on dates in the church year that have a particularly paschal resonance, underscores the fact that baptism is rooted in the *whole* Pasch (passage or journey) of Christ—from his birth, through death and resurrection, to the giving of the Spirit.[19] The evangelists, as we saw, use the metaphor of baptism to represent this whole paschal journey, with its ascent into death to take away the sins of the world, and its rising to take a re-forged humanity into the very selfhood of God. When placed within this story-frame, as the liturgy intends, the baptism of ordinary human beings must be seen as the immersion of the human self in Christ's own baptismal Pasch, such that this self is transformed and transfigured according to the 'mind that was in Christ Jesus'. The mind of Christ is *kenotic*, Paul tells us. It is a mind that is willing to lose everything in order to become the vessel of God's infinite love for the world (Phil 2.5-8; cf. 2 Cor 4.7).

The movement immediately after the baptismal rites, in which the neophytes share in the Eucharist with all the faithful, shows that baptism finds its completion in the Eucharist. Having been baptised, the neophytes are now part of the body of Christ, the church, in which the one Spirit of Christ dwells and ministers. The sharing in a common loaf and a common cup, themselves symbols of Christ's paschal giving, performs the newness of the neophyte's position tangibly. No longer is the candidate primarily a citizen of the 'here' and 'now' as those words are commonly understood, forever at the mercy of particular class, race, gender or family identities. Now the baptised one has become part of a heavenly citizenry in which the only significant mark of identity is that given by Christ in the Spirit (Eph 2.19; Col 3.11; Eph 1.13). Those who communicate in Christ's body and blood do so under the rubric of *God's* 'here' and 'now', a here and now which is not yet entirely arrived in being, and yet traverses being in the manner of its arrival. Baptism is therefore

---

[17] The reader is reminded that the root-meaning of the word sacrament is 'promise'. See chapter 1.

[18] Power, *Sacraments*, p. 223.

[19] At the Easter Vigil, on the day of Pentecost, on All Saints Day, and at the feast of the Baptism of Jesus. See, for example, Episcopal Church USA, *Book of Common Prayer and Administration of the Sacraments and Other Rites and Ceremonies of the Church* (New York: Oxford University Press, 1990), p. 312; United Methodist Church, *The United Methodist Book of Worship* (Nashville, TN: The United Methodist Publishing House, 1992), p. 84; *Rite of Christian Initiation of Adults*, Study ed. (Strathfield, NSW: St. Pauls Publications, 2003), pp. xi, xiii.

the gateway into a realm that is, at once, ordinary and familiar and yet also strange and unfamiliar. The latter comes to contest the former's ultimacy even to the point of transformation.

2.2 The Significance of Sponsors

The rites we are considering are agreed, also, on the need for 'sponsors' or 'godparents' for the candidates. Whether the candidates are young children, older children who can speak for themselves, or fully responsible adults, it is widely recognised that the church has a responsibility to form and prepare candidates for baptism through the agency of mentors especially set aside for that ministry. In the case of young children, almost all the rites assume that at least one of the parents will also be a 'god-parent', already formed in a mature faith and ready to share what they have learned with their children. Without the active participation of such a parent, it is unlikely that the word sown by others will find the constant tending it needs to take root and grow to maturity. 'Those who are born of the flesh are flesh,' says the evangelist, 'and those who are born of the Spirit are spirit.' (Jn 3.6). In another place he says 'to all who received him, to those who believed in his name, he gave the right to become children of God—children born of natural descent, nor of human decision or a husband's will, but born of God' (Jn 1.12). It is one thing to have biological parents, but it is quite another to find spiritual parents who will offer themselves to do God's work. Those who form candidates for baptism are like midwives: they labour with God to bring forth the Christ-self in those under their care (Gal 4.19). At baptism that Christ-self is born eschatologically—'from above,' in water and by the power of the Spirit (Jn 3.5). Yet, as one expects with things eschatological, baptism merely *inaugurates* a process of becoming which will last a lifetime. Thus, sponsors are needed well beyond the moment of birth, to teach by word and example the pattern of Christ's own life (Phil 3.17; Heb 13.7).

2.3 The Turning from Evil to Christ

So, imagine them all there about the font or baptismal pool—candidates, parents, sponsors, and at least one minister of the church.[20] Around about, in prayerful support, are the people who belong to that community, those who will become the neophyte's sisters and brothers in faith. In the rites we are examining, what usually happens next is a renunciation of the devil and his works (or, in demythologised form, simply evil and its more personal manifestation, sin), a performative turning to Christ, and then a declaration of faith in the form of the Apostle's Creed. That the candidates (or, in the case of young children, their sponsors) should turn *from* sin and evil and *to* Christ is a

---

[20] In Roman and Anglican churches, the ordinary minister of baptism is a bishop, especially if a rite of 'confirmation' is to follow. In Protestant churches, it is the presbyter or (in some traditions) a deacon who presides at baptism.

clear recognition of the centrality of repentance in any baptismal celebration. Without repentance, as we saw earlier, there is no way to really *receive* and *accept* forgiveness. Without a letting go of the old way of life, there will be no room for the new in a candidate's self-definition. Without a dying of the old self, the new self who is Christ can never begin to arrive.

The imagery of turning, present in almost all the rites we are citing, also suggests that *facing* Christ is an important moment in the arrival of saving faith. Sequentially, the facing of Christ immediately precedes the saying of the creed. This suggests that faith itself is a gift from Christ (Eph 2.8). For faith is never understood, in the New Testament, to be a 'work' that begins in the will of the human soul. It is, rather, the shape of a life that finds both its genesis and its final destination in another, in Christ (Heb 12.2). The baptismal candidate is therefore encouraged to perform in baptism what she or he will develop as a foundational *habitus* for the rest of their life: a fixing of his or her eyes on the face of Christ as the *ikon* of God who alone is able to live the faith/ful life, and trusting Christ alone to carry them in his train to justification and reconciliation with God (Col 1.15, 19; Rom 5.1, 2).

2.4 The Declaration of Faith

The owning of faith in the form of a communal affirmation of the Apostle's Creed witnesses to the fact that Christian faith is never simply the invention of the individual, but is transmitted and learned through the mediation of the Church. As we have noted in a number of places already, it is Louis-Marie Chauvet who is most insistent upon this point. While the Word of salvation may come from 'elsewhere', *extra nos,* and while we may wish to insist upon the excessive freedom of God from human formulations, it is nevertheless true that the word of a specifically *Christian* faith only comes to its fullest presentation within the corporality of the church as the body of Christ.[21] Robert Jenson agrees. When Christ addresses us, he does so in the available body of the materiality of word and sacrament. Therefore, in looking for the substance of faith, we are to gaze neither at idols nor at nothing. Rather, 'the whole object-reality of our community is the body of Christ. When we pray, we properly look right at each other. When we gather, we gather around the bread and the cup. When we meditate, it is on the gifts of the water. When we seek God's peace, it is in the kiss of the fellow believer.'[22]

We are not born with faith in Christ, and we do not invent it. We *learn* faith from the corporeal forms in which the church bears it: through its sociality as a community; through its traditions and cultural symbols, which reach back to the Scriptures; and through its appropriation of cosmic elements like bread, wine, water and oil, into the storying of the gospel. All of which is to say, again, that faith is fundamentally *sacramental*, a visible word of promise adhering to

---

[21] Chauvet, *Symbol and Sacrament*, p. 152.
[22] Jenson, *Visible Words*, pp. 45-6.

bodies and a bodily memory. Thus, *'there is no faith unless somewhere inscribed, inscribed in a body*—a body from a specific culture, a body with a concrete history, a body of desire.'[23] Those who say the Apostle's Creed immediately before baptism acknowledge this fact and own it for themselves. By saying the faith in words that have belonged to the baptismal liturgy for most of the church's long history, the candidate says 'the faith of the church is my faith; it does not come from me, and yet I own it, receiving its inscription upon my body and soul from this time forth.'

The rite of baptism is a symbolic performance of that auto-inscriptive process. Being plunged into water in the name of the triune God is clearly a metaphor for being plunged into the body of signifiers that is the church. Thus, *'one becomes a Christian only by entering an institution and letting this institution stamp its 'trademark,' its 'character,' on one's body.'*[24] I agree with Chauvet in his opinion that a sacramental faith like this provides the only effective guard or stumbling block against the excessive individualism and spiritualism that characterizes some of the more marketable segments of today's church. Communities that teach a faith that is essentially private and internal, a 'personal relationship' with a spiritualised Jesus, are in danger of becoming Gnostic rather than Christian.[25] Psychologically, one suspects that Jesus is being made-over in the image of an individual's often-pathological need or desire—not that there is anything wrong with desire as such! Yet, as I argued in chapter five, in order for desire to become *Christian* it needs to be disciplined and formed by a participation in the sacramental practices of the church, which are non-identical repetitions of the paschal faith of Christ. The Apostle's Creed, with its trinitarian form and pattern, transmits and preserves that faith without in any way closing down the invitation to a creative and unique reception of its truths on the occasion of its recital.

2.5 The Immersion in Water

So then, to the washing itself. The rites we are considering insist that the preferred modes for baptism are by immersion in, or by the generous pouring of, water. Sprinkling will not do, because it fails to evoke the reality it is supposed to symbolise, namely, the death and burial of the candidate in Christ's own death and burial. Just before the baptism (and sometimes before the renunciations), the principal minister will say a prayer of thanksgiving over the water which functions to imbue its use with a multi-layered biblical meaning.

---

[23] Chauvet, *Symbol and Sacrament*, p. 154.
[24] Chauvet, *Symbol and Sacrament*, p. 155.
[25] Chauvet, *Symbol and Sacrament*, p. 153. For a detailed discussion of the Gnostic tendency in contemporary ecclesial life, see also John Dominic Crossan, 'Our Own Faces in Deep Wells: A Future for Historical Jesus Research,' *God, the Gift, and Postmodernism*, eds. John D. Caputo and Michael J. Scanlon (Bloomington: Indiana University Press, 1999), pp. 282-310.

Most of the contemporary rites appear to adapt Luther's celebrated 'flood-prayer', with its fivefold evocation of water as: (1) the place of primal beginnings under the brooding of the fertile Spirit; (2) the deluge by which wickedness was done away with and a new covenant forged with Noah; (3) the sea and/or river by which Israel made its passage from slavery in Egypt to freedom in the promised land; (4) the place of Jesus' own baptism, which signifies his being chosen by God for the paschal vocation of death and resurrection; and (5) the place of our own passage into a new beginning, a new covenant, a promised inheritance, and a place with Christ in his passage from death to resurrection.[26] The prayer usually culminates with an epiclesis calling on the Spirit to *arrive* and *act* for the salvation of the candidates as they are baptised right then and there. The concluding ascription of glory to the Trinity prefigures the baptismal act itself. The epiclesis is of crucial significance, for the water does not save the candidate in and of itself (1 Pet 1. 21, 22). One of the distinguishing features of Christian baptism, as opposed to the baptism of John, is its insistence that baptism in water effects a participation in the more primal baptism 'with' or 'in' the Spirit.[27] This is particularly clear in the Johannine writings. Jesus is looked for as one who will baptise not with water alone, but with the Holy Spirit. For John the new birth of baptism in water is understood as a participation in the new birth that comes from the Spirit (Jn 1.33; 3.5-8). That gospel's favourite image for the Spirit is water. The Spirit is said to be a stream of 'living water' that wells up to quench one's spiritual thirst (Jn 7.37-39; cf. 4.13).

Still, the Spirit does not act on her own, anymore than Jesus acts upon his own. The Johannine narrative connects the giving of the Spirit with Christ's 'glorification', that is, with his death and resurrection (7.39. cf. 12.23, 24). That glorification is further understood to be an event both from, and within, the life of the Father (Jn 13.31, 32). Thus we must say that the primary agent of baptism into the death and resurrection of Christ is the Father, in the Son, by the Holy Spirit. That is the significance of the threefold naming of the Trinity as the candidate is immersed in water. By agreeing to be baptised 'in' the names of this God, the neophyte also agrees to be received into the filial *communio* of this three-fold God, a *communio* that also encompasses the church. The evangelist has Jesus pray that all the believers will be one 'just as you are in me and I am in you. May they also be in us so that the world may believe you have sent me.' (Jn 17.21). The union of the Christian with God in the whole of life is therefore signified here at the beginning. It is not an undifferentiated union, after the manner of Greco-Roman longing. It is a union that remains illocutionary and perlocutionary, that is, relational and

---

[26] See, for example, Inter-Lutheran Commission on Worship, *Lutheran Book of Worship* (Minneapolis/Philadelphia: Augsburg Publishing House/Board of Publication, 1978), p. 122.
[27] Kavanagh, *The Shape of Baptism*, p. 25.

transformative. For baptism changes everyone: God, those baptised, and all who gather to witness the event in faith. In baptism, God is changed because a uniquely new identity is taken to the heart of the trinitarian *perichoresis*. God cedes something of the divine identity in order to make room for this other in God's divinity. At the same time, the neophyte also changes, dying with Christ in order to receive from him a new self and a new name, his or her specifically *Christian* name. From now on, that neophyte will belong not only to him or herself, but also, more primarily, to God in Christ and to the church in which the Spirit of Christ has come to dwell.[28] The witnesses are changed as well. For as God adopts a new child, the children of God acquire a new brother or sister, along with all the rights and responsibilities attending the fact. The neophyte is no longer merely the neighbour whom Christians are enjoined to love, but a member of the body which Christ has given to all in common. Thus, when the one suffers, all suffer; and when the one rejoices, all rejoice (1 Cor 12. 12, 13, 26). It is truly said that becoming a member in Christ is like acquiring a new family. Families, as Lévinas understood, are precisely those realities in which the divine call of responsibility reoccurs in the face of each brother and sister, always preceding one's ability to choose.[29]

2.6 The Signing and Anointing

Immediately following the baptism, the new Christian is anointed with oil in the sign of the cross. As we noted earlier, the New Testament understands such marking in a twofold sense. At one level, it is a receiving of the marks of crucifixion into the very flesh of one's body. Thus, the candidate is reminded that he or she has died with Christ to the basic principles of the world at large, and now approaches that world with the more specific outlook and vocation of Christ and his church (Gal 6.14, 17). At another level, the oil is a sign of anointing by the Spirit into the vocation and mission of Christ as prophet, priest, and king (Lk 3.21, 22; 4.14-21). From now on, the neophyte is enjoined to share with his or her brothers and sisters in the vocation of Christ's witness to the coming reign of God. The oil thus 'seals' the covenant with God in Christ, and symbolises, again, the giving of the Spirit to sustain the neophyte in that covenant until the promised inheritance arrives in its fullness (2 Cor 1.22; Eph 1.13, 14).

The candidate may then be arrayed in a garment of white (an *alb*), symbolising his or her membership of the company of people now clothed with Christ (Col 3.10; Rom 13.14; cf. Rev 6.11; Mk 16.5). A candle may be given also, lit from the paschal candle, thus calling the new Christian to become a vessel for Christ, the light of the world (Jn 8.12; cf. Mt 5.14). At this point, or immediately following the anointing, the principal minister (accompanied, in some rites, by other sponsors and members of the congregation) may lay his or

---

[28] Chauvet, *Symbol and Sacrament*, p. 439.
[29] Lévinas, *Totality and Infinity*, p. 214.

her hands on the kneeling neophyte and say a prayer of *confirmation*. It is usual to adapt the words of Isaiah 11.2, which calls on the Spirit to strengthen the convert in their newfound faith, and to bring forth in them the fruit of that conversion.

When the prayer of confirmation is integrally linked, as it should be, with the baptism and anointing, this part of the liturgy is brief and very much supplementary to the meanings already enunciated. But the rites also allow for the possibility that such a prayer may be used in order to confirm a person who, having already been baptised at some time in the middle to distant past, may not be baptised again. In this case, the confirmee joins with the candidates for baptism in all the parts of the liturgy except for the washing in water (and, in some instances, the anointing with oil). While some rites see confirmation as a once-only event which follows on from the once-only event of infant baptism, others see it as a rite which may be repeated at any time in a Christian's life as they re-embrace or re-affirm their baptismal faith. Almost all the churches under consideration provide rites for a congregational reaffirmation of the baptismal covenant, often at the Paschal Vigil. Here the rite of baptism with confirmation is followed, except that the congregation is sprinkled with water, as a reminder of baptism, where the baptism itself would ordinarily take place.

2.7 The Welcoming and Responsibilities

The specifically baptismal rites conclude with a formal reception into the ecclesial community and a set of vows in which the newly baptised (or their sponsors, in the case of young children) promise to follow Christ and do his will in all the business of life, from attendance to the word of God, through worship in the fellowship of the church, to an ethics and mission which may bear Christ's name with integrity.[30] Importantly, the congregation responds with a statement of its own responsibilities: to persevere in being a church that loves, welcomes and witnesses after the way and will of Jesus Christ, thus maintaining an environment in which the newly baptised are likely to flourish in faith, hope and love.

That such promises are sometimes presented as a sequentially ordered 'response' to God's offer of grace in baptism is appropriate, theologically, since the avowal of human beings is always already a manifestation of their respons/ibility before the God who calls, commands and promises.[31] But this should not be allowed to obscure the fact that the covenantal call-and-response is a structural feature of the liturgy *as a whole*. The renunciations and the declaration of faith occur before the washing, sequentially, yet they are each, manifestly, expressions of respons/ibility in the face of God's initiative. The

---

[30] Some rites place the post-baptismal promises before the prayer of confirmation. See, for example, Church of Scotland, *Book of Common Order of the Church of Scotland*, 2nd (emended) ed. (Edinburgh: Saint Andrew Press, 1996), pp. 103-05.

[31] See the discussion of responsibility in chapter 4.

thanksgiving prayer is the paradigm example. Here the president blesses God for all God has done in salvation yet, precisely in doing so, she or he becomes a mouthpiece for God in calling forth a *new* event of blessing. Even the washing itself should be seen as both grace *and* faith, separate movements that yet cohere in the same movement. Here the trinitarian God, who comes from an immemorial past as well as an eschatological future, nevertheless gifts a candidate with life under the conditions of that person's (or the sponsor's) *present and freely chosen submission.* Theologically we must say that grace comes first, and that faith is the response that the gift makes possible. But God's time is infinitely 'more' than our time. The sequence of the rite is therefore only relatively important. As in the book of Acts, the baptising Spirit comes sometimes *before* water baptism, sometimes *at* water baptism, and sometimes *after* water baptism, so it should be understood that divine time will not neatly 'fit' into our own linear sequences (Acts 2.38; cf. Acts 8.14-17; 10.44-48; Acts 19.1-6). What *is* clear, however, is that baptism inaugurates a new covenant between God and the human person, which is also a covenant between that person and the church.

2.8 Participation in the Eucharistic Meal

All the rites recommend (even where they cannot command) that the liturgy of baptism lead immediately to the reception of the neophytes at the prayers of the baptised and the table of the Lord. This reflects a clear understanding in the New Testament that initiation by baptism into Christ and his church has, as its immediate outcome, the living of a communal life in which both the sufferings and the promises of Christ are shared by all. As we saw earlier, baptism represents the blessing of grace, forgiveness and acceptance from a triune God. It calls into being human selves that are also able to bless, thus imitating the blessed and blessing Christ in his own baptism. The actual performance of blessing is, literally, *Eucharist*: an act of thanksgiving in which the promised blessing of God is both *proclaimed* to others in a doxological recitation of salvation history, and *asked* of God as a human act of eschatological invocation.[32] Anthropologically, the sharing of a ritual meal symbolises the exchange or mixing of selves in a common in/corp/oration of all that is said in the interlocution of the face-to-face.[33] This is all the more so in the Eucharist, for there the community receives its identity from the crucified and risen Jesus, who transmits his blessed and blessing self to the community through the recitation of the eucharistic prayer. By the saying of this prayer immediately before the meal, Christ inscribes himself upon broken bread and wine poured out. Thus, by eating the bread and sharing the wine, the community takes into its heart and soul, into its very interior, the blessed and blessing self of Christ. It *becomes* what it was given to become in baptism: *a blessed community of*

---

[32] Jenson, *Visible Words*, p. 68.
[33] Osborne, *The Christian Sacraments of Initiation*, p. 164.

blessing.

The Eucharist recalls baptism in another way also. The rite of baptism, as we saw, places the neophyte before the face of the crucified and risen Jesus through its use of the words 'I turn to Christ'. The marking of the neophyte's face with the sign of the cross underscores the effect of this facing: he or she now bears, within their own body, the whole Pasch of Christ. The language of facing is also present in the celebration of the Eucharist, which looks toward a more eschatological face-to-face. This is particularly clear in Luke's institution narrative, where Jesus says:

> I have eagerly desired to eat this Passover with you before I suffer. For I tell you, I shall not eat it again until it finds fulfilment in the kingdom of God . . . Take this [cup] and divide it among you. For I tell you I will not drink again of the fruit of the vine until the kingdom of God comes (Lk 22.15-18).

The eucharistic prayer of Christian liturgy usually concludes with an eschatological supplication, which acknowledges that the facing of Christ across the banqueting-table of heaven has not yet arrived in its fullness, and asks that God would continue to work in the community and the world to bring about that end. That supplication stands in the tradition of Paul, as we have seen, who looks forward to the day when we shall see Christ 'face to face' and be utterly transformed into the very image of Christ as a consequence (1 Cor 13.12; cf. 2 Cor 3.18; 4.6). In the meantime, the baptismal inauguration into a very *human* community of facing, the church as the body of Christ, is maintained and encouraged by the regular practice of the eucharistic meal. Here the community is encouraged to live out the baptismal covenant through the offering of a sacrificial hospitality to each other after the manner of Christ's sacrifice. As in the trinitarian communion, each cedes their place to the other and each receives his or her identity from the other so, in the eucharistic fellowship, its members are called to treat each other with both deference and respect. This is clear from Luke's decision to place the disciple's controversy about 'who is the greatest' within the narrative of the Supper (22.24-27). There Jesus turns the usual social pecking-order on its head. The one who *serves* at table is greater than the one who is *served*. The one who is greatest in the kingdom of heaven is the one who sacrifices his or her own status in order to enhance the dignity of others. In this Jesus offers himself, his own eucharistic Pasch, as the figure and example for a decidedly *communitarian* ethics. Paul makes a similar point in 1 Cor 11, where he castigates the richer members of the community for their failure to recognise the Christic dignity of the poor, even at the supper itself (11.17-34). The Eucharist is therefore a repetition of the new *placement* of the self which baptism makes possible. Both, as Ford notes, place us before others and shape a particular *habitus* of facing.[34]

---

[34] Ford, *Self and Salvation*, p. 163.

The Eucharist must therefore be understood as a repeatable version of the unrepeatable covenant of baptism, perhaps even a 'reaffirmation of baptism'.[35] Ford says it well:

> A eucharistic self is a baptised self in the routine of being blessed and blessing. Baptism is the archetypal Christian sign of personal identity, non-identically repeating Jesus' baptism, his death and resurrection, and the baptism of every other Christian. This is the initiating sacrament of blessing: being named and blessed in the name of the Father, Son, and Holy Spirit. It signifies the reality and the availability of the abundance; it invites and initiates into a eucharistic practice in order to sustain a life of flourishing within the infinite love and joy of God.[36]

In baptism the candidate is joined to the paschal Christ in a completely 'new' covenant of grace through faith. Here Christ stoops to take a scandalously sinful body, while the candidate receives a new, eschatological, self from Christ through the action of the Spirit. Baptism is the beginning, the inauguration of the relationship. Eucharist, on the other hand, is an imbibing of Christ in bread and wine, which recalls and repeats the blessed Pasch of baptism in a different register. The repeatable pattern of the Eucharist functions to remind both God *and* the faithful of their covenant promises in Christ, and maintains both parties in the faithful, engaged, dynamic relationship that was begun, but certainly not completed, in that event.[37] The weekly celebration of the Eucharist is itself *productive* of baptismal selves insofar as it recalls, in an eschatological memorial, the baptismal Pasch of Jesus in which Christians participate by means of their own baptisms. The eucharistic self is therefore a baptismal self first of all, a *'non-identical repetition of the baptismal self.'*[38] The open invitation of Christ to feed on his body and drink of his blood is first of all a call and summons to covenant with God in baptism.

Liturgically, the common celebration of the Eucharist references baptism in a number of ways. Osborne notices the following. First, the modern liturgy of the word began as a 'mass for the catechumens,' those who were preparing for baptism. By listening to the Word read and proclaimed, they learned to have faith. Having heard, the catechumens were blessed and dismissed before the Eucharist began. They would join the community at table only after they had received baptism. Second, the saying of a creed at Eucharist recalls the declaration of faith that candidates have to make in order to be baptised. In their baptismal form, they are patterned in the form of question and answer: 'Do you believe? Yes, I believe.' Historically, the creeds used at Eucharist grew out of

---

[35] Osborne, *The Christian Sacraments of Initiation*, p. 231.
[36] Ford, *Self and Salvation*, pp. 162-63.
[37] Jenson points out that a part of the function of *anamnesis* in the Supper is to remind *God* of God's *own* promises, an element taken over from the Jewish celebration of Passover. Jenson, *Visible Words*, pp. 72-3.
[38] Ford, *Self and Salvation*, p. 162.

the liturgy of baptism, not the other way around. Third, the 'prayers of the people' in the regular mass should be understood as the prayers of the baptised because they were originally part of the service which the catechumens missed out on until they had received baptism. Fourth, many Sunday liturgies include a sprinkling or 'asperging' with water as part of the preparation for Eucharist. The connection with baptism is obvious. The purpose of the sprinkling is clearly to remind the congregation of its baptismal identity in the same way that fonts placed in entranceways or at the front of churches do. Fifth, the singing of the *Agnus Dei* at communion in the Eucharistic liturgy establishes a clear baptismal reference because of its origin in Jn 1.29-31. There the Baptist witnesses to the paschal lamb who takes away the sin of the world, but also baptises with the Holy Spirit.[39] Thus, we may agree with Kavanagh when he says that 'In baptism, the eucharist begins, and in the eucharist baptism is sustained . . . The eucharist is thus most profoundly the constantly reiterated 'seal' of baptism, as baptism is its unique and unrepeatable introit.'[40] Without participation in the meal of the kingdom, Christian initiation is incomplete. But without baptism, participation in the supper could only ever bear witness to a certain kind of lack, for in that case the meal would recall and reinforce a covenant that has never been agreed!

3. The Formative Context of Baptismal Liturgy: The Catechumenate

We have seen that the rite of baptism occurs in a rich and deeply interwoven context of theology, symbol, history, and communal action. But there is a particularly important dimension to that context that I should like to examine in more detail: the period of preparation known as the 'catechumenate.' As we have seen, almost all the rites examined for this chapter assume that candidates for baptism have already undergone a significant period of preparation, under the guidance of 'sponsors', 'god-parents' and ministers of the gospel. It is also assumed that these sponsors have themselves been baptised, and now wish to share with the candidates *out of the experience of having been formed in a deeply baptismal faith themselves*. The introduction to the new Uniting Church rite says, for example, that

> The Tenth Assembly commended to congregations and faith communities the *Becoming Disciples* process, known universally as the catechumenate. It is a major mission strategy which puts the formation of adult disciples at the centre of congregational life. Its focus is those who have never been baptised and who have heard the call of Christ in the life of a local congregation. It is based in the worshipping life of a local Church, and involves learning and practising the

---

[39] Osborne, *The Christian Sacraments of Initiation*, pp. 226-27.
[40] Kavanagh, *The Shape of Baptism*, pp. 122, 127.

Christian life over a substantial period prior to baptism. It may also be adapted for the reaffirmation of baptism or confirmation of those already baptised.[41]

This 'catechumenate,' as I hinted in the last section, is a 2nd to 6th century practice that is currently being revived in the English-speaking churches in very exciting ways. Historically, it was a process of education and formation specifically designed to bring about the 'conversion' of adults and their families to Christ through baptism.[42] The word 'catechumenate' comes from 'catechesis' or instruction. Both words have as their root the Greek '*echo*', suggesting that a major goal of the process is that catechumens so internalise the life and teaching of Jesus that their own selves will become 'echoes'—non-identical repetitions, one might say—of this unique life.[43] Conversions then, as now, were occasionally quick (or seemed to be), but were more often characterized by a long process of action and reflection.

For the ancient churches, the initial period of conversion was co-extensive with the catechumenate, and occurred in four stages. First, there was a period of preparation, with an emphasis on learning the Word of God, testing the authority of that word in one's life, and struggling against the influence of other sources of authority within society and culture. In some traditions, this first period could last as long as three years, and usually had a strong association with the participation of the catechumens in a regular liturgy of the Word.[44] It has already been suggested that the origins of our modern services of the Word may be found there, with their emphasis on biblical readings, homiletic instruction, petitionary prayer, and a blessing from the teacher at the end.[45] The second stage continued the foci of the first stage, but in a more intensive way. Once teachers and sponsors were satisfied that the catechumen was living a Christian life visibly and constantly, the catechumen would be 'elected' or set aside to receive baptism. Public rituals of renunciation, moral scrutiny and exorcism become prominent as key formation strategies. Usually preceding the celebration of Easter, over a period of six to eight weeks, these disciplines formed the nucleus of what later became the season of Lent. 'It was a time less of negative penitence than of positive preparation for the whole Church to relive and thus renew its own conversion in the passage of its catechumens into

---

[41] 'The Sacrament of Baptism' in Uniting Church in Australia, *Uniting in Worship 2* (Sydney: Uniting Church Press, 2005), p. 64 note 7.

[42] My knowledge of the ancient catechumenate is largely derived from Thomas M. Finn, *Early Christian Baptism and the Catechumenate: West and East Syria* (Collegeville, Minnesota: Liturgical Press, 1992), and Thomas M. Finn, *From Death to Rebirth: Ritual and Conversion in Antiquity* (New York/Mahwah, New Jersey: Paulist Press, 1997), chapters 6-9.

[43] Finn, *Early Christian Baptism and the Catechumenate*, p. 4.

[44] Kavanagh, *The Shape of Baptism*, p. 56.

[45] Kavanagh, *The Shape of Baptism*, p. 57.

life in Christ through baptism.'[46]

The third stage of conversion was the rite of baptism itself, which usually took place at the vigil for Easter. The contemporary rites of baptism we have been describing owe a great deal to this more ancient practice. The pool or font was understood to be both a tomb and a womb, a place of death and burial for the old way of life, but also the place of rebirth to the gift of new life from Christ.[47] It was assumed that the primary actor in the baptismal liturgy was God as Trinity. The ordained minister was seen as God's instrument.[48] The faith of the church was assumed of the candidates, as formation in that faith was regarded as the *express goal* of the catechumenate by which they had been prepared. They declared this faith in a credal form following their renunciation of Satan and, in some places, an anointing for healing.[49] Gregory of Nyssa warned that for unconverted candidates 'the water is but water, for the gift of the Holy Spirit in no ways appears in him who is thus baptismally born.'[50] That is not to say that children were not baptised from the beginning; there the faith of their parents, and of the church, 'substituted'.[51] More often than not, children would be baptised along with their newly catechised parents. By the fourth century, the post-baptismal rites included intercessions and the saying of the Lord's Prayer by the neophytes, intercessions for the neophytes, their vesting in white garments, their receiving of a candle, and (sometimes) their crowning with garlands to signify a 'marriage' with Christ. But the most important of these rites was that of an anointing with oil, seen from earliest times as a participation in Christ's anointing by God as prophet, priest and king. It was used to signify the arrival of a new 'Christ' self, and so was called 'Christening'. The anointing was also seen as a 'seal'—a mark of ownership by Christ, a 'deposit' for future blessing, and a sign of the new covenant. It emphasised the continuing work of the Spirit in the formation of the Christian following baptism, and was usually administered in the shape of the cross.[52] Finally, the new Christian(s) would be offered the kiss of peace and welcomed to the Eucharist for the very first time.

But conversion did not end with baptism! A fourth and final phase of conversion in this early church setting was known as 'post-baptismal mystagogy', which literally means 'formation in the mysteries'. The neophytes would continue to receive instruction about the nature of their faith, this time with an emphasis on living out the implications of the baptismal promises in all

---

[46] Kavanagh, *The Shape of Baptism*, p. 59.
[47] Finn, *Early Christian Baptism and the Catechumenate*, p. 10.
[48] Finn, *Early Christian Baptism and the Catechumenate*, p. 13.
[49] Kavanagh, *The Shape of Baptism*, p. 45.
[50] Cited in Finn, *Early Christian Baptism and the Catechumenate*, p. 14.
[51] Finn, *Early Christian Baptism and the Catechumenate*, p 15. Compare Osborne, *The Christian Sacraments of Initiation*, p. 75.
[52] Finn, *Early Christian Baptism and the Catechumenate*, p. 18.

the business of life. Thus, there was much discussion about ethics and mission—not that discussion was the only mode of teaching. As with the catechumenal phase, the mystagogues also *did* things. They participated in the many and various aspects of the church's charitable mission. They learned to hear the call of Christ in the poor, and recognise his face amongst the marginalised. Crucially, the mystagogues participated regularly in the weekly Eucharist. This celebration was regarded as indispensable for their formation, for it provided them with a symbolic and linguistic cosmos by which to interpret the world in which they lived and acted. In the Eucharist the mystagogues learned *how* to be Christians through a covenantal encounter with the one *in whom* they were Christians: Christ. For the Eucharist was seen, from the beginning, as a weekly renewal of the baptismal covenant. By imbibing the Word of God in the material form of bread and wine, and making themselves available to become Christ's body in the world, the worshippers repeated over again the story of their Paschal plunge into Christ's death and resurrection. Here they *received* what they had already become in baptism, at the same time *becoming* what they received in the Eucharist: the body of Christ. In this sense, any who would follow Christ to the end are mystagogues, not only those who continue in a particular course of instruction during the Eastertide following their baptisms. As we have seen, each of us continues in conversion as we continue in the apostolic teaching, the community, the prayers, and the breaking of the bread.

4. Critical Remarks toward a Contemporary Practice of Baptismal Formation

These historical conversion practices are being adapted and revitalised as a crucially important context for baptism by contemporary churches.[53] The reasons for this are several, I think. First, there is a widespread recognition that the church has become lax in its formation of a specifically Christian identity in those who come for baptism. So often the rite is performed, but in a perfunctory way that makes a mockery of the solemn vows actually uttered in the rite by God, congregation, candidates, and sponsors. The practice of baptising the children of unconverted parents—parents for whom Christ is clearly not

---

[53] There is a growing body of literature, much of it coming from officially appointed committees and commissions. See, for example, *Rite of Christian Initiation of Adults, Welcome to Christ: A Lutheran Introduction to the Catechumenate,* (Minneapolis: Augsburg Press, 1997), Peter Ball and Malcolm Grundy, *Faith on the Way: A Practical Parish Guide to the Adult Catechumenate* (London/New York: Mowbray, 2000), Daniel T. Benedict Jr., *Come to the Waters: Baptism and Our Ministry of Welcoming Seekers and Making Disciples* (Nashville: Discipleship Resources, 1996), Robert E. Webber, *Ancient-Future Evangelism: Making Your Church a Faith-Forming Community* (Grand Rapids, Michigan: Baker Books, 2003), (especially part 1).

'Lord'—is particularly problematic. How can the church take responsibility for the formation of young Christian lives when their most influential teachers, their parents, are either unwilling or unable to share in that responsibility? Clearly this practice continues as a consequence of the mistaken belief (or wish) that the church's faith remains the orienting hermeneutic for our culture at large.[54] Or perhaps it continues out of an anthropological need in parents to somehow mark the birth of their children ritually.

Chauvet has written that Christian pastors must greet such requests with nothing less than an evangelical invitation to 'taste and see' what genuine faith is all about, to begin on the catechumenal journey toward conversion in Christ. Of course, that call needs to be issued in a thoroughly evangelical way, that is, through a gentle invitation that communicates care and respect. Should that invitation be refused, the requestants should nevertheless depart with a sense that the church has listened to their deepest desires, and helped them to identify what it is that they long for. In any case, the church must be firm in its resolve to see baptism as a rite which assumes that a genuinely churchly faith is present and active in the both the candidates and their sponsors.[55]

There are, of course, ways in which the deeply ritual needs of parents can be addressed, apart from baptism itself. Liturgies of blessing and thanksgiving for the gift of a child are now available in the worship books of almost every English-speaking church. These, no less than an ordinary service of the Word, declare the promises of God to all who hear. In such services, even parents with little Christian faith are encouraged to see the birth of their children as both a gift from God and an invitation to live their lives as an offering of thanks to that God. But they do not call on parents, congregations and godparents to make the promises appropriate only to a committed baptismal faith.

The move to a catechumenate obviously assumes that the 'norm' for initiation into the Christian community is *believer* baptism (or, at least, the baptism of those who can answer for themselves).[56] The reasons for this are clear, I trust, from what has been written already in this book. Biblically, Christian covenant involves two movements: both divine promise *and* a human decision to accept and perform that promise in a life of responsible blessing. Since the embodiment of that covenant is necessarily individual as well as communal, only people capable of making an informed *decision* about God's promises may truly *perform* that covenant in a thoroughly interlocutionary way. That should *not* be taken to imply, however, that there is no way to justify the baptism of children under this biblical approach to covenant. 'Believer' baptism, where grace and faith correlate in a single ritual action and within a single human self, is clearly the norm. Let that be clear. But there are good reasons, both theological and phenomenological, to support the continuation of

---

[54] Jenson, *Visible Words*, pp. 166-67.
[55] Chauvet, *The Sacraments*, pp. 195-98.
[56] Kavanagh, *The Shape of Baptism*, p. 109.

infant baptism, albeit under certain conditions.

Phenomenologically, we learned from Lévinas and Derrida that ordinary, historical, space and time are far from seamless in their total unfolding. Historical experience often contradicts or fractures itself in such a way that one catches a glimpse of something that is somehow 'more' than history. These *lacunae*, we learned, are traces of history's supplement: an immemorial origin or impossible future which makes history possible as history, and yet is excessively 'more' than a strictly historical epistemology is able to account for. In theological terms, as we learned from Marion, Jüngel and Kearney, God's time and space are not entirely coincident with human time and space. While God has indeed come to us in the trinitarian history of the Christ event, and in that event's unfolding through the church and its mission, the coming of God will complete itself in ways which ultimately fractures and relativises the ultimacy of historical experience. For God's becoming is an eschatological becoming. When it is fulfilled, as Moltmann says, the whole of human history will be completely refigured, from its first memory to its last, according to a unique moment of absolute correlation between God's history and our own.[57]

Now, while the baptism of human selves certainly occurs within human history, that history is also relativised by the fact of *God's* involvement. Baptism represents an incursion of eschatological or 'more real' time and space into historical or 'real' time and space. The observable effect of that incursion is that apparently impossible things suddenly become possible, like the future becoming present or the past becoming future, like the 'there' becoming the 'here' and the selfhood of Christ becoming the selfhood of the baptised. The linearity of time and space, in short, may be (and, in the case of baptism, certainly *is*) disrupted and turned all topsy-turvy. We saw an example of that with baptism and the coming of the Spirit in the New Testament. Sometimes the Spirit appeared to come even *before* the baptism had taken place.

Now what all that implies for the baptism of children is that the present faith of sponsors may indeed come to 'substitute' for the not-yet-present faith of the candidate. Put otherwise, the not-yet-present faith of the child baptised—precisely because it is also the faith of the church—may become present at the point of baptism *in and through* the faith of his or her sponsors. What is foundational to such baptism, making possible that which is ordinarily impossible, is the theologically 'prior' substitution of Christ's faith for the faith of both candidate *and* sponsors. For according to the New Testament, as we have seen already, human faith lives from the faith of Christ. Our faith is effective and real with regard to God's commands and promises only because Christ creates a space within his own faith for ours. He *substitutes* for us in the sense of drawing our uncertain faith and obedience into his own *accomplished* faith and obedience. Because both the faith of sponsors and the not-yet-present

---

[57] Jürgen Moltmann, *The Way of Jesus Christ: Christology in Messianic Dimensions*, trans. Margaret Kohl (London: SCM Press, 1990), p. 333.

faith of the child candidate live from the faith of Christ in his life, death, and resurrection, saving faith may indeed come to belong to the uncomprehending child at the point of his or her baptism.

Despite that possibility, we must nevertheless continue to view the baptism of infants as exceptional rather than normative for the practice of the church, even as we must view the coming of the Spirit *at* baptism as normative, even though there are clearly occasions where this is not the case. Thus, as Kavanagh wisely advises, infant baptism should only be practised in communities where the norm is clearly *adult* baptism.[58] Only communities such as this, who know from their practised catechumenate that baptism is a serious act of mutual vowing between God and a human being, are competent to provide a sufficiently nurturing environment for the growth of faith in an initially uncomprehending child.

A second reason for the renewal of the baptismal catechumenate is clearly its enormous *ritual* power to form Christian disciples who are willing to both lose, and find themselves anew, in the depths of Christ's life, death, and resurrection. According to Kavanagh, the invention of the catechumenate was a 'stupendous achievement' primarily because of its power to bind and integrate a community of faith into the life of God:

> The sacraments were seen as a totality coextensive with the Church's life itself, a life carried on in a series of events which arose out of and in turn shaped all the members of the local church—catechumens, penitents, inquirers, clergy, and faithful. The liturgy was seen not as a matter of exquisite ecclesiastical ceremonial to occupy clergy and religious but as the way a Christian people live in common. Whatever such a people did *as* a people was liturgical, an act of corporate worship of God. What this meant was sacramental—understood as any thing or act that relates one to God.[59]

As we have seen already, sacraments are God's body, the visibility of God's word of address in the materiality of the church.[60] In the sacraments, Christ is present to himself in the same way that our own bodies are present to ourselves—through the distance of relationship.[61] In any relationship, there is a period of 'getting-to-know' the other person before any meaningful commitment or vow can be made. The catechumenate is that period in which the candidates 'get-to-know' Christ-in-the-Church so that they are finally able to make an informed decision about whether or not to vow themselves to him for life. The Christ they get to know is not a Gnostic Christ, a purely 'spiritual' reality that they somehow access in a mystical and interior mode. For Christ is the church, that community which has already joined itself to him in baptism,

---

[58] Kavanagh, *The Shape of Baptism*, p. 110.
[59] Kavanagh, *The Shape of Baptism*, p. 118.
[60] Jenson, *Visible Words*, p. 29. See also Power, *Sacraments*, pp. 86-8.
[61] Jenson, *Visible Words*, p. 47.

and therefore become the primary mode of his visibility in the world. One cannot face Christ without facing the church; one cannot face the church without facing Christ. Of course, the church can never claim to represent Jesus to the point of exhaustion. Jesus is far more than the church: in the Spirit he stands over and against what is present in the name of an eschatological remainder, the reign of God. Yet the church is precisely that community which does not claim to constitute itself from itself; instead, the church takes the pose of someone who is praying, waiting always for the Word of another to reveal its identity and purpose. It is in *this* sense, and this sense only, that the church is Christ: in it's sharing of Christ's vocation as the hearer and doer of the Father's will (Jn 5.19-20). Thus, the catechumens learn to become Christ by imitating a church that is itself imitating Christ (Eph 5.1; Heb 13.7). Christ, we are told, 'learned obedience' through his suffering; in the midst of his distress he called out to God and was heard because of his 'reverent submission' (Heb 5.7, 8). Like Christ, the catechumens must struggle to renounce the spirits of their age—the moral and ideological powers—in order to find that place of submission to Christ in which they may be 'saved'. They learn how to do that from those who go before them, who face them *in persona Christi*. By watching, listening, and *imitating*, they learn both how to die and how to live. They learn to be baptised with Christ in his death and his resurrection.

We must be careful to define what we mean by this idea of imitation (*mimesis*). Baptism is a ritual, certainly; it repeats the baptism of Christ's Pasch, and it does so in liturgical forms that share a similar shape across both time and space. Yet, as we have seen, both the preparation and the baptism of each new Christian is nevertheless a genuinely *new* event, a repetition that is qualitatively different from every other baptism. David Power writes that the original Pasch of Jesus always takes form according to the possibilities inherent in local symbols and languages, yet it does this in a way which disrupts any attempt to bring the Pasch into a simple or linear experience of time.[62] Because the rite of baptism, for example, remembers a past event which was itself an irruption of God's entirely new future, it cannot do otherwise than inscribe this future onto the bodies of those who are baptised. *Mimesis*, then, has more to do with the non-identical repetition of a unique 'gift' (Marion) than with the eternal return of the 'same' in the form of conventional ideology or ritual. The gift, having once been given, continues to give itself in forms that promise only that the gift is still being given. All such forms are therefore iconic or sacramental. They are witnesses to a gaze which they may not 'enworld' apart from their own *prior* 'enworlding' by the gaze of God. In the language of the Reformation, the sacraments are signs of 'promise'. They are the arrival of a promise that, precisely as promise, nevertheless looks to an untameable 'future' for its full realization and fulfilment.[63]

---

[62] Power, *Sacraments*, p. 92.
[63] Power, *Sacraments*, pp. 223-24.

The appropriate mode for the reception of such a gift is the persistently asymmetrical pose of prayer: a continuous waiting and hoping toward a future which, paradoxically, has already arrived in the prayer of Christ that pose reproduces. *Mimesis* is like a memory in the body of a place we have never been and a time we have never known. Bodily memories, as is well known, are memories that affect all that we do in a persistent habitus of behaviour and belief; yet, unlike 'mental' memories, they do not often present themselves in consciousness. Bodily memory is tacit memory, sitting under the surface of consciousness in a way that defies the control of the ego. Those who are baptised into Christ Jesus are scarified, ritually and psychosomatically, with the marks of the cross (signing), the tomb (immersion in water), and the resurrection (the Paschal candle and the alb). These memories are powerful. As Power notes, people who are baptised beyond infancy will carry stories of their catechumenate and baptism for all their lives, especially if those memories are reinforced by the oft-repeated bodily actions common to both baptism and the Eucharist.[64]

All of which is to say that the rituality of catechumenate and baptism are certainly *not* designed to maintain people in the individual and collective identities received from their culture, language and society. If baptismal rituals do only this, then they have failed to be genuinely Christian. A ritual is a *Christian* ritual only if it is able to contest the values and perspectives of conventional reality in the name of a parabolically 'more real' reality, namely the paschal story of the crucified and risen Jesus as it comes to us in the mission of the Spirit. The rites of baptism should never be *comfortable* for either the candidates or their congregational supporters. Even when one has already been baptised oneself, walking the road with a catechumen should be an arduous task. For the call to the catechumen—'die to the world and rise with Christ'— is also a call to the community in which he or she is learning the faith. No one who watches over the process may avoid being implicated by the process: for the one who faces the catechumen *in persona Christi* is likely to find that Christ is already facing them through the face and form of the catechumen (Mt 25.34-40), calling even the most mature and committed Christians to a deeper, more consistent, conversion to Christ.

Christian conversion is, of course, a life-long process that baptism inaugurates and the other rituals of the church reinforce. As a fundamentally illocutionary process, it is effected primarily in and through spatio-temporal relationships of *facing*. In turning to face Christ, the self undergoes a painful passage *away from* 'the world, the flesh, and the devil' and *towards* the church, the Spirit embodied, and the coming reign of God. The language of turning, facing and procession or passage is clearly *embodied* language that seeks to transfigure the performances of the self in space and time, as well as in thought or belief. Theologically, this suggests that the church would do well to carefully

---

[64] Power, *Sacraments*, p. 126.

plan the *choreography of the body* in its baptismal ceremonies, and not to simply revise texts to the exclusion of all else. There are compelling *pedagogical* reasons for doing so. Paul Connerton has shown that the memory of the body is more lasting and effecting than the memory of cognition alone. When beliefs or attitudes are correlated with analogous bodily actions, they are more likely to become 'sedimented' into the tacit or habitual processes of self-performance.[65] This shows that the revision of baptismal texts will not necessarily lead to a renewal of baptismal faith. In the words of Byron Anderson, 'Liturgical renewal will not take hold unless we stop revising texts and start incorporating them.'[66] This is to make a distinction between 'what' knowledge and 'how' knowledge:

> I learn what it means to be a Christian as, year in, year out, I hear and tell the stories and traditions of that community. I learn how to be a Christian by enacting those stories and traditions in the ritual actions of the Christian community, in the dying and rising experienced in baptism, in the grateful reception of bread and wine, in kneeling, bowing or standing for prayer.[67]

Thus, human selves will only gain the competence to perform or enact the Christian life if they are first prepared to allow the rituals of the community to 'perform' them: to manipulate and scarify their body-selves in concert with the more 'cognitive' inscription which comes through the hearing and reading of texts. That is why it is important to incorporate ritual performances into the period of the catechumenate itself, rituals that are able to reinforce the conversion from sin and evil to Christ. We noted how the ancient church did this, with rituals of election, scrutiny and exorcism. In the modern era, new rituals are being created.

The Roman church rendered a great service with the publication of its *Rite of Christian Initiation of Adults*. Alongside the rite of baptism itself, this process includes several other ceremonies specifically designed to assist in the formation of catechumens. The first of these, the 'rite of acceptance into the catechumenate' includes an impressive array of rituals that deliberately foreshadow the rite of baptism, as it shall be celebrated at the Easter Vigil. After the candidates have declared their intention to 'try on' the Christian faith and life, they may be 'exorcised' of the influence of evil in their lives. This involves the celebrant breathing upon the candidates, a sign of the Holy Spirit, and praying that God may 'drive away the spirits of evil.' Now, whether one believes that evil may be ontologically personified or not, it is clear that this intentionally theatrical form of the rite is likely to gain far more traction in the memory of its witnesses than some snippet of demythologised, post-Marxist rhetoric about structural evil! The rite of exorcism prepares the candidates for

---

[65] Cited in Anderson, *Worship and Christian Identity*, pp. 77-8.
[66] Anderson, *Worship and Christian Identity*, p. 78.
[67] Anderson, *Worship and Christian Identity*, p. 80.

the final renunciations that they shall make at their baptisms. The candidates may then be signed with the cross—not only on the forehead, as in baptism, but on every part of their bodies. This indicates for the candidate, in a very effective manner, that the life of baptised faith involves handing over every region of one's bodily existence to be crucified with Christ. The candidate is given a Bible (their new 'roadmap' for life). They may also be given a new name, a specifically 'Christian' name, thus signifying that that their allegiance to Christ is more important than their allegiance to either ethnic group or clan. For baptism requires a renunciation of every kind of self-identification save those which Christ will give in baptism. By these and other rites, the message of the catechumenate is reinforced and performed: baptism is a dying to self, and a receiving of the new, resurrected self in Christ.

I would argue for the inclusion of more specifically 'theatrical' moments in the liturgy of baptism as well. The ancients were very good at this and so, also (as we learned from Breton) were the 'fools for Christ' of the Slavic Middle Ages. But we moderns have become far too one-sided in our dependence upon words and cognition. The renunciations and the turning to Christ could be performed, for example, after the manner of that depicted in the Eastern Church's *Barberini Euchologion*. There the candidates not only renounce, but also ex/pel Satan by means of a dramatic blowing motion while facing the West; then they turn 180 degrees to the East and the rising sun, a graphic depiction of both repentance and the desire to be raised with Christ.[68] One could also mount an argument for the visible shedding of clothes before descending into the pool, as was done in Jerusalem under the patronage of Cyril. Nakedness is a figure of the loss we must sustain in order to embrace the new life. It recalls the nakedness of birth and, according to Cyril, the nakedness of Christ's vulnerability on the cross.[69] The performance would be even more effective if, as the candidates ascend from the pool, they were albed in white (to signify being clothed with Christ) and adorned with a wedding-band (as a sign of their marriage to Christ). Now, a practice like that would be a true prophecy against the consumerism and individualism of our age. I doubt, though, that many churches would accept it, even with plenty of preparatory education! Still, there are ways to do something *like* that. In some local churches the candidates change into a simple garment, in private and behind a screen, immediately before they are baptised, removing also any jewellery they are wearing. After being baptised they are towelled dry and adorned in an alb while the congregation sings a doxology.

Obviously, in order to stage these more theatrical rites, the architecture and adornment of churches would need some converting as well. To pick a paradigm example, some churches or monasteries still possess a purpose-built baptistery in which a genuine 'burial' under the water may take place. But

---

[68] Osborne, *The Christian Sacraments of Initiation*, p. 71.
[69] Osborne, *The Christian Sacraments of Initiation*, p. 73.

most, in the traditions I am examining, do not. So often, today, it is architecture and furnishing which holds the church back when it comes to liturgical reforms. Sprinkling persists because churches do not have pools, and because the fonts they possess are very small. The interim solution in many places is to take the congregation off to a Baptist or Pentecostal church building where a pool can be found. But this creates as many problems as it solves, for the art and architecture in such churches often clashes badly with the experience of faith a more catholic or ecumenical rite is trying to convey. A further difficulty is the fact that the borrowed building is not in any sense 'home' for the local community of faith into which the neophytes are being welcomed; therefore it cannot 'co-operate' with the ritual in its acts of hospitality. If the community's home building is near an outdoor pool, a river or a beach, it may be best to perform the strictly baptismal rites there, and then move quickly on to the church proper for the rites of welcome and of Eucharist. This practice would not be so very different from that recorded by Justin at the church of Rome (c. 150). The baptism he describes occurred at some distance from the church proper. The baptismal party then processed to the church, Easter candles ablaze, where most of the community had been waiting in some kind of vigil of the Word. The neophytes were welcomed there with fervent prayer and the kiss of peace.[70] However I would prefer, in the case of the modern stopgap manoeuvre, that the whole community be present at *both* halves of the liturgy.

Conclusion

This final chapter concentrated on baptism in the practice of the church. Having demonstrated that churchly practices in general, and liturgy in particular, are of especial importance to a genuinely covenantal theology, I went on to exegete the meaning of the covenant as it is established in the catholic or ecumenical rites of baptism. My aim was to demonstrate the ways in which the liturgy of baptism, insofar as it is part of a comprehensive pedagogy of baptismal formation, is able to form both God and human beings. Central to such formation is the *making of vows*: God toward human beings, and human beings toward God. The baptismal liturgy, as the culmination of an intentional catechumenate, not only teaches the disciple how to know God and make God known. It also draws that God, uniquely and vulnerably, into the spiritual life and practice of all who are baptised. Here the baptised lose themselves to God, but find themselves anew precisely as God refigures God's own self through the ecclesial becoming of the ever-vulnerable Christ.

By means of this confluence of pedagogy and ritual, the Christian avowal accomplishes a performative truth. This truth concerns and implicates both God and the Christian self, inscribing itself onto the baptismal body as a peculiarly

---

[70] Justin's *First Apology*, chapters 61 and 65, cited in Kavanagh, *The Shape of Baptism*, pp. 43-4.

paradoxical identity and vocation: to know, love and imitate a God who can never be exhaustively known, loved or imitated. Christian identity is irreducibly paradoxical because the Christian avowal towards God responds to that divine avowal towards human beings we have called the 'Pasch' of Christ, an event which conceals the meaning of history in the same movement as it is revealed. The Christian avowal responds to the Pasch in the form of the non-identical repetitions of baptism and Eucharist. In these uniquely Christian practices, the human person puts aside his or her pretensions toward a self-generated meaning or identity, trusting instead to an eschatological meaning and identity that arrives as from another, from the relational facing of God in Christ.

The meaning and identity of a specific Christian life should therefore be seen as both excessive and incomplete. It is excessive because its meaning has already been given in Christ, yet each personal recapitulation of Christ's Pasch reveals something 'more' in that gift, a never-exhausted supplement or surplus. A Christian life is also incomplete because what was given, and what is received anew in each new Christian avowal, is given from a future which has not yet arrived in its fullness. In the Christian sense, therefore, vows can never be made with the intention of taming or circumscribing the meanings of either God or the human self. Neither can they be used as a way to control or guarantee the future of the relationship they inaugurate. Christian vows are not contracts or protocols of exchange. Because they perform the self by favouring God—a trinitarian reality who is always already other-centred—Christian vows are radically relational. They anchor personal identity and meaning in the reality of an infinitely surprising alter-ego. As a Christian, I can only become myself in and as the becoming of another self. I have myself only as God has me: through the giving of myself into another's care. I have myself by vowing to surrender myself to the one who has already surrendered Godself to me. In this paradox is the uniquely Christian avowal; it is also, therefore, a unique metonym for the Christian life as a whole.

EPILOGUE

Trauma and Joy:
A Meditation on Mark's Baptism of Jesus[1]

> *In those days Jesus came from Nazareth of Galilee and was baptized by John in the Jordan. And just as he was coming up out of the water, he saw the heavens torn apart and the Spirit descending like a dove on him. And a voice came from heaven, 'You are my Son, the Beloved; with you I am well pleased.' And the Spirit immediately drove him out into the wilderness. He was in the wilderness for forty days, tempted by Satan; and he was with the wild beasts; and the angels waited on him.*
>
> Mark 1.9-13

1. The Holy Ambiguity of Baptism

There is a holy ambiguity to the sacrament of baptism. On the one hand, the waters represent an original wounding, trauma, and loss—surely the source and wellspring of all that we might refer to, with Jacques Derrida, as the 'work' of mourning.[2] Yet, on the other hand, the waters are also the power of God to inaugurate a new world, a world that may *appear to be* patterned upon the old, yet is not. For now this world is looked at as if from another person or place, such that our former experience of the world is transfigured into some kind of 'new experience with experience', as Jüngel has said.[3] This because we ourselves have become different or, more strictly speaking, we have finally come to ourselves, our true selves, by becoming another self, the self who is Christ. As St. Paul says in Galatians: 'Now I live, yet not I; it is Christ who lives within me.' So there is something, I suggest, of the oft-neglected themes of Holy Saturday in the story or memory of baptism. Only by mourning, by visiting the world of the dead, is Jesus able to gain the power to overcome death. Only by mourning and pining for a world that has *not yet arrived*, only

---

[1] This chapter was previously published as Garry J. Deverell, 'The Work of Mourning: Derridean Reflections Upon the Waters,' *Australian Journal of Liturgy* 10.3 (2006): 91-104.

[2] Jacques Derrida, *The Work of Mourning*, trans. Michael Naas and Pascale-Anne Brault (Chicago: University of Chicago Press, 2001), p. 50.

[3] Jüngel, *God as the Mystery of the World*, p. 32.

by being prepared to die in the midst of life, do the baptised come face to face with the Christ who can raise them from death into the strange new world of the kingdom of God. In baptism we mourn. Not for the loss of an Eden that has been devastated through sin, flood and fire. In baptism we mourn for a world that has not yet arrived, and can only arrive as we do the work of mourning, that is, speak and act as the material presence of an absent Christ, who died and rose again, and is coming to our world in glory to transform it utterly.

2. Water is Dangerous: It can take One's Life Away

One should understand that, in the ancient world, water was not so benign as we regard it today, flowing purely and freely from our taps as it does. In the ancient world, water very often symbolised chaos and evil. On the waves of the sea, many ancient people lost their lives. With the flooding of the rivers, they lost their harvests. In the ancient world, people knew that water was both necessary to life but also the bringer of death. 'Fear death by water' said the Buddha in T.S. Eliot's *The Wasteland*. What that meant for Eliot, as it means for us, is that the waters of baptism should not be regarded as tame, given only to feed and sustain life as we already know it. The waters of baptism are dangerous: they are designed to take our lives away. Without doing so, they cannot give us a new life. Consider that icon of Jesus' baptism in the traditions of the Eastern Church. Under Christ's feet is Leviathan, an ancient symbol of water's power to kill and destroy. In order to be baptised, Jesus had to be willing to submit himself to the chaotic power of Leviathan. For that is the only way to overcome Leviathan's power. Perhaps we moderns, stuck in the Enlightenment categories of control and safety, may only get in touch with the unsettling *force* of that ancient sensibility when something like a tsunami comes along to confront the heterogeneity of our mythologies.

3. Derrida: Mourning as the Work of any Life Lived before the Other

In the last book Jacques Derrida published before his death he spoke of mourning as a work (or, in my designation, a liturgy) that is inaugurated at the beginning of life, at the naming of a new life, not at its end with the funeral. For in naming someone we secretly acknowledge that the substance of that person is as much absent to us as it is present. The name can be present where the person is not. The name stands in for a person who is never entirely here with us in the now. The name signifies that the personhood of an/other is able to permanently elude our instinct for presence, still arriving, as it were, from an immemorial past or unimagined future. There is a paradox, therefore, in speaking to, for, or about the other, whether in life or in death. Such speech 'comes to tear itself toward that which, or the one who, can no longer receive it; it rushes toward the impossible'. Still, the impossible sometimes, 'by chance' says Derrida, becomes possible, when the one we name is the one in me, in you, in us.[4] As in death, a person whom we regard as very much alive is only ever present to us insofar as he or she works *in* us, in our *interiority*, as a name. So, there is death, and a life that is made possible by death, even from the very first naming.[5]

In Derrida-speak, this paradox is signified by the relationship between two ancient terms, the *punctum*, the prick or wound of the absolutely unique and singular, and the *stadium*, that mythological network of meanings by which we render the world habitable:

> The heterogeneity of the *punctum* is rigorous; its originality can bear neither contamination nor concession . . . This absolute other composes with the same, with its absolute other that is thus not its opposite, with the locus of the same and of the *stadium* . . . If the *punctum* is more or less that itself, dissymmetrical—to everything and in itself—then it can invade the field of the *stadium*, to which, strictly speaking, it does not belong.[6]

This means that the *punctum* can 'induce' a metonymy. 'As soon as it allows itself to be drawn into a network of substitutions, it can invade everything, objects as well as affects. This singularity that is nowhere in the field mobilizes everything everywhere; it pluralizes itself.' This is the force, power, or *dynamis* of the *punctum*.[7] It is this metonymic force of the *punctum* that allows us to speak of the unique other, to speak of and to it. It makes possible a 'relation without relation'.[8] The absent living resist and address our exteriorisations in a way that differs from the non-responsibility of a corpse only, perhaps, as a matter of degree.[9]

Mourning is therefore something that happens everyday. It is a recognition, in the midst of life, that the other who faces me is not one who can be finally appropriated into my own agenda for life. The other is mysterious, a particularity who resists my rendering of the world by a kind of absence-in-presence. The other, we might say, is like a parable that is able to question my personal mythologies, and in questioning to reconfigure, or reinvigorate, or make the same seem somehow different. Or, in the speech of Derrida, the other may be like a *punctum*, a prick of conscience or a wounding, which makes the lore of the tribe seem completely inadequate. Love, for example, is singular. For Derrida, love is not the love of a universal figure, but the singularity of a relation; 'it disorganises all studied discourses, all theoretical systems and philosophies.' The singular other can only appear by disappearing. Such love is, as Blanchot said, an 'absence-as-presence'. The other who appears this ways

---

[4] Derrida, *The Work of Mourning*, p. 45.
[5] Derrida, *The Work of Mourning*, p. 46.
[6] Derrida, *The Work of Mourning*, p. 57.
[7] Derrida, *The Work of Mourning*, p. 57.
[8] Derrida, *The Work of Mourning*, p. 58.
[9] Derrida, *The Work of Mourning*, p. 47.

is like the Referent in a photo. The Referent is not a real or a present. It is another who appears by not appearing.[10]

That should not be taken to imply, however, that the Christic other encountered in baptism—baptism as a mourning in and with Christ—may be taken as the quasi-transcendental legitimisation of any Nietzschean-styled permissiveness, where individuals may do whatever they want by way of flouting the law of the tribe. There are some, the most radically 'postmodern' amongst us, who would perhaps like it to be that way. For isn't it frankly true that most of us feel legitimately *exempt* from what is socially acceptable? Each of us have a sense of the 'higher law' in whose name we regularly break the law or contravene what our tribe would expect of us. Indeed, confessing such transgressions has today become passé. When slightly drunk at dinner parties, we will all put our hands up to confess. Speeding tickets, tax evasion, even sexual misdemeanours, these are 'no big deal'. If the television show *Seinfeld* is about anything, it is about watching other people actually do what most of us still baulk at doing, even though we have no real reason not to. *Seinfeld* is about the 'higher law' to which many of us subscribe today, the Nietzschean law of the will to power which says: I can do anything I like because, in the end, all that matters is what *I* make of myself.

4. The Rite of Baptism Today: Legitimization or Subversion of the *Status Quo*?

Today the church celebrates baptism within a social and cultural environment where baptism has been largely sanitised of its dangerous and subversive qualities. In the paedobaptist churches the rite is all-too-often reduced to a quaint and pleasant little naming ceremony. Friends and relatives gather in their finery on a bright Sunday morning; the child's forehead is wetted with a few tiny drops of water while his or her godparents are content to make promises they can neither comprehend nor keep. In the so-called 'baptist' churches, the rite is often reduced to its pre-Christian tribal meanings, i.e. baptism as a rite of passage into responsible adult membership of the tribe or congregation. Unfortunately, neither of these practices is adequate to the baptism undergone by Jesus, the baptism that is paradigmatic for Christians. For while the baptisms of the tribe pander to social and anthropological needs, the baptism of Jesus models the rather anti-social action of God, by which the baptised person is torn away from his or her 'natural' tribal roles in favour of a way of life which actually subverts and fractures what is commonly done. Christian baptism, then, is far more than a capitulation to the symbolic 'lore' of the tribe, such that the common*place* common*sense* is owned and internalised.

The mourning that makes us genuinely *Christian* in the sacrament of baptism is infinitely more difficult than the choice for either the lore of the tribe

---

[10] Derrida, *The Work of Mourning*, p. 48.

or the higher law of the will-to-power. Why? Because in baptism we confess a profounder and more painful truth: that *neither the 'symbolic' law of the tribe, nor the 'higher' law of the will-to-power* are able to accomplish a self that is capable of that freedom we call *joy*. The law of the tribe can only ever accomplish our guilt, while the higher law is simply a *fetish we have made for ourselves* in a desperate attempt to escape the horror of subject-less anonymity of which Emmanuel Lévinas wrote so profoundly.[11] In theological perspective, the impossible journey towards joy (or, in Lacanian terms, *jouissance*) goes by no other way than by a literally *unbearable* encounter with God who was in Christ. In this perspective, we can never really become ourselves apart from the traumatic interventions that the Bible calls creation and redemption. Christian baptism is therefore painful in the extreme because here we admit that it is not ourselves but another, God, who gives our life and livelihood; that we are not the masters of our destiny or the makers of our own salvation; that our fetishised lives therefore have no more substance than a house of cards.

To confess or avow the truth which comes from another, rather than from ourselves alone, is painful in the extreme, for here we touch the raw wound of that founding *trauma* that most of us spend our whole lives running from. *The founding trauma who is God*. 'In the beginning,' says the Book of Genesis, the universe was a void and formless waste. It was a watery Nothing. But over this dark Nothingness the Spirit of God brooded, and that Spirit spoke. 'Let there be light!' and there was. This is a story about the making of the world, certainly, but it is also about the making of the human self. It tells us that the Self is never itself without the traumatic intervention or presence of another. The call or voice of this other summons us from the womb-like Nothing of infinite solipsism into the real world of consciousness, inter-dependence and relationship. Thus, we are called to ourselves by an intervention, a creation, an interrupting trauma that leaves its mark on us forever.

In this, says Slavoj Žižek, Christianity and psychoanalysis are agreed: that the first event is the traumatic arrival of another, and that most us spend our lives running away from this event, pretending that we can found ourselves, or make our own salvation.[12] Ironically, the way to healing is to return to the founding trauma, and find there a God who is irrevocably *for* us, who longs for and promises our liberation. For Christians, this constitutes a return to the violence of the cross, that sacrifice to end all sacrifices in which is revealed, as René Girard has said, a God who asks for the worship of mercy rather than sacrificial appeasement.[13] This is not to say that a return to the founding trauma can be accomplished by human beings in and of themselves. For a trauma is exactly that archaic or eschatological event which *cannot* be in/corporated or

---

[11] Lévinas, *Existence and Existents*, p. 61.
[12] Žižek, *On Belief*, p. 47.
[13] René Girard, *Things Hidden since the Foundation of the World*, trans. Stephen Bann and Michael Metteer (London/New York: Continuum, 2003), p. 210.

re/membered. Yet, God is one who makes the return possible from the side of divinity. In the Spirit, God makes of Christ the *traverse* between the founding event and the event of baptism, such that baptism becomes a precisely *real* submersion of the self in the *yet more real* selfhood of Christ in his accomplished humanity, a humanity finally competent to perform the unique mercy of God. Here the human self is both lost and recovered more wholly than ever before; trauma is transfigured into joy. Joy, of course, is a vocative language, a language of prayer. Its primary motivation is neither to constitute the other as a version of the same, nor to reduce the transcendence of the other to a particular appearance. Joy simply *celebrates* the always-already-accomplished fact of the other as the salvific centre of the self.

5. Mourning and Hope

In this we catch a glimpse of the absurdly paradoxical *hope* inscribed in Christian baptism. For baptism is not only a letting-go of the fantasy-self, the lie of a self that is its own law and judge, but also the arrival of another self, a truer self given in love by God. Such arrivals are inscribed everywhere in Mark's story of Jesus' baptism, literally everywhere. The river in which Jesus is baptised is the Jordan. It is the river that, in the memory of Israel, marks their exodus from the land of slavery into the land of promise, their transformation from a loose collection of tribal nomads into a federated nation with a land and a holy vocation given by Yahweh. The baptism therefore recalls that God is one who liberates, who takes a broken people to his breast and gives them both a new name, and a new purpose. Note, also, that the baptism of Jesus is placed by Mark alongside a memory of the exile in Babylon. Isaiah interpreted that event as an intervention by God to change the people's hearts. The city's nobles had become obsessed with their own power and prestige. They had forgotten the claims of charity and mercy, and so God destroyed the city. In that context, the baptism of Jesus can be read as a renewal of the work of God in human society: after destruction and exile comes forgiveness and a new covenant, the advent of a new relationship between God and the people of God's affection.

Still, the most potent trace of arriving hope, in Mark's story, is when the heavens are ripped open as Jesus comes out of the water, and the Spirit of God descends upon him like a dove. Again, one does not necessarily understand these symbols unless one knows the stories of the Hebrew Bible. There one reads of a God who dwells in a holy of holies, an ark that is placed behind a curtain in the innermost chamber of the temple. Only the High Priest, or some specially appointed leader like Moses, may approach God there, and usually only once per year at *Yom Kippur*, the Day of Atonement. To my mind, the theatre of these Jewish rituals is about the irreducible otherness of God, the danger of assuming too close a familiarity with God. God is in heaven, hidden behind a veil that we may not open from our side. Yet, here in the baptism of Jesus, the veil that separates God from ourselves is not simply put aside, but *ripped to pieces.* Furthermore, it is done by *God*, from God's 'side,' if you like. In the Spirit, God actually *leaves* the holy of holies in heaven, and comes to dwell within the heart and spirit of one who is not simply a prophet, but a Son, a beloved one. No longer is God to be understood as the other beyond us, beyond our being in the heavens. From now on God is to be understood as the *other who is Christ*, a human being who walks amongst us, who speaks our language, who shows us what God is like as a child reveals the form and character of his or her parent. That is to renounce a religion of the 'sublime' in favour of what Žižek calls a radical religion of 'desublimation':

> not desublimation in the sense of a simple reduction of God to man, but desublimation in the sense of the decendence of the sublime Beyond to the everyday level. Christ is a 'ready-made God' (as Boris Groys put it), he is fully human, inherently indistinguishable from other humans in exactly the same way Judy is indistinguishable from Madeleine in [Hitchcock's] *Vertigo* . . . it is only the imperceptible 'something,' a pure appearance which cannot ever be grounded in a substantial property, that makes him divine.[14]

To put all this another way, what Mark proclaims about what happened to Christ is also something that may happen to all of us. After the collapse and breakdown of the false self that is part of a genuinely baptismal avowal, God promises to come to us with the gift of a new self: a self forged within by the cruciform activity of the Spirit who was in Christ and now bears, forever, Christ's form and character. In the Spirit, Christ himself comes to us as the love and vitality that empowers us to put off the old and embrace the gift of the new and truer self. *Galatians* again: 'Now I live, and yet not I; it is Christ who lives within me. The life I live in the body I live by faith in the Son of God, who loved me, and gave himself for me' (2.20).

Mark's story confronts the commonplace understanding and practice of baptism in two ways. First, it tells us that there is no such thing as a Christian baptism without the hard and soul-destroying work of what I have been calling mourning. In the first centuries of the Christian church, this was taken very seriously. Several years were given over to the catechumenal learning of the faith. Through a process of action and reflection, the catechumens wrestled against the demons of both self and tribe; and they did so in the power of a newly arriving self, figured for them in the mentor or sponsor who was, themselves, a figure of Christ. Second, the story tells us that baptism will bear its human fruit not because of our own will or determination, but because *God is faithful*. The Father sends the Spirit, the Spirit of his son Jesus, to hollow out the old self from the inside out, and replace it with a selfhood of God's own making and design. In this sense, baptism is not simply about the ceremonial occasion itself. It is rather a cipher and a ritual performance of the Christian life as a whole: a calling and a pledge to leave the false self behind, and to wrestle

---

[14] Žižek, *On Belief*, p. 90.

always to find the truth about things which is God's gift to everyone who asks for it. This second movement confronts our fantasies about either absorption into the tribe *or* the will-to-power. For here we learn the difficult and liberating truth that we have never been on our own, that even the breath that we take this moment is possible only because *God* has made it possible.

Baptism, then, is a mourning and a building, it is mourning *as* building. It is the Christian life. It is a promise from *God* that may only be received and performed by means of a *human* promising: to walk the way of the cross by which trauma is transfigured into joy. All of which is to say that it is perhaps the memory in me, in my body, of the encounter with Christ in baptism that gives me the courage to live responsibly. For what is my life if not a response and a metonymic substitution for these memories, memories so powerful and present that they make for me, and for all they love in me, a future?

Bibliography

Anderson, E. Byron. *Worship and Christian Identity: Practicing Ourselves*. Collegeville, Minnesota: Liturgical Press, 2003.
Austin, John Langshaw. *How to Do Things with Words*. William James Lectures. 2nd ed. Oxford: Clarendon Press, 1975.
Australia, Uniting Church in. *Uniting in Worship 2*. Sydney: Uniting Church Press, 2005.
Ball, Peter, and Malcolm Grundy. *Faith on the Way: A Practical Parish Guide to the Adult Catechumenate*. London/New York: Mowbray, 2000.
Barth, Karl. *Evangelical Theology: An Introduction*. Trans. Grover Foley. Grand Rapids, Michigan: Eerdmans, 1963.
—. *The Humanity of God*. Trans. John Newton Thomas and Thomas Wieser. Richmond, Virginia: John Knox Press, 1960.
Benedict Jr., Daniel T. *Come to the Waters: Baptism and Our Ministry of Welcoming Seekers and Making Disciples*. Nashville: Discipleship Resources, 1996.
Benveniste, Emile. *Indo-European Language and Society*. Les Editions de Minuit 1969. Trans. Elizabeth Palmer. London: Faber and Faber, 1973.
Bonhoeffer, Dietrich. *Life Together*. Gemeinsame Leben. Trans. John W. Doberstein. London: SCM Press, 1954.
Breton, Stanislas. *The Word and the Cross*. Trans. Jacquelyn Porter. New York: Fordham University Press, 2002.
Brueggemann, Walter. *The Covenanted Self*. Minneapolis: Fortress Press, 1999.
Caputo, John D. *Demythologising Heidegger*. Bloomington: Indiana University Press, 1993.
—. Toward a Postmodern Theology of the Cross: Augustine, Heidegger, Derrida. *Postmodern Philosophy and Christian Thought*. Ed. Merold Westphal. Bloomington: Indiana University Press, 1999.
Chauvet, Louis-Marie. *The Sacraments: The Word of God at the Mercy of the Body*. 1997. Collegeville, Minnesota: The Liturgical Press, 2001.
—. *Symbol and Sacrament: A Sacramental Reinterpretation of Christian Existence*. 1987. Trans. Patrick Madigan and Madeleine Beaumont. Collegeville, Minnesota: The Liturgical Press, 1995.
Childs, Brevard S. *Old Testament Theology in a Canonical Context*. Philadelphia: Fortress Press, 1985.
Church, United Methodist. *The United Methodist Book of Worship*. Nashville, TN: The United Methodist Publishing House, 1992.
Crichton, James D. *Lights in Darkness: Forerunners of the Liturgical Movement*. Collegeville, Minnesota: Liturgical Press, 1996.

Crossan, John Dominic. *The Dark Interval: Towards a Theology of Story.* Sanoma, California: Polebridge Press, 1998.

—. Our Own Faces in Deep Wells: A Future for Historical Jesus Research. *God, the Gift, and Postmodernism.* Eds. John D. Caputo and Michael J. Scanlon. Bloomington: Indiana University Press, 1999.

Cusa, Nicholas of. Trialogus De Possest. *A Concise Introduction to the Philosophy of Nicholas of Cusa.* Ed. Jasper Hopkins. Minneapolis: University of Minnesota Press, 1980.

De Vries, Hent. *Philosophy and the Turn to Religion.* Baltimore: John Hopkins University Press, 1999.

DeHart, Paul. *Beyond the Necessary God: Trinitarian Faith and Philosophy in the Thought of Eberhard Jüngel.* Atlanta: Scholars Press, 1999.

Derrida, Jacques. Faith and Knowledge: The Two Sources Of "Religion" At the Limits of Reason Alone. Trans. Samuel Weber. *Acts of Religion.* Ed. Gil Anidjar. London/New York: Routledge, 2002.

—. 'Force of Law: The Mystical Foundation of Authority.' *Cardozo Law Review* 11 (1990): 919-1045.

—. *The Gift of Death.* 1992. Trans. David Wills. Chicago: University of Chicago Press, 1995.

—. How to Avoid Speaking: Denials. Trans. Ken Frieden. *Language of the Unsayable: The Play of Negativity in Literature and Literary Theory.* Eds. Sanford Budick and Wolfgang Iser. New York: Columbia University Press, 1989.

—. Limited Inc. A B C. Trans. Samuel Weber and Jeffrey Mehlman. *Limited Inc.* Ed. Gerald Graf. Evanston, Illinois: Northwestern University Press, 1988.

—. *Of Grammatology.* 1967. Trans. Gayatri Chakravorty Spivak. corrected ed. Baltimore: John Hopkins University Press, 1997.

—. On a Newly Arisen Apocalyptic Tone in Philosophy. Trans. J.P. Jr. Leavy. *Raising the Tone of Philosophy: Late Essays by Emmanuel Kant, Transformative Critique by Jacques Derrida.* Ed. Peter Fenves. Baltimore: John Hopkins University Press, 1993.

—. *On the Name.* 1993. Trans. David Wood, Jr. John P. Leavey and Ian McLeod. Stanford, California: Stanford University Press, 1995.

—. *The Post Card: From Socrates to Freud and Beyond.* Chicago: University of Chicago Press, 1987.

—. Signature Event Context. Trans. Samuel Weber and Jeffrey Mehlman. *Limited Inc.* Ed. Gerald Graf. Evanston, Illinois: Northwestern University Press, 1988.

—. *The Work of Mourning.* Trans. Michael Naas and Pascale-Anne Brault. Chicago: University of Chicago Press, 2001.

Derrida, Jacques, and Geoffrey Bennington. *Circumfession/Derridabase.* Trans. Geoffrey Bennington. Chicago: University of Chicago Press, 1993.

Derrida, Jacques, and Jean-Luc Marion. On the Gift: A Discussion between

Jacques Derrida and Jean-Luc Marion, Moderated by Richard Kearney. *God, the Gift, and Postmodernism.* Eds. John C. Caputo and Michael J. Scanlon. Bloomington: Indiana University Press, 1999.

Deverell, Garry J. 'The Desire of God.' *The Heythrop Journal* 48.3 (2007): 343-70.

—. '"If It Be Your Will": Making Promises with Derrida, Ricoeur and Chauvet.' *Pacifica: Australasian Theological Studies* 16.3 (2003): 271-94.

—. 'The Making of the Body of Christ: Worship as a Technological Apocalypse.' *Australian Journal of Liturgy* 9.1 (2003): 19-35.

—. 'Uniting in Worship? Proposals Towards a Liturgical Ecumenics.' *Uniting Church Studies* 11.1 (2005): 21-36.

—. 'The Work of Mourning: Derridean Reflections Upon the Waters.' *Australian Journal of Liturgy* 10.3 (2006): 91-104.

Ebeling, Gerhard. *Introduction to a Theological Theory of Language.* Trans. R.A. Wilson. London: Collins, 1973.

—. *The Nature of Faith.* Trans. Ronald Gregor Smith. London: Collins, 1961.

Finn, Thomas M. *Early Christian Baptism and the Catechumenate: West and East Syria.* Collegeville, Minnesota: Liturgical Press, 1992.

—. *From Death to Rebirth: Ritual and Conversion in Antiquity.* New York/Mahwah, New Jersey: Paulist Press, 1997.

Ford, David F. *Self and Salvation: Being Transformed.* Cambridge: Cambridge University Press, 1999.

Fowler, James W. *Stages of Faith: The Psychology of Human Development and the Quest for Meaning.* Melbourne: Collins Dove, 1981.

Girard, René. *Things Hidden since the Foundation of the World.* Trans. Stephen Bann and Michael Metteer. London/New York: Continuum, 2003.

Gottwald, Norman K. *The Hebrew Bible: A Socio-Literary Introduction.* Philadelphia: Fortress Press, 1985.

Hart, David Bentley. *The Beauty of the Infinite: The Aesthetics of Christian Truth.* Grand Rapids, Michigan: William Eerdmans, 2003.

Hegel, Georg Wilhelm Friedrich. *Lectures on the Philosophy of Religion: The Lectures of 1827.* Trans. R.F. Brown, et al. One Volume ed. Berkeley: University of California Press, 1988.

Heidegger, Martin. *Being and Time: A Translation of Sein Und Zeit.* Trans. Joan Stambaugh. Albany: State University of New York Press, 1996.

—. *Contributions to Philosophy (from Enowning).* Trans. Parvis Emad and Kenneth Maly. Bloomington: Indiana University Press, 1999.

—. *Identity and Difference.* Trans. Joan Stambaugh. New York: Harper and Row, 1969.

—. *The Piety of Thinking: Essays by Martin Heidegger.* Trans. James G. Hart and John C. Maraldo. Bloomington: Indiana University Press, 1976.

—. *The Principle of Reason.* Trans. Reginald Lilly. Bloomington: Indiana University Press, 1991.

Horner, Robyn L. *Rethinking God as Gift: Marion, Derrida and the Limits of*

Phenomenology. New York: Fordham University Press, 2001.
Irwin, Kevin. *Liturgical Theology: A Primer*. Collegeville, Minnesota: Liturgical Press, 1990.
Jenson, Robert W. *Visible Words: The Interpretation and Practice of Christian Sacraments*. Philadelphia: Fortress Press, 1978.
Jüngel, Eberhard. *God as the Mystery of the World: On the Foundation of the Theology of the Crucified One in the Dispute between Theism and Atheism*. Trans. Darrell L. Guder. Edinburgh: T & T Clark, 1983.
Kavanagh, Aidan. *The Shape of Baptism: The Rite of Christian Initiation*. Collegeville, Minnesota: Liturgical Press, 1978.
Kearney, Richard. *The God Who May Be: A Hermeneutics of Religion*. Bloomington: Indiana University Press, 2001.
—. *Strangers, Gods and Monsters: Interpreting Otherness*. London/New York: Routledge, 2003.
Kristeva, Julia. *Tales of Love*. Trans. Leon S. Roudiez. New York: Columbia University Press, 1987.
Lathrop, Gordon W. *Holy Things: A Liturgical Theology*. Minneapolis: Fortress Press, 1993.
Lévinas, Emmanuel. *Existence and Existents*. Trans. Alphonso Lingis. The Hague: Martinus Nijhoff, 1978.
—. *Of God Who Comes to Mind*. Trans. Bettina Bergo. Stanford, California: Stanford University Press, 1998.
—. *Otherwise Than Being or, Beyond Essence*. 1974. Trans. Alphonso Lingis. Pittsburgh: Duquesne University Press, 1981.
—. *Time and the Other (and Additional Essays)*. Trans. Richard A. Cohen. Pittsburgh: Duquesne University Press, 1987.
—. *Totality and Infinity: An Essay on Exteriority*. Trans. Alphonso Lingis. The Hague: Martinus Nijhoff Publishers, 1979.
Luther, Martin. The Babylonian Captivity of the Church. Trans. A.T.W Steinhäuser. *Three Treatises*. Philadelphia: Fortress Press, 1970.
Marion, Jean-Luc. *God without Being: Hors-Texte*. Trans. Thomas A. Carlson. Chicago: University of Chicago Press, 1991.
—. *The Idol and Distance: Five Studies*. Paris: B. Grassett, 1977. Trans. Thomas A. Carlson. New York: Fordham University Press, 2001.
—. *In Excess: Studies of Saturated Phenomena*. Trans. Robyn Horner and Vincent Berraud. New York: Fordham University Press, 2002.
—. In the Name: How to Avoid Speaking Of "Negative Theology". *God, the Gift, and Postmodernism*. Eds. John C. Caputo and Michael J. Scanlon. Bloomington: Indiana University Press, 1999.
—. *Prolegomena to Charity*. Trans. Stephen Lewis. New York: Fordham University Press, 2002.
—. *Reduction and Givenness: Investigations of Husserl, Heidegger, and Phenomenology*. Trans. Thomas A. Carlson. Evanston, Illinois: Northwestern University Press, 1998.

Moltmann, Jürgen. *The Crucified God: The Cross of Christ as the Foundation and Criticism of Christian Theology*. Trans. John Bowden and R.A. Wilson. London: SCM Press, 1974.

—. *The Way of Jesus Christ: Christology in Messianic Dimensions*. Der Weg Jesu Christi: Christologie in messianischen Dimensionen. Trans. Margaret Kohl. London: SCM Press, 1990.

Nicholson, Ernest W. *God and His People*. Oxford: Clarendon Press, 1986.

Nietzsche, Friedrich Wilhelm. The Anti-Christ. Trans. Walter Arnold Kaufmann. *The Portable Nietzsche*. Ed. Walter Arnold Kaufmann. New York: Penguin Books, 1982.

—. The Gay Science. Trans. Walter Arnold Kaufmann. *The Portable Nietzsche*. Ed. Walter Arnold Kaufmann. New York: Penguin Books, 1982.

Osborne, Kenan B. *Christian Sacraments in a Postmodern World: A Theology for the Third Millenium*. New York/Mahweh, New Jersey: Paulist Press, 1999.

—. *The Christian Sacraments of Initiation: Baptism, Confirmation, Eucharist*. New York/Mahweh, New Jersey: Paulist Press, 1998.

Power, David Noel. *Sacraments: The Language of God's Giving*. New York: Crossroad/ Herder & Herder, 1999.

Rahner, Karl. *The Trinity*. 1967. Trans. Joseph Donceel. Tunbridge Wells, Kent: Burns and Oates, 1970.

Rees, Frank D. *Wrestling with Doubt: Theological Reflections on the Journey of Faith*. Collegeville, Minnesota: Liturgical Press, 2001.

Ricoeur, Paul. *Figuring the Sacred: Religion, Narrative, and Imagination*. Trans. David Pellauer. Ed. Mark I. Wallace. Minneapolis: Fortress Press, 1995.

—. From Interpretation to Translation. Trans. David Pellauer. *Thinking Biblically: Exegetical and Hermeneutical Studies*. Eds. André LaCocque and Paul Ricoeur. Chicago: Chicago University Press, 1998.

—. Lamentation as Prayer. Trans. David Pellauer. *Thinking Biblically: Exegetical and Hermeneutical Studies*. Eds. André LaCocque and Paul Ricoeur. Chicago: Chicago University Press, 1998.

—. The Nuptial Metaphor. Trans. David Pellauer. *Thinking Biblically: Exegetical and Hermeneutical Studies*. Eds. André LaCocque and Paul Ricoeur. Chicago: Chicago University Press, 1998.

—. *Oneself as Another*. Soi-meme comme un autre, 1990. Trans. Kathleen Blamey. Chicago: University of Chicago Press, 1992.

Rilke, Rainer Maria. *Letters to a Young Poet*. Trans. Joan M. Burnham. San Rafael, California: New World Library, 1992.

Rite of Christian Initiation of Adults. Study ed. Strathfield, NSW: St. Pauls Publications, 2003.

Saliers, Don E. *Worship as Theology: Foretaste of Glory Divine*. Nashville: Abingdon Press, 1994.

Sawicki, Marianne. *Seeing the Lord: Resurrection and Early Christian*

Practices. Minneapolis: Fortress Press, 1994.
Scarry, Elaine. *The Body in Pain: The Making and Unmaking of the World*. New York: Oxford University Press, 1985.
Schmemann, Alexander. *Introduction to Liturgical Theology*. New York: St. Vladimir's Seminary Press, 1966.
Scotland, Church of. *Book of Common Order of the Church of Scotland*. 2nd (emended) ed. Edinburgh: Saint Andrew Press, 1996.
Senn, Frank C. *Christian Liturgy: Catholic and Evangelical*. Minneapolis: Fortress Press, 1997.
Tracy, David. *The Analogical Imagination: Christian Theology and the Culture of Pluralism*. New York: Crossroad, 1981. 2000.
—. *Plurality and Ambiguity: Hermeneutics, Religion, Hope*. Chicago: Chicago University Press, 1987.
USA, Episcopal Church. *Book of Common Prayer and Administration of the Sacraments and Other Rites and Ceremonies of the Church*. New York: Oxford University Press, 1990.
Ward, Benedicta, ed. *The Sayings of the Desert Fathers*. Kalamazoo: Cistercian Publications, 1975.
Webber, Robert E. *Ancient-Future Evangelism: Making Your Church a Faith-Forming Community*. Grand Rapids, Michigan: Baker Books, 2003.
Welcome to Christ: A Lutheran Introduction to the Catechumenate. Minneapolis: Augsburg Press, 1997.
Williams, Rowan. *On Christian Theology*. Oxford: Blackwell, 2000.
Winquist, Charles E. *Desiring Theology*. Chicago: University of Chicago Press, 1995.
Worship, Inter-Lutheran Commission on. *Lutheran Book of Worship*. Minneapolis/Philadelphia: Augsburg Publishing House/Board of Publication, 1978.
Žižek, Slavoj. *On Belief*. London: Routledge, 2001.

Author Index

Anderson, E.B. 170, 194.
Augustine. 138.
Austin, J.L. 6–8.

Ball, P. 188.
Barth, K. 71, 161.
Benedict Jr., D.T. 188.
Bennington, G. 46, 57, 79.
Benveniste, E. 18–19.
Bonhoeffer, D. 109, 157.
Breton, S. 135, 138, 163.
Brueggemann, W. 106–7, 122–23, 126.

Caputo, J.D. 41, 57, 90.
Chauvet, L-M. 22–5, 27, 127, 132, 138–41, 146, 154, 156, 159, 171, 177–78, 180, 189.
Childs, B.S. 104–5, 123, 125.
Cohen, L. 5, 29.
Connerton, P. 194.
Crichton, J.D. 174.
Crossan, J.D. 159–60, 162–63, 178.
Cusa, Nicholas of. 84.

De Vries, H. 20, 46.
DeHart, P. 43–4, 71, 75, 86.
Derrida, J. 8–10, 16, 18–21, 26, 45–6, 54–8, 62, 120, 128, 144, 165, 199, 201–2.
Desert Fathers. 164.
Deverell, G.J. 5, 89, 142, 169, 199.

Ebeling, G. 44, 128, 139.
Eliot, T.S. 31, 200.

Finn, T.M. 186–87.
Ford, D.F. 102, 120, 132, 134–35, 158, 165, 171–72, 183–84.
Fowler, J.W. 126.

Girard, R. 203.

Gottwald, M.K. 121.
Grundy, M. 188.

Hart, D.B. 41.
Hegel, G.W.F. 72.
Heidegger, M. 15, 32, 40, 42, 64.
Hopkins, G.M. 149.
Horner, R.L. 62, 101.

Irwin, K. 171.

Jenson, R.W. 100, 103, 141, 151, 153–54, 177, 182, 184, 189, 191.
Jüngel, E. 25, 36–9, 43–4, 69–78, 92, 113, 118, 130–31, 136–37, 155, 157, 161–62, 199.
Justin Martyr. 196.

Kavanagh, A. 150, 152, 170, 172, 179, 185, 186–87, 189, 191.
Kearney, R. 35, 46, 67, 78–86, 103, 116, 127, 143, 154, 157, 174.
Kierkegaard, S. 16, 55–7, 94.
Kristeva, J. 114, 116, 118, 133, 146, 154.

Lathrop, G.W. 171.
Lévinas, E. 14–15, 21, 33–4, 42–3, 50–4, 91–7, 100–1, 156, 164, 180, 203.
Luther, M. 139, 179.

Marion, J.L. 21, 34–5, 38–9, 41–2, 44, 58–69, 94–9, 129, 131, 136–37, 145, 156, 165, 172.
Moltmann, J. 25, 190.

Nicholson, E.W. 121–22, 125.
Nietzsche, F.W. 38–9.
Nyssa, Gregory of. 187.

Osborne, K.B. 21-2, 150, 158, 166,

174, 182, 184–85, 187, 195.

Power, D.N. 21, 161, 166, 175, 191–93.

Rahner, K. 76.
Rees, F. 130.
Ricoeur, P. 6, 10–18, 35, 41, 78, 90, 101, 104–6, 108, 110, 113–15, 117, 160.
Rilke, R.M. 112.

Saliers, D.E. 170–71.

Sawicki, M. 142–43.
Scarry, E. 13, 103, 110–11, 142.
Schmemann, A. 170.
Senn, F.C. 174.

Tracy, D. 6, 174.

Webber, R.E. 188.
Williams, R. 155.
Winquist, C.E. 102.

Žižek, S. 67, 82, 132, 203, 205.

Paternoster Biblical Monographs
(All titles uniform with this volume)
Dates in bold are of projected publication

Joseph Abraham
Eve: Accused or Acquitted?
A Reconsideration of Feminist Readings of the Creation Narrative Texts in Genesis 1–3
Two contrary views dominate contemporary feminist biblical scholarship. One finds in the Bible an unequivocal equality between the sexes from the very creation of humanity, whilst the other sees the biblical text as irredeemably patriarchal and androcentric. Dr Abraham enters into dialogue with both camps as well as introducing his own method of approach. An invaluable tool for any one who is interested in this contemporary debate.
2002 / 0-85364-971-5 / xxiv + 272pp

Octavian D. Baban
Mimesis and Luke's on the Road Encounters in Luke-Acts
Luke's Theology of the Way and its Literary Representation
The book argues on theological and literary (mimetic) grounds that Luke's on-the-road encounters, especially those belonging to the post-Easter period, are part of his complex theology of the Way. Jesus' teaching and that of the apostles is presented by Luke as a challenging answer to the Hellenistic reader's thirst for adventure, good literature, and existential paradigms.
2005 */ 1-84227-253-5 / approx. 374pp*

Paul Barker
The Triumph of Grace in Deuteronomy
This book is a textual and theological analysis of the interaction between the sin and faithlessness of Israel and the grace of Yahweh in response, looking especially at Deuteronomy chapters 1–3, 8–10 and 29–30. The author argues that the grace of Yahweh is determinative for the ongoing relationship between Yahweh and Israel and that Deuteronomy anticipates and fully expects Israel to be faithless.
2004 / 1-84227-226-8 / xxii + 270pp

Jonathan F. Bayes
The Weakness of the Law
God's Law and the Christian in New Testament Perspective
A study of the four New Testament books which refer to the law as weak (Acts, Romans, Galatians, Hebrews) leads to a defence of the third use in the Reformed debate about the law in the life of the believer.
2000 / 0-85364-957-X / xii + 244pp

July 2005

Mark Bonnington
The Antioch Episode of Galatians 2:11-14 in Historical and Cultural Context

The Galatians 2 'incident' in Antioch over table-fellowship suggests significant disagreement between the leading apostles. This book analyses the background to the disagreement by locating the incident within the dynamics of social interaction between Jews and Gentiles. It proposes a new way of understanding the relationship between the individuals and issues involved.

2005 / 1-84227-050-8 / approx. 350pp

David Bostock
A Portrayal of Trust
The Theme of Faith in the Hezekiah Narratives

This study provides detailed and sensitive readings of the Hezekiah narratives (2 Kings 18–20 and Isaiah 36–39) from a theological perspective. It concentrates on the theme of faith, using narrative criticism as its methodology. Attention is paid especially to setting, plot, point of view and characterization within the narratives. A largely positive portrayal of Hezekiah emerges that underlines the importance and relevance of scripture.

2005 / 1-84227-314-0 / approx. 300pp

Mark Bredin
Jesus, Revolutionary of Peace
A Non-violent Christology in the Book of Revelation

This book aims to demonstrate that the figure of Jesus in the Book of Revelation can best be understood as an active non-violent revolutionary.

2003 / 1-84227-153-9 / xviii + 262pp

Robinson Butarbutar
Paul and Conflict Resolution
An Exegetical Study of Paul's Apostolic Paradigm in 1 Corinthians 9

The author sees the apostolic paradigm in 1 Corinthians 9 as part of Paul's unified arguments in 1 Corinthians 8–10 in which he seeks to mediate in the dispute over the issue of food offered to idols. The book also sees its relevance for dispute-resolution today, taking the conflict within the author's church as an example.

2006 / 1-84227-315-9 / approx. 280pp

Daniel J-S Chae
Paul as Apostle to the Gentiles
His Apostolic Self-awareness and its Influence on the Soteriological Argument in Romans
Opposing 'the post-Holocaust interpretation of Romans', Daniel Chae competently demonstrates that Paul argues for the equality of Jew and Gentile in Romans. Chae's fresh exegetical interpretation is academically outstanding and spiritually encouraging.
1997 / 0-85364-829-8 / xiv + 378pp

Luke L. Cheung
The Genre, Composition and Hermeneutics of the Epistle of James
The present work examines the employment of the wisdom genre with a certain compositional structure and the interpretation of the law through the Jesus tradition of the double love command by the author of the Epistle of James to serve his purpose in promoting perfection and warning against doubleness among the eschatologically renewed people of God in the Diaspora.
2003 / 1-84227-062-1 / xvi + 372pp

Youngmo Cho
Spirit and Kingdom in the Writings of Luke and Paul
The relationship between Spirit and Kingdom is a relatively unexplored area in Lukan and Pauline studies. This book offers a fresh perspective of two biblical writers on the subject. It explores the difference between Luke's and Paul's understanding of the Spirit by examining the specific question of the relationship of the concept of the Spirit to the concept of the Kingdom of God in each writer.
2005 / 1-84227-316-7 / approx. 270pp

Andrew C. Clark
Parallel Lives
The Relation of Paul to the Apostles in the Lucan Perspective
This study of the Peter-Paul parallels in Acts argues that their purpose was to emphasize the themes of continuity in salvation history and the unity of the Jewish and Gentile missions. New light is shed on Luke's literary techniques, partly through a comparison with Plutarch.
2001 / 1-84227-035-4 / xviii + 386pp

July 2005

Andrew D. Clarke
Secular and Christian Leadership in Corinth
A Socio-Historical and Exegetical Study of 1 Corinthians 1–6
This volume is an investigation into the leadership structures and dynamics of first-century Roman Corinth. These are compared with the practice of leadership in the Corinthian Christian community which are reflected in 1 Corinthians 1–6, and contrasted with Paul's own principles of Christian leadership.
2005 / 1-84227-229-2 / 200pp

Stephen Finamore
God, Order and Chaos
René Girard and the Apocalypse
Readers are often disturbed by the images of destruction in the book of Revelation and unsure why they are unleashed after the exaltation of Jesus. This book examines past approaches to these texts and uses René Girard's theories to revive some old ideas and propose some new ones.
2005 / 1-84227-197-0 / approx. 344pp

David G. Firth
Surrendering Retribution in the Psalms
Responses to Violence in the Individual Complaints
In *Surrendering Retribution in the Psalms*, David Firth examines the ways in which the book of Psalms inculcates a model response to violence through the repetition of standard patterns of prayer. Rather than seeking justification for retributive violence, Psalms encourages not only a surrender of the right of retribution to Yahweh, but also sets limits on the retribution that can be sought in imprecations. Arising initially from the author's experience in South Africa, the possibilities of this model to a particular context of violence is then briefly explored.
2005 / 1-84227-337-X / xviii + 154pp

Scott J. Hafemann
Suffering and Ministry in the Spirit
Paul's Defence of His Ministry in II Corinthians 2:14–3:3
Shedding new light on the way Paul defended his apostleship, the author offers a careful, detailed study of 2 Corinthians 2:14–3:3 linked with other key passages throughout 1 and 2 Corinthians. Demonstrating the unity and coherence of Paul's argument in this passage, the author shows that Paul's suffering served as the vehicle for revealing God's power and glory through the Spirit.
2000 / 0-85364-967-7 / xiv + 262pp

Scott J. Hafemann
Paul, Moses and the History of Israel
The Letter/Spirit Contrast and the Argument from Scripture in 2 Corinthians 3
An exegetical study of the call of Moses, the second giving of the Law (Exodus 32–34), the new covenant, and the prophetic understanding of the history of Israel in 2 Corinthians 3. Hafemann's work demonstrates Paul's contextual use of the Old Testament and the essential unity between the Law and the Gospel within the context of the distinctive ministries of Moses and Paul.
2005 / 1-84227-317-5 / xii + 498pp

Douglas S. McComiskey
Lukan Theology in the Light of the Gospel's Literary Structure
Luke's Gospel was purposefully written with theology embedded in its patterned literary structure. A critical analysis of this cyclical structure provides new windows into Luke's interpretation of the individual pericopes comprising the Gospel and illuminates several of his theological interests.
2004 / 1-84227-148-2 / xviii + 388pp

Stephen Motyer
Your Father the Devil?
A New Approach to John and 'The Jews'
Who are 'the Jews' in John's Gospel? Defending John against the charge of antisemitism, Motyer argues that, far from demonising the Jews, the Gospel seeks to present Jesus as 'Good News for Jews' in a late first century setting.
1997 / 0-85364-832-8 / xiv + 260pp

Esther Ng
Reconstructing Christian Origins?
The Feminist Theology of Elizabeth Schüssler Fiorenza: An Evaluation
In a detailed evaluation, the author challenges Elizabeth Schüssler Fiorenza's reconstruction of early Christian origins and her underlying presuppositions. The author also presents her own views on women's roles both then and now.
2002 / 1-84227-055-9 / xxiv + 468pp

July 2005

Robin Parry
Old Testament Story and Christian Ethics
The Rape of Dinah as a Case Study

What is the role of story in ethics and, more particularly, what is the role of Old Testament story in Christian ethics? This book, drawing on the work of contemporary philosophers, argues that narrative is crucial in the ethical shaping of people and, drawing on the work of contemporary Old Testament scholars, that story plays a key role in Old Testament ethics. Parry then argues that when situated in canonical context Old Testament stories can be reappropriated by Christian readers in their own ethical formation. The shocking story of the rape of Dinah and the massacre of the Shechemites provides a fascinating case study for exploring the parameters within which Christian ethical appropriations of Old Testament stories can live.

2004 / 1-84227-210-1 / xx + 350pp

Ian Paul
Power to See the World Anew
The Value of Paul Ricoeur's Hermeneutic of Metaphor in Interpreting the Symbolism of Revelation 12 and 13

This book is a study of the hermeneutics of metaphor of Paul Ricoeur, one of the most important writers on hermeneutics and metaphor of the last century. It sets out the key points of his theory, important criticisms of his work, and how his approach, modified in the light of these criticisms, offers a methodological framework for reading apocalyptic texts.

2006 / 1-84227-056-7 / approx. 350pp

Robert L. Plummer
Paul's Understanding of the Church's Mission
Did the Apostle Paul Expect the Early Christian Communities to Evangelize?

This book engages in a careful study of Paul's letters to determine if the apostle expected the communities to which he wrote to engage in missionary activity. It helpfully summarizes the discussion on this debated issue, judiciously handling contested texts, and provides a way forward in addressing this critical question. While admitting that Paul rarely explicitly commands the communities he founded to evangelize, Plummer amasses significant incidental data to provide a convincing case that Paul did indeed expect his churches to engage in mission activity. Throughout the study, Plummer progressively builds a theological basis for the church's mission that is both distinctively Pauline and compelling.

2006 / 1-84227-333-7 / approx. 324pp

David Powys
'Hell': A Hard Look at a Hard Question
The Fate of the Unrighteous in New Testament Thought
This comprehensive treatment seeks to unlock the original meaning of terms and phrases long thought to support the traditional doctrine of hell. It concludes that there is an alternative—one which is more biblical, and which can positively revive the rationale for Christian mission.
1997 / 0-85364-831-X / xxii + 478pp

Sorin Sabou
Between Horror and Hope
Paul's Metaphorical Language of Death in Romans 6.1-11
This book argues that Paul's metaphorical language of death in Romans 6.1-11 conveys two aspects: horror and hope. The 'horror' aspect is conveyed by the 'crucifixion' language, and the 'hope' aspect by 'burial' language. The life of the Christian believer is understood, as relationship with sin is concerned ('death to sin'), between these two realities: horror and hope.
2005 / 1-84227-322-1 / approx. 224pp

Rosalind Selby
The Comical Doctrine
The Epistemology of New Testament Hermeneutics
This book argues that the gospel breaks through postmodernity's critique of truth and the referential possibilities of textuality with its gift of grace. With a rigorous, philosophical challenge to modernist and postmodernist assumptions, Selby offers an alternative epistemology to all who would still read with faith *and* with academic credibility.
2005 / 1-84227-212-8 / approx. 350pp

Kiwoong Son
Zion Symbolism in Hebrews
Hebrews 12.18-24 as a Hermeneutical Key to the Epistle
This book challenges the general tendency of understanding the Epistle to the Hebrews against a Hellenistic background and suggests that the Epistle should be understood in the light of the Jewish apocalyptic tradition. The author especially argues for the importance of the theological symbolism of Sinai and Zion (Heb. 12:18-24) as it provides the Epistle's theological background as well as the rhetorical basis of the superiority motif of Jesus throughout the Epistle.
2005 / 1-84227-368-X / approx. 280pp

Kevin Walton
Thou Traveller Unknown
The Presence and Absence of God in the Jacob Narrative
The author offers a fresh reading of the story of Jacob in the book of Genesis through the paradox of divine presence and absence. The work also seeks to make a contribution to Pentateuchal studies by bringing together a close reading of the final text with historical critical insights, doing justice to the text's historical depth, final form and canonical status.
2003 / 1-84227-059-1 / xvi + 238pp

George M. Wieland
The Significance of Salvation
A Study of Salvation Language in the Pastoral Epistles
The language and ideas of salvation pervade the three Pastoral Epistles. This study offers a close examination of their soteriological statements. In all three letters the idea of salvation is found to play a vital paraenetic role, but each also exhibits distinctive soteriological emphases. The results challenge common assumptions about the Pastoral Epistles as a corpus.
2005 / 1-84227-257-8 / approx. 324pp

Alistair Wilson
When Will These Things Happen?
A Study of Jesus as Judge in Matthew 21–25
This study seeks to allow Matthew's carefully constructed presentation of Jesus to be given full weight in the modern evaluation of Jesus' eschatology. Careful analysis of the text of Matthew 21–25 reveals Jesus to be standing firmly in the Jewish prophetic and wisdom traditions as he proclaims and enacts imminent judgement on the Jewish authorities then boldly claims the central role in the final and universal judgement.
2004 / 1-84227-146-6 / xxii + 272pp

Lindsay Wilson
Joseph Wise and Otherwise
The Intersection of Covenant and Wisdom in Genesis 37–50
This book offers a careful literary reading of Genesis 37–50 that argues that the Joseph story contains both strong covenant themes and many wisdom-like elements. The connections between the two helps to explore how covenant and wisdom might intersect in an integrated biblical theology.
2004 / 1-84227-140-7 / xvi + 340pp

Stephen I. Wright
The Voice of Jesus
Studies in the Interpretation of Six Gospel Parables
This literary study considers how the 'voice' of Jesus has been heard in different periods of parable interpretation, and how the categories of figure and trope may help us towards a sensitive reading of the parables today.
2000 / 0-85364-975-8 / xiv + 280pp

Paternoster:
thinking faith

Paternoster
9 Holdom Avenue,
Bletchley,
Milton Keynes MK1 1QR,
United Kingdom
Web: www.authenticmedia.co.uk/paternoster

July 2005

Paternoster Theological Monographs

(All titles uniform with this volume)
Dates in bold are of projected publication

Emil Bartos
Deification in Eastern Orthodox Theology
An Evaluation and Critique of the Theology of Dumitru Staniloae
Bartos studies a fundamental yet neglected aspect of Orthodox theology: deification. By examining the doctrines of anthropology, christology, soteriology and ecclesiology as they relate to deification, he provides an important contribution to contemporary dialogue between Eastern and Western theologians.

1999 / 0-85364-956-1 / xii + 370pp

Graham Buxton
The Trinity, Creation and Pastoral Ministry
Imaging the Perichoretic God
In this book the author proposes a three-way conversation between theology, science and pastoral ministry. His approach draws on a Trinitarian understanding of God as a relational being of love, whose life 'spills over' into all created reality, human and non-human. By locating human meaning and purpose within God's 'creation-community' this book offers the possibility of a transforming engagement between those in pastoral ministry and the scientific community.

__2005__ / 1-84227-369-8 / approx. 380 pp

Iain D. Campbell
Fixing the Indemnity
The Life and Work of George Adam Smith
When Old Testament scholar George Adam Smith (1856–1942) delivered the Lyman Beecher lectures at Yale University in 1899, he confidently declared that 'modern criticism has won its war against traditional theories. It only remains to fix the amount of the indemnity.' In this biography, Iain D. Campbell assesses Smith's critical approach to the Old Testament and evaluates its consequences, showing that Smith's life and work still raises questions about the relationship between biblical scholarship and evangelical faith.

2004 / 1-84227-228-4 / xx + 256pp

Tim Chester
Mission and the Coming of God
Eschatology, the Trinity and Mission in the Theology of Jürgen Moltmann
This book explores the theology and missiology of the influential contemporary theologian, Jürgen Moltmann. It highlights the important contribution Moltmann has made while offering a critique of his thought from an evangelical perspective. In so doing, it touches on pertinent issues for evangelical missiology. The conclusion takes Calvin as a starting point, proposing 'an eschatology of the cross' which offers a critique of the over-realised eschatologies in liberation theology and certain forms of evangelicalism.
2006 / 1-84227-320-5 / approx. 224pp

Sylvia Wilkey Collinson
Making Disciples
The Significance of Jesus' Educational Strategy for Today's Church
This study examines the biblical practice of discipling, formulates a definition, and makes comparisons with modern models of education. A recommendation is made for greater attention to its practice today.
2004 / 1-84227-116-4 / xiv + 278pp

Darrell Cosden
A Theology of Work
Work and the New Creation
Through dialogue with Moltmann, Pope John Paul II and others, this book develops a genitive 'theology of work', presenting a theological definition of work and a model for a theological ethics of work that shows work's nature, value and meaning now and eschatologically. Work is shown to be a transformative activity consisting of three dynamically inter-related dimensions: the instrumental, relational and ontological.
2005 / 1-84227-332-9 / xvi + 208pp

Stephen M. Dunning
The Crisis and the Quest
A Kierkegaardian Reading of Charles Williams
Employing Kierkegaardian categories and analysis, this study investigates both the central crisis in Charles Williams's authorship between hermetism and Christianity (Kierkegaard's Religions A and B), and the quest to resolve this crisis, a quest that ultimately presses the bounds of orthodoxy.
2000 / 0-85364-985-5 / xxiv + 254pp

Keith Ferdinando
The Triumph of Christ in African Perspective
A Study of Demonology and Redemption in the African Context
The book explores the implications of the gospel for traditional African fears of occult aggression. It analyses such traditional approaches to suffering and biblical responses to fears of demonic evil, concluding with an evaluation of African beliefs from the perspective of the gospel.
1999 / 0-85364-830-1 / xviii + 450pp

Andrew Goddard
Living the Word, Resisting the World
The Life and Thought of Jacques Ellul
This work offers a definitive study of both the life and thought of the French Reformed thinker Jacques Ellul (1912-1994). It will prove an indispensable resource for those interested in this influential theologian and sociologist and for Christian ethics and political thought generally.
2002 / 1-84227-053-2 / xxiv + 378pp

David Hilborn
The Words of our Lips
Language-Use in Free Church Worship
Studies of liturgical language have tended to focus on the written canons of Roman Catholic and Anglican communities. By contrast, David Hilborn analyses the more extemporary approach of English Nonconformity. Drawing on recent developments in linguistic pragmatics, he explores similarities and differences between 'fixed' and 'free' worship, and argues for the interdependence of each.
2006 / 0-85364-977-4 / approx. 350pp

Roger Hitching
The Church and Deaf People
A Study of Identity, Communication and Relationships with Special Reference to the Ecclesiology of Jürgen Moltmann
In *The Church and Deaf People* Roger Hitching sensitively examines the history and present experience of deaf people and finds similarities between aspects of sign language and Moltmann's theological method that 'open up' new ways of understanding theological concepts.
2003 / 1-84227-222-5 / xxii + 236pp

July 2005

John G. Kelly
One God, One People
The Differentiated Unity of the People of God in the Theology of Jürgen Moltmann

The author expounds and critiques Moltmann's doctrine of God and highlights the systematic connections between it and Moltmann's influential discussion of Israel. He then proposes a fresh approach to Jewish–Christian relations building on Moltmann's work using insights from Habermas and Rawls.

2005 / 0-85346-969-3 / approx. 350pp

Mark F.W. Lovatt
Confronting the Will-to-Power
A Reconsideration of the Theology of Reinhold Niebuhr

Confronting the Will-to-Power is an analysis of the theology of Reinhold Niebuhr, arguing that his work is an attempt to identify, and provide a practical theological answer to, the existence and nature of human evil.

2001 / 1-84227-054-0 / xviii + 216pp

Neil B. MacDonald
Karl Barth and the Strange New World within the Bible
Barth, Wittgenstein, and the Metadilemmas of the Enlightenment

Barth's discovery of the strange new world within the Bible is examined in the context of Kant, Hume, Overbeck, and, most importantly, Wittgenstein. MacDonald covers some fundamental issues in theology today: epistemology, the final form of the text and biblical truth-claims.

2000 / 0-85364-970-7 / xxvi + 374pp

Keith A. Mascord
Alvin Plantinga and Christian Apologetics
This book draws together the contributions of the philosopher Alvin Plantinga to the major contemporary challenges to Christian belief, highlighting in particular his ground-breaking work in epistemology and the problem of evil. Plantinga's theory that both theistic and Christian belief is warrantedly basic is explored and critiqued, and an assessment offered as to the significance of his work for apologetic theory and practice.

2005 / 1-84227-256-X / approx. 304pp

Gillian McCulloch
The Deconstruction of Dualism in Theology
With Reference to Ecofeminist Theology and New Age Spirituality
This book challenges eco-theological anti-dualism in Christian theology, arguing that dualism has a twofold function in Christian religious discourse. Firstly, it enables us to express the discontinuities and divisions that are part of the process of reality. Secondly, dualistic language allows us to express the mysteries of divine transcendence/immanence and the survival of the soul without collapsing into monism and materialism, both of which are problematic for Christian epistemology.

2002 / 1-84227-044-3 / xii + 282pp

Leslie McCurdy
Attributes and Atonement
The Holy Love of God in the Theology of P.T. Forsyth
Attributes and Atonement is an intriguing full-length study of P.T. Forsyth's doctrine of the cross as it relates particularly to God's holy love. It includes an unparalleled bibliography of both primary and secondary material relating to Forsyth.

1999 / 0-85364-833-6 / xiv + 328pp

Nozomu Miyahira
Towards a Theology of the Concord of God
A Japanese Perspective on the Trinity
This book introduces a new Japanese theology and a unique Trinitarian formula based on the Japanese intellectual climate: three betweennesses and one concord. It also presents a new interpretation of the Trinity, a co-subordinationism, which is in line with orthodox Trinitarianism; each single person of the Trinity is eternally and equally subordinate (or serviceable) to the other persons, so that they retain the mutual dynamic equality.

2000 / 0-85364-863-8 / xiv + 256pp

Eddy José Muskus
The Origins and Early Development of Liberation Theology in Latin America
With Particular Reference to Gustavo Gutiérrez
This work challenges the fundamental premise of Liberation Theology, 'opting for the poor', and its claim that Christ is found in them. It also argues that Liberation Theology emerged as a direct result of the failure of the Roman Catholic Church in Latin America.

2002 / 0-85364-974-X / xiv + 296pp

Jim Purves
The Triune God and the Charismatic Movement
A Critical Appraisal from a Scottish Perspective
All emotion and no theology? Or a fundamental challenge to reappraise and realign our trinitarian theology in the light of Christian experience? This study of charismatic renewal as it found expression within Scotland at the end of the twentieth century evaluates the use of Patristic, Reformed and contemporary models of the Trinity in explaining the workings of the Holy Spirit.
2004 / 1-84227-321-3 / xxiv + 246pp

Anna Robbins
Methods in the Madness
Diversity in Twentieth-Century Christian Social Ethics
The author compares the ethical methods of Walter Rauschenbusch, Reinhold Niebuhr and others. She argues that unless Christians are clear about the ways that theology and philosophy are expressed practically they may lose the ability to discuss social ethics across contexts, let alone reach effective agreements.
2004 / 1-84227-211-X / xx + 294pp

Ed Rybarczyk
Beyond Salvation
Eastern Orthodoxy and Classical Pentecostalism on Becoming Like Christ
At first glance eastern Orthodoxy and classical Pentecostalism seem quite distinct. This ground-breaking study shows they share much in common, especially as it concerns the experiential elements of following Christ. Both traditions assert that authentic Christianity transcends the wooden categories of modernism.
2004 / 1-84227-144-X / xii + 356pp

Signe Sandsmark
Is World View Neutral Education Possible and Desirable?
A Christian Response to Liberal Arguments
(Published jointly with The Stapleford Centre)
This book discusses reasons for belief in world view neutrality, and argues that 'neutral' education will have a hidden, but strong world view influence. It discusses the place for Christian education in the common school.
2000 / 0-85364-973-1 / xiv + 182pp

Hazel Sherman
Reading Zechariah
The Allegorical Tradition of Biblical Interpretation through the Commentary of Didymus the Blind and Theodore of Mopsuestia
A close reading of the commentary on Zechariah by Didymus the Blind alongside that of Theodore of Mopsuestia suggests that popular categorising of Antiochene and Alexandrian biblical exegesis as 'historical' or 'allegorical' is inadequate and misleading.
2005 / 1-84227-213-6 / approx. 280pp

Andrew Sloane
On Being a Christian in the Academy
Nicholas Wolterstorff and the Practice of Christian Scholarship
An exposition and critical appraisal of Nicholas Wolterstorff's epistemology in the light of the philosophy of science, and an application of his thought to the practice of Christian scholarship.
2003 / 1-84227-058-3 / xvi + 274pp

Damon W.K. So
Jesus' Revelation of His Father
A Narrative-Conceptual Study of the Trinity with Special Reference to Karl Barth
This book explores the trinitarian dynamics in the context of Jesus' revelation of his Father in his earthly ministry with references to key passages in Matthew's Gospel. It develops from the exegeses of these passages a non-linear concept of revelation which links Jesus' communion with his Father to his revelatory words and actions through a nuanced understanding of the Holy Spirit, with references to K. Barth, G.W.H. Lampe, J.D.G. Dunn and E. Irving.
2005 / 1-84227-323-X / approx. 380pp

Daniel Strange
The Possibility of Salvation Among the Unevangelised
An Analysis of Inclusivism in Recent Evangelical Theology
For evangelical theologians the 'fate of the unevangelised' impinges upon fundamental tenets of evangelical identity. The position known as 'inclusivism', defined by the belief that the unevangelised can be ontologically saved by Christ whilst being epistemologically unaware of him, has been defended most vigorously by the Canadian evangelical Clark H. Pinnock. Through a detailed analysis and critique of Pinnock's work, this book examines a cluster of issues surrounding the unevangelised and its implications for christology, soteriology and the doctrine of revelation.
2002 / 1-84227-047-8 / xviii + 362pp

July 2005

Scott Swain
God According to the Gospel
Biblical Narrative and the Identity of God in the Theology of Robert W. Jenson
Robert W. Jenson is one of the leading voices in contemporary Trinitarian theology. His boldest contribution in this area concerns his use of biblical narrative both to ground and explicate the Christian doctrine of God. *God According to the Gospel* critically examines Jenson's proposal and suggests an alternative way of reading the biblical portrayal of the triune God.
2006 / 1-84227-258-6 / approx. 180pp

Justyn Terry
The Justifying Judgement of God
A Reassessment of the Place of Judgement in the Saving Work of Christ
The argument of this book is that judgement, understood as the whole process of bringing justice, is the primary metaphor of atonement, with others, such as victory, redemption and sacrifice, subordinate to it. Judgement also provides the proper context for understanding penal substitution and the call to repentance, baptism, eucharist and holiness.
2005 / 1-84227-370-1 / approx. 274 pp

Graham Tomlin
The Power of the Cross
Theology and the Death of Christ in Paul, Luther and Pascal
This book explores the theology of the cross in St Paul, Luther and Pascal. It offers new perspectives on the theology of each, and some implications for the nature of power, apologetics, theology and church life in a postmodern context.
1999 / 0-85364-984-7 / xiv + 344pp

Adonis Vidu
Postliberal Theological Method
A Critical Study
The postliberal theology of Hans Frei, George Lindbeck, Ronald Thiemann, John Milbank and others is one of the more influential contemporary options. This book focuses on several aspects pertaining to its theological method, specifically its understanding of background, hermeneutics, epistemic justification, ontology, the nature of doctrine and, finally, Christological method.
2005 / 1-84227-395-7 / approx. 324pp

Graham J. Watts
Revelation and the Spirit
A Comparative Study of the Relationship between the Doctrine of Revelation and Pneumatology in the Theology of Eberhard Jüngel and of Wolfhart Pannenberg

The relationship between revelation and pneumatology is relatively unexplored. This approach offers a fresh angle on two important twentieth century theologians and raises pneumatological questions which are theologically crucial and relevant to mission in a postmodern culture.

2005 / 1-84227-104-0 / xxii + 232pp

Nigel G. Wright
Disavowing Constantine
Mission, Church and the Social Order in the Theologies of John Howard Yoder and Jürgen Moltmann

This book is a timely restatement of a radical theology of church and state in the Anabaptist and Baptist tradition. Dr Wright constructs his argument in dialogue and debate with Yoder and Moltmann, major contributors to a free church perspective.

2000 / 0-85364-978-2 / xvi + 252pp

Paternoster:
thinking faith

Paternoster
9 Holdom Avenue,
Bletchley,
Milton Keynes MK1 1QR,
United Kingdom
Web: www.authenticmedia.co.uk/paternoster

July 2005